THE DREMEL® GUIDE TO COMPACT POWER TOOLS

By Len Hilts

Consulting Editor: Jay Hedden,
Editor, *Workbench Magazine*

Photography: Gene Hamilton

Published by Dremel, Division of
Emerson Electric Co.
Racine, Wisconsin 53406

i

TABLE OF CONTENTS

Chapter Six

A compact version of the big belt sanders, this tool enables you to shape, sand, polish, clean and sharpen items in wood, soft metals and plastics, using either the continuous belt or the disc.

Chapter Seven

For those times when you need a third hand in the workshop, look to the D-Vise. It holds the work in any position and frees your hands to operate tools with greater safety and accuracy. And for special jobs, there are the Chainsaver, for sharpening chain saws; the Engraver, for all kinds of engraving; and the Woodburner, for decorative work on wood.

Chapter Eight

Here is a 4-inch tilt arbor table saw that can do bevel cuts, miter cuts, tongue-and-grooving and other wood joints, as well as all the other work you expect of a table saw, making cuts up to 1 inch in depth.

Chapter Nine

You have the capability of assembling a complete compact workshop, using the Dremel tools. Here are suggested layout plans, workbench ideas, and even fold-up storage ideas for people with limited space.

Chapter Ten

Routine care and maintenance can extend the life of your tools and keep them working at peak efficiency. Here are tips on how to give your compact power tools the care they deserve and how to make minor repairs.

Chapter Eleven

Before you start a project, discover the working properties of the materials you will handle. Then you can select the right accessories to do the work most efficiently.

Chapter Twelve

An idea is only an idea until it is translated into a plan. Here you find out how to plan the pieces, joinery, and materials; how to scale plans, and how to make and use templates.

INTRODUCTION

Welcome to the world of Dremel power tools.

The purpose of this book is to introduce you to the wonderfully practical collection of Dremel tools — compact, handy, easy-to-use tools with an almost endless list of uses in your home and workshop. Whether you are an apartment dweller or a homeowner faced with the usual run of repairs and installations, a wood carver, a model builder, or a person who likes to make things in wood or metal or glass, these tools will add a new dimension to your life.

In these pages, we propose to tell you about each of these tools: what they can do, how to use them and the handy attachments which extend their usefulness. We will present a wide range of projects that should whet your do-it-yourself appetite. And in case our projects are not exactly what you are looking for, we tell you how to convert your own ideas into practical plans from which you can work.

The book is written from the viewpoint of the beginner, but also covers material aimed at the more experienced craftsman. What this means is that we have tried to explain technical terms. Too often,

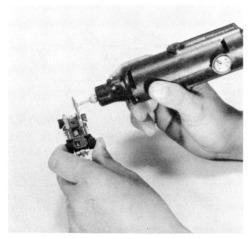

A wire brush accessory can be used in the Moto-Tool to clean electrical contacts, as on this slot car racer.

Pre-drilling holes for screws is one of the hundreds of jobs around the house the Moto-Tool makes easy.

how-to books and articles assume a basic level of understanding on the part of the reader. They might casually refer to the "chuck" of the tool, assuming that everyone must know what a chuck is. The term is common among people who know tools. But the fact is that some readers may not yet have discovered either tools or the chuck. We want to help them get started.

On the other hand, we know that it is no fun for an experienced hand to wade through pages of very basic material he or she already understands. So we have carefully constructed the text to give the beginner a gradual understanding of how to use these tools and, at the same time, to give the advanced worker a new and perhaps deeper insight into their operation. The very high speed of the Moto-Tool, for example, gives it capabilities not found in other tools, and in this book we will tell you how to use this speed to your advantage.

An Overview

The first thing you discover as you page through the book is that we are not talking about a random collection of tools, but about a whole compact workshop of tools, power- ful enough to provide you with a wide range of capabilities. Yet these tools are so compact that they offer the possibility of a workshop which can be rolled into a closet when not in use. Later in the book, we show you how to build just such a disappearing shop if work space and storage space are your problems.

With these tools, you can work with wood, metal, glass, plastics and nearly any other material. The variable speed allows you to run at slow speeds for materials like plastics, and at high speeds for hard materials such as steel. You can do

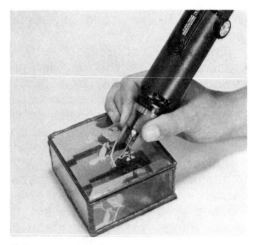

Using an engraving accessory, you can etch delicate designs on glass, plastic, or ceramic items.

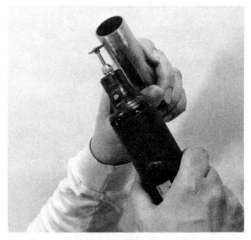

You can put together a workshop of compact tools, including a disc-belt sander, lathe and a Moto-Shop.

Another application: The Moto-Tool can be used to clean copper tubing or pipe prior to sweat soldering.

things you once thought were possible only with a complete full-scale metal or woodworking shop. You can make thousands of items for yourself and for gifts. You can develop all those ideas you have had, and translate those feelings of "why doesn't somebody do this" into "I just did it." Get an idea for a novel set of bookends, a unique salt and pepper set, an artistic coaster? Here is your chance to do something about it.

The possibilities are endless: bird houses, lamps, candle holders, picture frames, inlaid chess boards, chessmen, doll furniture, model railroad accessories, shadow boxes for the wall, inlaid jewel boxes — the list is bounded only by your own imagination.

But these tools are not just for the craftsman. They put power in the hands of the artist who wants to carve relief plaques in fine wood, and in the hands of the jeweler who translates precious metals and stones into rings and other things of beauty. The furniture maker can revive the ancient art, now disappearing, of artistically carving furniture.

In between all of these creative jobs, these tools turn into little

Freehand carving with the Moto-Tool is a favorite artform for professionals and amateurs alike.

Restore door knobs, furniture hardware and other painted-over items to their original bright look.

Remove rust and dirt from shop and garden tools using one of the wire brush accessories.

Quickly sharpen scissors on the Disc-Belt Sander, as shown, or on the disc sander of the Moto-Tool.

workhorses around your house. Hang pictures and install shelves with them. Pre-drill the holes for drapery rods. Makes repairs — and even replacement parts — for damaged furniture. Sharpen scissors and tools. Clean the rust from pipe threads. Get the old hard, cracked putty off window panes to replace it with new putty that will seal out winter drafts. Put new hinges on cabinets. Or even go so far as to redesign kitchen and bathroom cabinet doors by using the router to cut new patterns in plain decors. Or to add distinctive inlays to these doors for a personalized, handcrafted look.

The Moto-Tool has gained the reputation of being the tool which does jobs that other tools will not.

The Tools

One chapter in the book is devoted to each of the major tools in the Dremel workshop collection. These include:

The Moto-Tool and its wide range of interchangeable high speed bits and accessories is the basic tool of the compact workshop. Known for years by professional and amateur craftsmen as the tool which would do things that others would not.

The Moto-Flex Tool is a Moto-Tool type tool with a 34-inch flexible shaft and ball bearing hand piece. It can be mounted on a swivel base or hung from hanger built into the tool. It has been popular with wood carvers, gemologists, taxidermists, gunsmiths and model makers because of its ability to work in tight places and around abrasive materials.

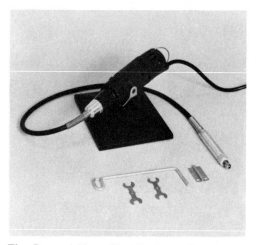

The Dremel Moto-Flex Tool provides the power and speed of the Moto-Tool and the utility of a 34-in. flexible shaft.

The Moto-Tool drill press, created by the addition of an accessory stand which converts the Moto-Tool into a compact-sized drill press with many of the features of a full-sized model. It makes accurate drilling easy.

The Moto-Tool router attachment, a neat tool for running

The Moto-Tool Drill Press is assembled by attaching the Drill Press Attachment to the Moto-Tool.

The Moto-Tool router attachment converts the Moto-Tool into a practical router for recessing, grooving, edging.

The ideal table saw for the compact workshop, the Dremel uses 4-inch blades and has a tilt arbor.

The Moto-Shop is a combination tool, with a scroll saw, a disc sander, and a flexible shaft attachment.

The Dremel Disc/Belt sander has a belt 1 inch wide for belt sanding, and a 5-inch disc for disc work.

The Dremel lathe can be used for turnings on stock up to 6 inches long and 1-1/2 inches in diameter.

Upper left in this picture is the Moto-Tool in the base mount attachment. Below it are two D-Vises.

grooves, shaping edges and making signs, cutting recesses for hinges and other door hardware, inlays and small furniture joints.

The Moto-Shop, a cleverly designed combination tool featuring a scroll saw, a disc sander, and a flexible shaft attachment.

The Moto-Lathe, with head and tail stock centers and a face plate. With it, you can make all kinds of small turnings.

The Dremel Table Saw, a 4-inch tilt arbor motorized table saw that can do a myriad of things including bevel cuts, miter cuts, tongue-and-grooves, and of course, everyday straight saw cuts.

The Dremel Disc-Belt Sander, with which you can sand, shape, polish, clean, and sharpen. Use it on woods, metals and some plastics, using either the belt or the disc.

The Dremel D-Vise, a handy bench vise with a ball swivel that allows vise positioning around a 360 degree axis and over a 180 degree range. It gives you a third hand in your workshop.

Other Dremel tools which provide added dimension to the workshop include a wood burner, an engraver, and a chain saw sharpener.

A glance at this impressive list should tell you why we think of these tools as "a compact workshop." Individually, each tool provides an important capability; combined, they become a full workshop. You may have one or two of these tools now, but as you expand your creativity, you'll find uses for others. The chapter on each tool previews how to set it up, how to use it, and a description of the attachments available for use with it. With this information, you should have little trouble in purchasing the exact tools you need for whatever project you have in mind.

Model railroad enthusiast uses the drill press to take some flashing from a newly-cast part.

Moto-Flex handpiece makes carving, drilling, sanding and grinding possible in tight places.

When assembling plastic models, make the job professional by grinding off burrs and flashing left by molding.

A bit of history

Dremel tools have a long history. Back in 1931, Mr. A.J. Dremel retired after an active life of invention and manufacture, during which he had conceived such revolutionary items as the power lawn mower, the electric hair clipper and the electric massager, which have all become standard products today. But after less than a year he was back in business again. This time to design, develop and manufacture the hand grinder that developed into the present day Moto-Tool. It was a new kind of tool — high speed and low torque — that spun interchangeable bits up to 30,000 revolutions per minute exploiting speed instead of brute power. He added specially designed cutter accessories, to do all kinds of cutting, grinding and polishing jobs. It soon became known around the world.

Hobbyists and craftsmen have known it. So have dentists and dental technicians in laboratory work. Industry has used it in the making of molds and dies. It can be found in virtually every machine shop, where it is used for sharpening cutting tools. To wood carvers, it is the standard power carver. And you may even find it at your nearby pet care shop, where it is frequently used for pedicures.

Through the nearly 50 years since its introduction, this tool has undergone a continuous development. As new materials and manufacturing techniques became available, they were used in newer models. Engineers at Dremel developed a steady stream of attachments to broaden the applications of the Moto-Tool — the router, the drill press, the flexible shaft, and others. These attachments gave the Moto-Tool wide capabilities and led to a new concept: *The Compact Workshop.* Then compact versions of standard workshop tools — the table saw, the disc belt sander, and the lathe — were added to the line to fulfill this concept.

As you can see, the tools in the Dremel workshop aren't new and untried. They have a long history of design, development and use behind them.

The projects

In the pages immediately following each chapter, you will find projects which employ the tool described in that chapter. These projects have been designed not only to help familiarize you with the uses of the tool, but also to provide useful and enjoyable items for you to make.

Our approach to the projects was broad. Selection was difficult, since there are hundreds of things you could make with each tool. We tried to design projects which used a range of materials — wood, metal, plastic, glass — and also provided practice in using the tools in a number of ways.

Then, to enable you to design, engineer and create your own projects, we added two special chapters at the back of the book. In Chapter Eleven, you will find a basic guide to materials. In it is useful information on the working properties, uses and limitations of a wide range of materials. Some are hard to cut; some work easily. Some can be bought readily from local sources. Others can be had only in specialty shops or by mail order. When selecting a material for use in a project, you should find sound guidance here.

In Chapter Twelve, we do our best to turn you into a designer/draftsman/engineer. If you have an idea, it should be created on paper before it can come alive in the workshop. We show you how to make drawings and give you some tips on measurements, templates, etc. Most useful

Introduction

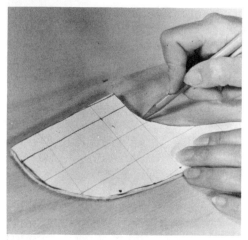

Make a template to enlarge scale drawings or transfer them from sketches and plans to the workpiece.

In Chapter Ten, you will find information on installing new brushes and other servicing of Dremel tools.

Projects come at the end of each chapter and cover a wide variety of items from toys to wine racks.

of all, perhaps, are the instructions on how to scale a design up or down in size. None of this is too technical in nature. It's aim is to be practical.

Your Own Workshop

Chapter Nine is dedicated to the idea that you need a practical place to work. In it, we show ways of laying out a complete compact workshop, using some or all of the Dremel tools. You'll find several different work benches you can build, with a lot of emphasis on easy storage. There is a standard compact workshop, a folding workshop,

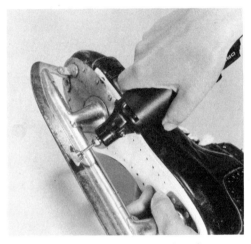

The Quick Fix pages present handy ideas such as this, using a wire brush to remove rust from a skate blade.

The best way to protect valuable items is to engrave your social security number on them.

and even one that rolls away into a closet between jobs.

We had the apartment dweller in mind with this last project. One of the best aspects of compact tools is that by their small scale, they naturally fit right into the apartment craftsman's life. If he can find one corner of a room free from time to time, he can pursue his craftsmanship. We think this concept can bring the joy of creativity to a lot of people who otherwise couldn't experience it.

Service

Chapter Ten covers the care and self servicing of your workshop tools. A little thoughtful care is great preventive medicine, and will give your workshop a long and happy life. Following the advice here, you'll find the care easy.

Chapter Ten explains all about motors and shows in step-by-step fashion how to replace the motor brushes yourself in some models. No trip to the repair shop is needed for these units. There is a Moto-Tool repair kit containing everything you need.

The Quick Fixes

There are hundreds of ways that Dremel compact tools can help solve everyday problems around the house, and to pass some of these ideas along to you, we have included special pages in each chapter. Look for pages headlined *Quick Fixes.* Each features a collection of half a dozen or so good ideas capsuled in single photographs with captions. Some of these are new ways to solve old problems. Others are simply quicker ways to do tasks you are now doing with other tools.

And now it is time to go to work. Turn to Chapter One and find out about the Moto-Tool.

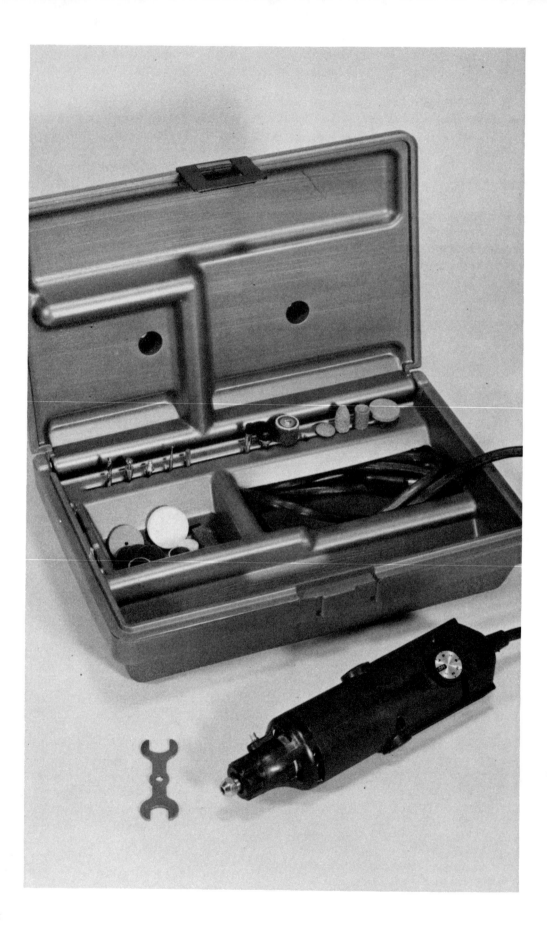

CHAPTER ONE

The Moto-Tool

The Moto-Tool is a handful of high-speed power. It serves as a carver, a grinder, polisher, sander, cutter, power brush, drill, and more.

The Moto-Tool has a small, powerful electric motor, is comfortable in the hand, and is made to accept a large variety of accessories including abrasive wheels, drill bits, wire brushes, polishers, engraving cutters, router bits, and cutting wheels. Accessories come in a variety of shapes and permit you to do a number of different jobs. As you become familiar with the range of accessories and their uses, you will learn just how versatile the Moto-Tool is. You'll see dozens of uses you hadn't thought of before now.

The real secret of the Moto-Tool is its speed. To understand the advantages of its high speed, you have to know that the standard portable electric drill runs at speeds up to 2,800 revolutions per minute. The Moto-Tool operates at speeds up to 30,000 revolutions per minute. The typical electric drill is a low-speed, high-torque tool; the Moto-Tool is just the opposite — a high-speed, low-torque tool. The chief difference to the user is that in the high-speed tools, the speed combined with the accessory mounted in the chuck does the work. You don't apply pressure to the tool, but simply hold and guide it. In the low-speed tools, you not only guide the tool, but also apply pressure to it, as you do, for example, when drilling a hole.

It is this high speed, along with its compact size and wide variety of special accessories, that makes the Moto-Tool different from other power tools. The speed enables it to do jobs low-speed tools cannot do, such as cutting of hardened steel, engraving of glass, etc.

Getting the most out of your Moto-Tool is a matter of learning how to let this speed work for you.

You should not think of the Moto-Tool as a small version of a standard electric drill. While it does do some of the same jobs as an electric drill, it is basically different in concept, design and use. Craftsmen who have used it for years think of it as a "special tool for special jobs," and as "the tool that does jobs which the others don't."

For example, if you want to cut a neat 2-inch square hole in a furnace duct, the Moto-Tool will do the job quickly and easily. Practically no other tool will. Or if a door in your home is slightly misaligned because the house has settled, the latch bolt may no longer enter the strike plate properly, making the door difficult to close or lock. Use the Moto-Tool to cut away just enough of the strike plate so that the latch bolt operates properly.

1

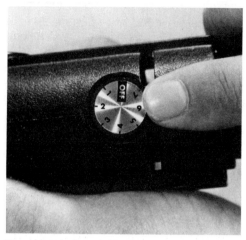

The speed of variable speed models of the Moto-Tool is controlled by setting this dial on the housing.

If you need it, constant-speed models also can have speed control by the addition of a foot control unit.

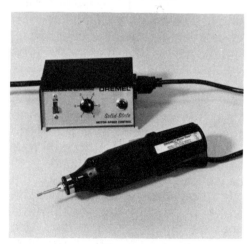

If you choose, dial the speed you need on constant-speed models with this table-top control accessory.

You can do it in minutes. There are literally hundreds of special applications such as these for the Moto-Tool in every home.

In addition to these special applications, think of the Moto-Tool for shaping or removing wood, metal and plastics. This is how wood carvers use the tool, and while you may not be interested in wood carving, there are many times when you want to cut a recess, round a sharp corner, or enlarge an opening.

And then there are the grinding and polishing jobs done by the Moto-Tool. You can sharpen tools, scissors and cutlery, get rid of burrs and unwanted sharp edges, accumulated rust, grind new shapes, etc.

The point is to think of the Moto-Tool for the many jobs it can do because of its own unique properties and capabilities. When you have a job to do, think of the Moto-Tool as one possible solution.

In this chapter we will cover the Moto-Tool — how to set it up, how to use it most effectively, and how to select the right accessory bits for each task. In later chapters, we'll show it fitted with special accessories that convert it to a drill press, a router and other special purpose tools.

A look at the tool

The Moto-Tool is an uncomplicated device, both in construction and operation. The motor is enclosed in a conveniently sized housing. There isn't much to see on the outside of the housing except a nameplate, a power cord, and the chuck, which is a clamping head made to hold the accessories.

There are two basic types of Moto-Tools: constant speed and variable speed models. On constant speed models, there is an ON-OFF switch. When the switch is on, the tool runs at 30,000 RPM (25,000 RPM for Model 245). On variable speed models, there is a small numbered dial which you turn to select the operating speed needed. You can refer to the charts in this chapter to determine the proper speed, based on the material being worked and the type of cutter or other accessory being used. These charts enable you to select both the correct accessory and the optimum speed at a glance.

If you have a constant speed model, you will be able to use many accessories to do a wide assortment of jobs. For the majority of applications, all models of the Moto-Tool should be used at top speed.

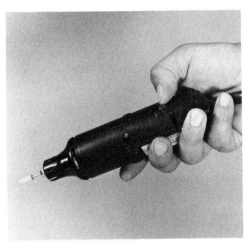

The constant-speed model, which runs at 30,000 RPM (25,000 for Model 245) has an ON-OFF switch on the housing.

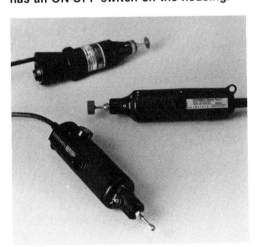

Most work is done at top speed on all Moto-Tool models. Lower speeds are needed only for certain tasks.

Dial Settings for Approximate Revolutions Per Minute Moto-Tool Variable Speed Models No. 350, 370 and 380

Dial Setting	Motor Speed
1	4,000 RPM
2	5,000 RPM
3	6,500 RPM
4	8,000 RPM
5	11,000 RPM
6	16,500 RPM
7	25,000 RPM

(Note: You can dial intermediate settings. For example, a dial setting of 1-1/2 would produce a motor speed of approximately 4,500 RPM.

Dial Settings for Approximate Revolutions Per Minute, using the No. 219 Manually Operated Speed Control with constant speed Moto-Tools, Model Nos. 245, 250, 260, 270 and 280

Dial Setting	Motor Speed
1	500 RPM
2	4,000 RPM
3	12,000 RPM
4	22,000 RPM
5	28,000 RPM

(Note: You can dial intermediate settings. For example, a dial setting of 2-1/2 would produce a motor speed of approximately 8,000 RPM.

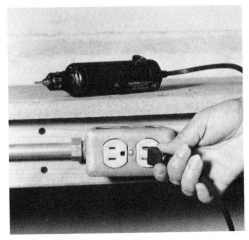

Moto-Tools must be plugged into 3-prong grounded electrical outlets, with hole for plug's grounding pin.

However, for those applications which require lower speeds, such as polishing operations and the use of wire brush accessories, you can add a speed control which will enable you to dial the speeds you want. There are two speed controls available. No. 217 is foot-operated and No. 219 is a table top unit on which you dial the speed you want.

These speed controls must not be used with the variable speed control Moto-Tools, Model 350, 370 and 380.

Electrical considerations

The Moto-Tool is designed for use on the average home electrical circuit. The electrical characteristics are shown on the label of the tool.

The power cord. The power cord of the Moto-Tool has three prongs, two blades and a round grounding pin. This cord is a safety feature which grounds the tool while in use to protect you from electrical shock in the event of a short circuit. The cord contains three wires, two for power and one to contact the ground in a properly grounded wall outlet.

If your wall outlets already have grounded outlet boxes which ac-

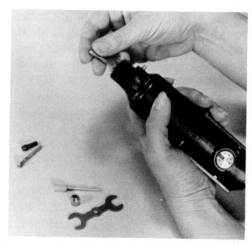

The chuck of the Moto-Tool, consisting of a collet and chuck cap, firmly grips accessories.

The chuck lock pin is depressed to lock the shaft so the cap can be tightened when changing accessories.

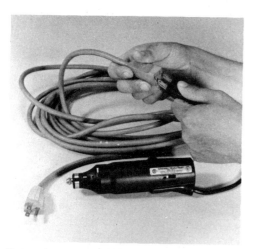

Extension cords used with compact tools must be the heavy-duty 3-conductor type shown here.

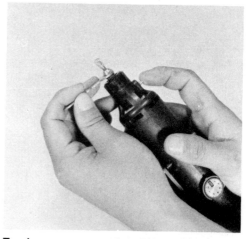

To change accessories, hold the lock pin down as shown and then loosen the chuck cap with the wrench.

cept the three-pronged plugs, you simply plug the Moto-Tool in and go to work. If your outlets have only two-slot receptacles, this means your electrical system hasn't been updated by the installation of grounded outlets. Then you must use an adapter which plugs into the wall outlet and accepts a three-prong plug.

It is important to ground this adapter before plugging the Moto-Tool into it. You do this by removing the small screw which holds the faceplate on the wall outlet. Hold the faceplate in place while you plug in the adapter with its grounding tab or pigtail aligned over the screw hole. Then insert the screw through the tab into the hole in the faceplate and tighten it. This connects the adapter to the ground of your electrical system.

Never use the Moto-Tool or any other electrical equipment which comes with a three-pronged plug until you have grounded the adapter in this manner. It is for your own safety. If your wall outlet already accepts the three-pronged grounded plug, as we said, then the adapter isn't necessary.

Extension cords. When you use an extension cord with the Moto-Tool or any grounded power tool, be sure to use the three-conductor type, with proper three-pronged connectors at each end.

Canadian regulations. Please note that adapters to convert a two-slot receptacle to a three-pronged grounding unit are not allowed in Canada by the Canadian electrical code.

Setting up the Moto-Tool

To begin work with the Moto-Tool, you select the accessory needed, clamp it in the chuck, and turn the switch on.

The chuck. The chuck is the business end of the Moto-Tool and firmly grips each of the accessories you will use. It consists of two parts, the chuck cap and a collet. If you look just above the chuck on the body of the Moto-Tool, you see a small pin or flat plate (depending on the model) protruding slightly. This is the chuck lock pin.

To insert an accessory in the chuck, you perform the following steps:

1. Remove the tool's plug from the electrical outlet.
2. Depress the chuck lock pin.
3. While holding it down, turn the

To remove or change collets, unscrew the chuck cap then pull out the collet under it with your fingers.

Place the new collet in the tool and put the chuck cap back on. Tighten it moderately with the wrench.

When changing accessories, just loosen the chuck cap. There is no need to completely remove it.

Four sizes of collets are available for the Moto-Tool to accommodate different-sized accessory shanks.

Abrasive points wear during use and may get out of balance. You can restore shape by dressing as shown.

For best control in close work, grip the Moto-Tool like a pencil between your thumb and forefinger.

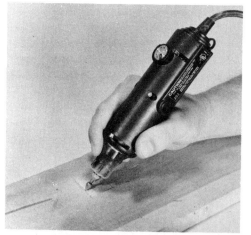

Get feel of carving with high speed cutters by practice on scrap wood. Cut with side of cutter, not the tip.

Use a back-and-forth motion, using only light pressure. Let the speed of the cutter do the work.

shaft by grasping the chuck cap between your fingers. After a partial turn of the shaft, you will feel the lock pin engage, and the shaft will turn no farther.

4. Continue to hold the lock pin down and use the chuck wrench which comes with the Moto-Tool to loosen the chuck cap. The wrench fits easily over the hexagonal sides of the chuck cap.

5. You do not need to remove the chuck cap when changing accessories if the accessories have the same size of shank. Just loosen it enough so the accessory in the chuck can be removed and another inserted in its place.

6. Insert the new accessory into the collet.

7. Use the chuck wrench to tighten the chuck cap while holding the lock pin down. Don't tighten it too much — just enough so the collet grips the shank of the accessory firmly. The Moto-Tool is now ready to use.

NOTE: New collets sometimes are closed too tight to allow easy insertion of an accessory shank. If you have difficulty in inserting an accessory the first time the collet is used, first check to see that the shank of the accessory is the correct size for the collet. If it is, then the problem is that the collet is too tight. To correct this, remove the collet and expand it slightly by pushing the pointed end of a pencil into it. Expand it *only enough* to allow the easy entry of the accessory shank.

Always be sure to unplug the Moto-Tool when you change accessories, change collets, or service it. The ON-OFF switch is placed for convenience during operation but because it is so handy, it could accidentally be turned on during an accessory change, causing injury.

Never depress the lock pin when the Moto-Tool is running, as this could cause damage to the tool.

The collet. There are four different-sized collets available for use with the Moto-Tool. Each one accommodates a shank of a different diameter.

Remove the collet from your Moto-Tool and examine it. To do this, remove the chuck cap and pull the collet out. You see that the collet is a slim steel tube with small slits in its sides, and that the outer end is larger than the shank. The larger outer end is tapered so that when the chuck cap is tightened, it presses the four slitted "fingers" of the collet together to grip the shank (arbor) of any accessory placed in the collet. The grip of these fingers is sufficient to prevent the shank from slipping even under the pressure of cutting, grinding or filing. When the chuck cap is loosened, the fingers spring back from the shank, releasing it.

To replace a collet, simply pull out the old one after removing the chuck cap, and insert the unslotted end of the new one into the hole. Then replace the chuck cap.

It is essential to use the correct size of collet for each accessory. Refer to the accompanying collet chart for sizes and part numbers and for the numbers of drill bits which may be used with each collet.

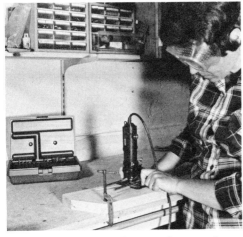

Always keep the work area clean and free of odd pieces and parts. And always wear safety goggles.

This is the "handgrip" method of holding the tool, used for operations such as wire brushing.

Numbered drill bits may be purchased in large hardware stores and machine tool supply houses.

Don't force a large shank into a small collet, since this will damage the collet.

Balancing Accessories

For precision work, it is important that all accessories be inserted in the Moto-Tool so that they are perfectly straight in the collet and thus in balance as they run. Occasionally, you may insert an accessory so that it doesn't sit straight in the col-

When using the saw or cutoff wheels, always use the two-handed grip and have the work firmly clamped.

Be careful as you hold the tool not to cover the air vents with your hand. It may cause overheating.

Collet Sizes, and Drills to be Used in Each Collet

Collet No.	Collet Size	Numbered Drills*	Description —
480	1/8″	1/8″ to #41	Use only with Moto-Tool Nos. 245,
481	3/32″	#39 to #51	250, 260 (Series 3 and later), 270
482	1/16″	#50 to #64	(Series 2 and later), 280 (Series 2
483	1/32″	3/64″ to #78	and later), 370, 380, and Moto-Flex Tool 232 and 332.
434	1/8″	1/8″ to #39	These are earlier collets. Use only
435	3/32″	#40 to #51	with Moto-Tool Nos. 260, 270, and
436	1/16″	#52 to #58	280, Series 1 or earlier.
437	1/32″	#59 to #80	

*Small drill bits in decimal sizes are referred to as Numbered Drills, and sold by these numbers. E.g.: The next size smaller than 1/8″ is #31, which is .120 in. diameter. No. 32 is .110 in diameter. See Chapter Eleven for a complete Numbered Drill Table.

let. You usually can see that the shaft is off center, but if you don't you should be able to tell that something is wrong by the sound and feel of the tool as soon as you turn it on. The accessory will wobble slightly as it turns, creating a vibration.

When this happens, unplug the tool, loosen the chuck cap slightly, and rotate the accessory about a quarter of a turn. This should seat it properly, and you can then re-tighten the chuck cap. Repeat the process if you don't achieve a balance the first time.

A collet will sometimes have a burr or tiny piece of dirt stuck in it which may cause the accessory to wobble. To correct this, remove the collet. Insert a drill of the proper size into the collet, then pinch the four collet jaws tight on it. Slide the drill in and out several times, which permits the drill flutes to remove any burrs or dirt.

If you ever find it impossible to get the accessory in balance, you can assume that the accessory shaft probably has been bent in use, and the accessory should be discarded. It isn't possible to straighten a bent shaft so that it will run in balance at very high speeds.

Abrasive wheel point accessories will wear and change shape during use and thus get out of balance. They can be rebalanced easily. Do this by clamping the wheel point in the collet in the normal manner. Then turn on the Moto-Tool, and hold a dressing stone (Part No. 415) lightly against the spinning abrasive point. This will remove any high spots and true up the abrasive point.

It is a good idea to balance abrasive wheel points before each use.

Accessories to avoid

Keep in mind that the Moto-Tool is a high speed instrument, very different from other tools. The accessories used in it should be designed for balance in high speed operation. You will get the best results by using only Dremel accessories, which have been carefully made for this kind of service.

There are certain types of accessories which should never be used with the Moto-Tool:

Never, for example, use any grinding wheel more than 1 inch in diameter. The extremely high speed of the Moto-Tool may cause large wheels to fly apart, endangering you.

Also, do not use drill bits with shanks larger than 1/8-inch in diameter. Any bit smaller than this may be used as long as it does not protrude more than 1 inch from the end of the collet.

There are miniature flap and disc sanders on the market (not made by Dremel) which will fit the Moto-Tool. Be extremely careful of these. We do not recommend their use. Some of these sanding devices are designed for a maximum rotation of about 15,000 RPM, and these may fly apart when used at higher speeds or will vibrate badly enough to cause tool damage. (Heavy vibration will damage the bearings and commutator). Other flap sanders create a high wind load which overloads the Moto-Tool motor, resulting in overheating and premature

With the Moto-Tool holder, you can use both hands to hold the work and bring it to the spinning accessory.

failure.

You should always wear safety glasses when using the Moto-Tool. The very high speed of the tool can hurl tiny fragments into your eyes and cause severe injury.

Safety considerations

Your Moto-Tool is a high-speed instrument which will perform hundreds of jobs for you. But, like any other instrument, it should be used with respect. Know how to use it, and also know *what not to do* with it. Here are some important operating guides for safe use:

The work area. Work in a clean, uncluttered area so that odd pieces and parts don't get in the way and cause accidents. Don't let the Moto-Tool get wet, or use it in a wet or damp location. Water and electricity are a dangerous combination. Don't use power tools in flammable or explosive atmospheres — in a room full of gas or solvent fumes, for example. Sparking at the motor brushes is normal and could initiate an explosion or fire. And don't use power tools with chemicals or corrosive materials. Finally, always work with plenty of light.

Your clothing. Whenever you work with any power tools, avoid

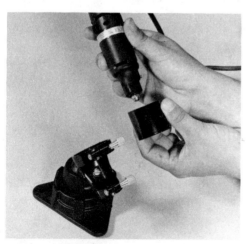

For Moto-Tool Model 260, you must have an adapter sleeve in order to be able to use the tool holder.

loose clothing such as neckties, loose sleeves or cuffs. These can get caught up in the spinning tool and cause injury. Remove jewelry, especially loose jewelry, before you start work. This would include neck chains, loose bracelets or chains on your wrist — anything which might accidentally contact the moving parts of the tool. When working outside or in a damp basement with any electrical tools, including the Moto-Tool, wear rubber-soled shoes and rubber gloves to prevent electrical shock. On wet ground or damp cement, your body may become grounded by contacting the moist surface and literally become a part of the electrical circuit.

Safety equipment. Each of the accessories for your Moto-Tool is designed to cut or abrade the material you are working on, and will throw off tiny bits of the material as it works. Because you are looking toward the work and are not far from it, there is a serious danger that these particles might fly into your eyes, causing serious injury.

There is absolutely no need to endanger your safety when working with power tools, because good safety equipment is readily available and inexpensive. Always wear safety glasses to protect your eyes when using any tool which cuts, abrades or removes material. You also can wear a face mask to protect your skin from flying particles.

Many times you will work with materials which fill the air with dust as you cut or abrade them. A typical example would be when cleaning paint from an item. Another would be when you use the Moto-Tool to clean or level the grout between ceramic tiles. In recent years, we have learned that serious lung problems can result from breathing particulate matter such as this, even occasionally. Protect yourself by wearing a dust mask whenever you create dust as you work.

Handling the tools. Be sure the switch on any tool is in the OFF position before plugging it in. Don't keep your finger on the switch when you carry a tool that is plugged in. You might trip, stumble or bump into something and accidentally turn it on. If you should accidentally drop the Moto-Tool while it is running, *let it fall.* The housing is strong and most likely will survive the fall. More important, however, is the fact that if you grab for the falling tool, your hand might contact the spinning cutter and injure you severely.

Don't force the tool to do a job beyond its capabilities. The tool will not do the job properly, and the situation often is hazardous. The easiest and safest way is to use the right tool for the job. The Moto-Tool is the right tool for hundreds of jobs — and the wrong tool for just about as many.

The work itself. Make sure the work is secure before you begin. Use clamps or a vise to hold it down. Work which is loose or held by one hand while you hold the tool in the other can suddenly wrench loose. This may destroy the work you have been doing, make cuts or gouges you don't want, and perhaps injure you. You do your best work when you have complete control over both the tool and the piece on which you are working.

Have the work conveniently in front of you, so that you don't have to reach when using the Moto-Tool. If you are sitting, you lose some control and can't see the work as well when you reach beyond a convenient distance. If you are standing, you not only lose control but may also lose your footing and balance by reaching. This is doubly hazardous if you are working on a ladder.

When to work. You do your best work when fully alert. Accidents and mistakes occur when you are tired, not feeling well, and after taking drugs, alcohol or medications. Something as simple as a pill to relieve sinus congestion can markedly disturb your vision and judgment, making it unwise to use any power tools. This is not only a matter of safety but also of quality work. A mistake can ruin what you are working on and force you to start over later.

Using the Moto-Tool

The first step in learning to use the Moto-Tool is to get the "feel" of it. Heft it in your hand and feel its weight and balance. Feel the taper

The Finger Grip Attachment was designed to allow the user accurate control close to the workpiece.

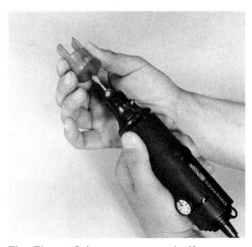

The Finger Grip snaps on and off easily, and must be taken off before you change accessories.

of the housing as it slims down to the chuck end. This taper permits the Moto-Tool to be grasped much like a pen or pencil.

With the Moto-Tool unplugged, hold it in your left hand (if you are right-handed), gripping it in your thumb and forefinger. Now turn the tool until your thumb rests on the chuck locking pin. Press the pin, while turning the chuck with your right hand. As you turn the chuck, you will feel the locking pin engage. You won't be able to turn the chuck any farther.

Keeping pressure on the locking pin, apply the wrench to the chuck. It should loosen readily. You can now remove the accessory in the chuck and insert a new one. The chuck cap need not be removed, only loosened.

Insert the shank (arbor) of the new accessory as far as it will go into the collet. Take care to see that the shank is straight in the collet, and then tighten the chuck cap with the wrench.

Now transfer the Moto-Tool to your right hand (if you are right-handed), gripping it like a pencil between your thumb and forefinger. If you have a variable speed model, turn it on by slowly turning the speed dial and allowing the tool to

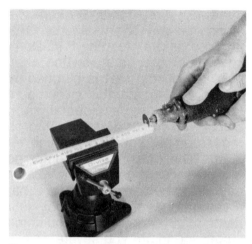

Emery cutting wheel cuts plastic pipe. Most plastics must be cut at low speeds to reduce heat buildup.

Wire brushing must be done at speeds below 15,000 RPM. Here, copper pipe is cleaned before sweat soldering.

Higher speeds, usually maximum, are best for most work, including cutting steel. which is shown here.

Mandrel No. 402 has a small screw at its tip, and is used with emery cutting wheels and sanding discs.

gradually gain speed. If you have a constant speed model, turn the switch to ON.

When you turn on the tool for the first time, hold it away from your face. Accessories can be damaged during handling, and can fly apart as they come up to speed. This is not common, but it does happen.

It is best to practice on scrap materials in the beginning to get the feel of the way the Moto-Tool cuts. Keep in mind that the work is done by the speed of the tool and by the accessory in the chuck. You should not lean on or push the tool into the work. Instead, lower the spinning accessory lightly to the work and allow it to touch the point at which you want cutting (or sanding or etching, etc.) to begin. Concentrate on guiding the tool over the work using very little pressure from your hand. Allow the accessory to do the work.

Usually, it is best to make a series of passes with the tool rather than attempt to do all the work in one pass. To make a cut, for example, pass the tool back and forth over the work, much as you would a small paint brush. Cut a little material on each pass until you reach the desired depth. For most work, the deft, gentle touch is best. With it, you have the best control, are less likely to make errors, and will get the most efficient work out of the accessory.

The pencil grip we described is one way to hold the Moto-Tool. It permits accurate work and good control. A second way is to grip the tool much as you would the hand-grip on a bicycle, with your hand wrapped around the housing and the chuck extending just beyond your thumb and forefinger. This grip must be used for cutoff wheels and saws for maximum control and is often used with polishing, brushing, and grinding accessories. This grip, for example, permits you to bring the saw wheel into play at the proper angle to cut such materials as copper tubing or model railroad rails.

When using the saw wheel (No. 400, 406) or cutoff wheel, (No. 409) *always* have the work securely clamped. Never attempt to hold the work with one hand while using either of these accessories. The reason is that these wheels will grab if they become slightly canted in the groove. Your second hand should be used to steady and guide the hand holding the tool. When a cutoff wheel grabs, the wheel itself usually breaks. When the steel saw wheel grabs, it may jump from the groove and you could lose control

Mandrel No. 401 is used with the felt polishing tip and wheels. Thread the tip on to the screw carefully.

The felt tip must thread down straight on the screw mandrel, and be turned all the way to the collar.

of the tool.

Whenever you hold the tool, be careful not to cover the air vents with your hand. This blocks the air flow and causes the motor to overheat.

There are times when it is most convenient to hold the Moto-Tool in one hand and bring the work to it. This might be true, for example, when polishing a small metal hinge. However, it is always safest to clamp the piece you are working on rather than to hold it in your hand. There is less chance for mistakes when the work is clamped, and the speed of the wheel won't move or throw the work. You have better control over both the work and the tool. As noted a few paragraphs back, *never* hold a workpiece in your hand when using the saw or cutoff wheel.

One excellent solution to the problem of holding the work in your hand is the Moto-Tool Holder (Accessory No. 2217), which is a swivel based clamp made to hold the Moto-Tool as you work, leaving both of your hands free. With the holder mounted on a workbench top, you can swivel the Moto-Tool into the right position, then lock it in place by means of a base lock ring. You can then turn the Moto-Tool on and use both hands to control the work piece as you move it against the spinning accessory. This is an ideal way to use abrasive and polishing wheels when working on small pieces.

(Note that the Moto-Tool holder fits all Moto-Tool models as purchased except Model No. 260. For this model, an adapter sleeve, Part No. 550090, is required.)

The Finger Grip. The Finger Grip attachment (Part No. 616) was developed to enable the user to grip the Moto-Tool closer to the work area without endangering his fingers. It allows very accurate control over the movement of accessories for precision work. A shaped plastic piece that fits over the tapered end of the tool, it snaps on and off easily when you want to change accessories.

The operating speeds

For the great majority of applications, the Moto-Tool is most efficient when operated at or near top speed. However, certain materials — some plastics, for example — require a relatively slow speed because at high speeds the friction of the tool generates heat and

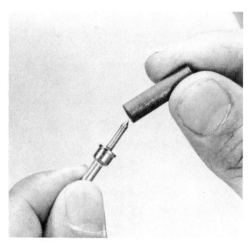

The machine-screw threading on Mandrel No. 424 threads into polishing point No. 427.

This and other threaded mandrels must be screwed firmly down to the collar before being used.

causes the plastic to melt.

Slow speeds (usually 15,000 RPM or less) usually are best for polishing operations employing the felt polishing accessories. They may also be best for working on delicate projects such as "eggery" work, delicate wood carvings, and fragile model parts. You should always do polishing with wire brush accessories at slower speeds, and never higher than 15,000 RPM.

Higher speeds are better for carving, cutting, routing, shaping, cutting dadoes or rabbets in wood. Hardwoods, metals, and glass require high speed operation, and drilling should also be done at high speeds.

The point to remember is this: You can do the great majority of your work with the constant speed model at its regular speed of 30,000 RPM. But for certain materials and types of work, you need slower speeds — which is the reason the variable speed models and the speed control units were developed.

To aid you in determining the optimum operational speeds for different materials and different accessories, we have constructed a series of tables. By referring to these tables, you can discover the recommended speeds for each type of material and for each type of accessory. Look these tables over and become familiar with them.

Ultimately, the best way to determine the correct speed for work on any material is to practice for a few minutes on a piece of scrap, even after referring to the chart. You can quickly learn that a slower or faster speed is more effective just by observing what happens as you make a pass or two at different speeds. When working with plastic, for example, start at a slow rate and increase the speed until you observe that the plastic is melting at the point of contact. Then back the speed off slightly to get the optimum working speed.

Some rules of thumb in regard to speed:

1. Plastics and materials that melt at low temperatures should be cut at low speeds.

2. Polishing, buffing and cleaning with a wire wheel should be done at speeds below 15,000 RPM to prevent damage to the wheel.

3. Soft wood should be cut at high speeds.

4. Iron or steel should be cut at top speed if using a tungsten carbide accessory, but at slower speeds if using high speed steel cutters. If a high speed steel cutter starts to chatter — this normally means it is running to slow.

5. Aluminum, copper alloys, lead alloys, zinc alloys, and tin may be cut at any speed, depending on the type of cutting being done. Use paraffin or other suitable lubricant on the cutter to prevent the cut material from adhering to the cutter teeth.

Increasing the pressure on the tool is *not* the answer when it is not cutting as you think it should. Perhaps you should be using a different cutter, and perhaps an adjustment in speed would solve the problem. But leaning on the tool seldom helps.

The Moto-Flex Tool

The Dremel 232 and 332 Moto-Flex Tools perform the same functions as other Moto-Tools, but have some distinct advantages. They have more powerful motors and are fitted with neoprene coated flexible shafts 34 inches long. They are mounted on swivel bases but also have hangers so they may be wall mounted instead of bench mounted, if you prefer.

The Model 232 has a constant-speed motor which turns at 28,000 RPM. The 332 Moto-Flex Tool is a variable speed version with speeds from 7,500 to 25,000 RPM.

Both Moto-Flex Tools have the same collets as the Moto-Tool, and take all of the same accessories. They are especially convenient for working in tight places where the full-size Moto-Tool won't fit, such as in porting and relieving engines, for example. The flexible shaft provides excellent finger-tip control for very accurate cutting, grinding, polishing, carving, and sanding. The small pencil grip hand piece creates less fatigue when the tool is used for long periods of time.

Another important advantage is that the work is done away from the fan and bearings of the motor. If you work in abrasive materials, such as fiber glass, stone or glass, this feature eliminates the problem of fine abrasive materials working their way into the vital parts of the motor.

Accessories for the Moto-Tool

As you can see from the illustrations in this chapter, the number and variety of accessories for the Moto-Tool are almost limitless. There is a category of accessory

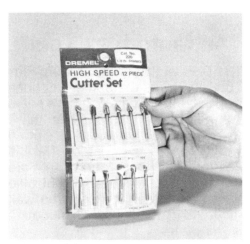

Cutters and other accessories can be purchased individually or in sets in convenient plastic wallets.

suited to almost any job you might have to do — and a variety of sizes and shapes within each category which enables you to get the perfect accessory for every need.

Collets. If you expect to use a variety of accessories, we recommend that in the beginning you purchase a complete set of four collets. Store these so that you will have the proper size of collet for any accessory or drill bit you might want to use.

Mandrels. A mandrel is a shank with a threaded or screw head, and mandrels are required when you use polishing accessories, cutting wheels, sanding discs, and polishing points. The reason mandrels are used is that sanding discs, cutting wheels and similar accessories must be replaced frequently. The mandrel is a permanent shank, allowing you to replace only the worn head when necessary, thus saving the expense of replacing the shaft each time. If each sanding disc or cutting wheel had its own shank, the cost would be much greater. There are three mandrels:

No. 401. This is a screw mandrel used with the felt polishing tip and felt polishing wheels. The end is threaded, and screws into a hole in the center of the polishing accessory. When the polishing accessory has become worn, it can be replaced by threading it off the mandrel and threading a new one in its place.

No. 402. This is a mandrel with a small screw at its tip, and is used with emery cutting wheels, sanding discs, and polishing wheels. The accessory is fitted to the end of the mandrel and held in place by tightening the tiny screw.

No. 424. This is a mandrel with a threaded tip which threads into the polishing point accessory No. 427.

There are eleven categories of accessories for the Moto-Tool. A brief description of each category

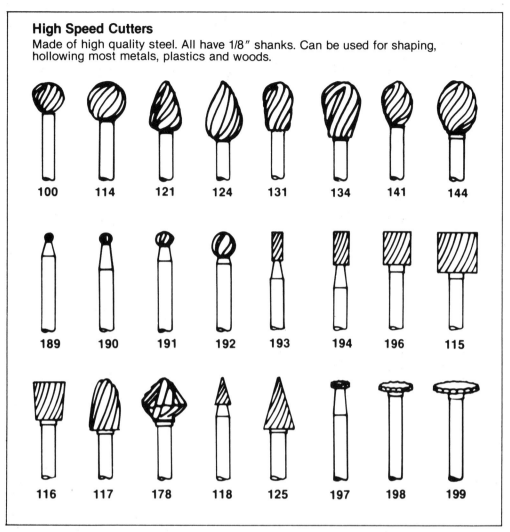

High Speed Cutters
Made of high quality steel. All have 1/8″ shanks. Can be used for shaping, hollowing most metals, plastics and woods.

100 114 121 124 131 134 141 144

189 190 191 192 193 194 196 115

116 117 178 118 125 197 198 199

High speed cutters, in 24 sizes and shapes, are used for carving and shaping wood, soft metal and plastics. All have 1/8-inch shanks. Nos. 197, 198, and 199 are small cutting wheels for slot cuts.

follows, so that you can become familiar with them. Later, we will discuss specific applications and methods for each type of accessory.

High speed cutters. Available in several dozen shapes, high speed cutters are used in carving, cutting, and slotting in wood, plastics, and soft metals such as aluminum, copper, and brass. These are the accessories to use for freehand routing or carving in wood or plastics, and for precision cutting.

Tungsten carbide cutters. These are tough, long-lived cutters for use on hardened steel, fired ceramics, and other very hard materials. They

can be used for engraving on tools and garden equipment.

Small engraving cutters. This group has a wide variety of sizes and shapes, and are made for intricate work on ceramics (greenware), wood carvings, jewelry, and scrimshaw. They often are used in making complicated printed circuit boards. They should not be used on steel and other very hard materials but are excellent on wood, plastics, and soft metals.

Abrasive wheel points. Round, pointed, flat — you name the shape and there is one available in this category. These are made of aluminum oxide and cover virtually every possible kind of grinding application. Use them for sharpening lawn mower blades, screwdriver tips, knives, scissors, chisels and other cutting tools. Use them to remove flash from metal castings, deburring any metal after cutting, smoothing welded joints, grinding off rivets, and removing rust. Check the pictures of these accessories to determine which shapes you might need.

In machine shops, high speed steel drills and cutters normally are ground on aluminum oxide wheels.

Silicon carbide grinding points. Tougher than the aluminum oxide

points, these are made especially for use on hard materials such as glass and ceramics. Typical uses might be the removal of stilt marks and excess glaze on ceramics and engraving on glass.

For quick identification around your workbench, silicon carbide accessories are always gray-green in color. Aluminum oxide accessories can be any color but are most often brown, white or blue.

Polishing accessories. These include an impregnated polishing point and an impregnated polishing wheel for bringing metal surfaces to a smooth finish; a felt polishing tip

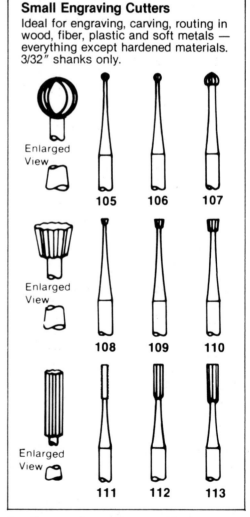

Tungsten Carbide Cutters

Carbide cutters outlast high speed cutters many times over. 1/8″ shanks with maximum cutting head of 1/8″.

9901 9902 9903 9904

9905 9906 9907 9908

9909 9910 9911 9912

Tough carbide cutters outlast others and hold sharpness longer. Twelve sizes and shapes are available.

Small Engraving Cutters

Ideal for engraving, carving, routing in wood, fiber, plastic and soft metals — everything except hardened materials. 3/32″ shanks only.

Enlarged View

105 106 107

Enlarged View

108 109 110

Enlarged View

111 112 113

Small engraving cutters are ideal for engraving intricate lettering and designs on wood, plastic, metals.

and felt polishing wheel, and a cloth polishing wheel, all used for polishing plastics, metals, jewelry, small parts. Also included in this group is a polishing compound (No. 421) for use with the felt and cloth polishers.

Polishing points make a very smooth surface, but a high luster is obtained using felt or cloth wheels and polishing compound.

No polishing compound is needed when using the rubber polishing points in either set No. 201 or 202. Use them for general or fine polishing on precious and semi-precious stones, metals, ceramics, plastics and glass.

Sanding accessories. Sanding discs in fine, medium and coarse grades are made to fit mandrel No. 402. They can be used for nearly any small sanding job you might have, from model making to fine furniture finishing. In addition, there is the drum sander, a tiny drum which fits into the Moto-Tool and makes it possible to shape wood, smooth fiber glass, sand inside curves and other difficult places, and other sanding jobs. You replace the sanding bands on the drum as they become worn and lose their grit. Bands come in fine and coarse grades.

Mounted Aluminum Oxide Wheel Points

Highest industrial quality with long abrasive life. 1/8″ shanks. Ideal for sharpening, deburring and general purpose grinding.

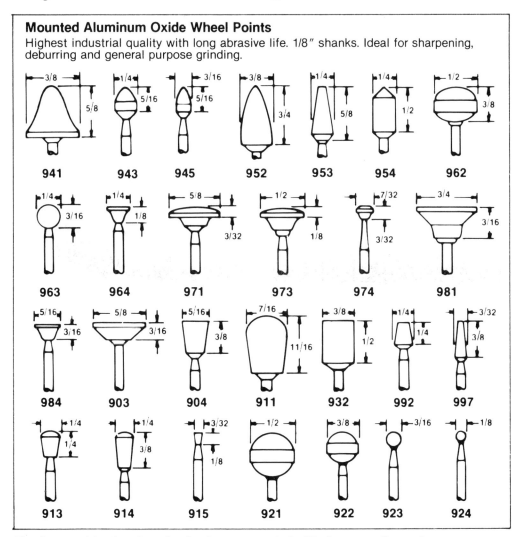

Aluminum oxide abrasive wheel points are made in 27 shapes to fit nearly every possible grinding use. Use them for sharpening tools, deburring castings, grinding down sharp points or edges on metal parts.

Miscellaneous Accessories
Plain Shaped Aluminum Oxide Wheel Points

Ideal for sharpening, deburring and general purpose grinding. All have 1/8" shanks.

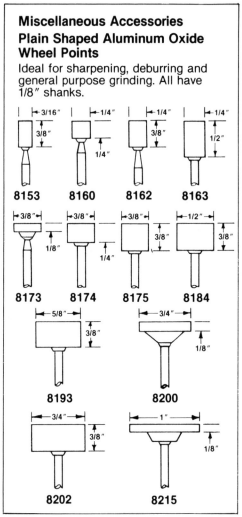

Plain shaped aluminum oxide wheel points have 1/8 inch shanks, come in 12 sizes.

Silicon Carbide Grinding Points

Made especially for grinding on hard steel, ceramics, glass and other hard materials. 1/8" shanks.

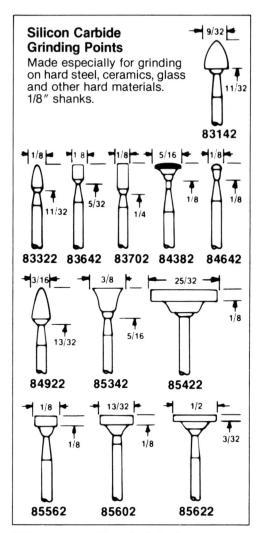

When you need to grind steel, glass or ceramics, these silicon grinding points are the answer.

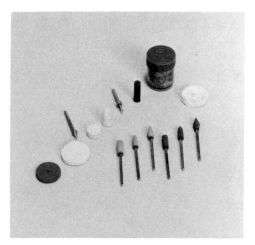

The polishing group includes felt, cloth, rubber and impregnated accessories and polishing compound.

Wire brushes. Three different shapes of wire brushes are available. These should not be used at speeds greater than 15,000 RPM. They remove rust from tools and other metal surfaces, and clean and burnish metal parts. Use for such jobs as cleaning electrical connectors to assure good conduction.

Bristle brushes. These are excellent cleaning tools on silverware, jewelry and antiques. The three shapes make it possible to get into tight corners and other difficult places. Bristle brushes can be used with polishing compound for faster cleaning or polishing.

Optimal R.P.M. for Selected Materials

The specific materials used to determine optional rpm were:

soft wood	— sugar pine, yellow pine, mahogany
hard wood	— maple, oak
plastic	— methyl methacralate (Plexiglass)
ferrous metal	— 1020 cold rolled, 4140
nonferrous metal	— 2024 T-4 aluminum, half hard brass, half hard copper
fibre	— Formica (industrial electrical grade)
stone	— Berea sand stone
shell	— bivalve
ceramic	— clay bisque
glass	— cast, bottle, untempered

The accessories selected for these tests were divided into seven (7) categories and their optimal operating speeds were determined for selected materials from the above list. The determined speeds were found to be extremely sensitive to tool pressure, pressure angle, tool feed direction relative to cutter rotation (for example, climb cutting) and tool feed direction relative to grain direction (in the case of woods).

Aluminum Oxide Wheel Points (RPM)

Catalog Number	Plastic	Nonferrous Metals	Stone	Shell
915, 923, 924, 945, 997, 8153	6,500	16,500	16,500	8,500
913, 914, 943, 953, 954, 963, 964, 974, 992, 8160, 8162, 8163	6,500	11,000	14,000	8,500
904, 922, 932, 941, 952, 984, 8173, 8174, 8175	5,250	9,500	9,500	7,250
911, 921, 962, 973, 8184	4,000	8,000	9,500	7,250
903, 971, 8193	4,000	8,000	8,000	6,500
981, 8200, 8202	4,000	6,500	8,000	6,500
8125	4,000	6,500	6,500	6,500

Rubber Polishing Points (RPM)

Catalog Number	Ferrous Metal	Nonferrous Metal	Stone	Ceramics
461, 462, 463		6,500	6,500	
464, 465, 466			4,000*	5,000

Excessive cutter wear at speeds over 25,000 RPM

Silicon Grinding Points (RPM)

Catalog Number	Ferrous Metal	Stone	Ceramics	Glass
83322, 83642, 83702, 84642	14,000	8,500	11,000	11,000
83142, 84382	14,000	6,500	11,000	8,000
84922	9,500	8,000	11,000	9,500
85422	7,250	6,500	11,000	6,500
85562	14,000	8,000	11,000	8,000
85342, 85602	11,000	6,500	11,000	8,000
85622	11,000	4,000	11,000	8,000

Small Engraving Cutters (RPM)

Catalog Number	Soft Wood	Hard Wood	Plastic	Nonferrous Metal	Fibre
105, 108	25,000	25,000	18,000	20,000	16,500
106, 109	25,000	25,000	14,000	20,000	16,500
107, 110	25,000	25,000	11,000	16,500	11,000
111	25,000*	25,000*	18,000*	20,000	16,500
112	25,000*	25,000*	14,000*	20,000	16,500
113	25,000*	25,000*	11,000*	16,500	11,000

Speed for light cuts, caution burning on deep grooves

Cutting Accessories (RPM)

Catalog Number	Soft Wood	Hard Wood	Ferrous Metals
400	25,000	25,000	
406	25,000	25,000	
409			25,000

High Speed Router Bits (RPM)

Catalog Number	Soft Wood	Hard Wood
610	16,500	16,500
612, 613, 614, 632, 640	16,500	14,000*
650, 652	25,000	25,000*
654	25,000	14,000*

Depending on cutting direction relative to grain

High Speed Cutters (RPM)

Catalog Number	Soft Wood	Hard Wood	Plastics	Ferrous Metal	Nonferrous Metal
100, 121, 131, 141	25,000	25,000	16,500	11,000	20,000
114, 124, 134, 144	25,000	16,500	11,000	9,500	14,000
189, 190	25,000	25,000	11,000	25,000	25,000
118, 191, 193	25,000	25,000	11,000	16,500	25,000
192, 194	25,000	25,000	11,000	14,000	16,500
116, 117, 125, 196	25,000	16,500	11,000	8,000	11,000
115, 178	25,000	25,000	11,000	6,500	9,500
197	20,000	14,000	11,000	11,000	16,500
198	20,000	14,000	14,000	11,000	16,500
199	20,000	14,000	9,500	8,000	11,000

Tungsten Carbide Cutters (RPM)

Catalog Number	Soft Wood	Hard Wood	Plastic	Ferrous Metal	Nonferrous Metal
9901, 9902, 9903, 9904, 9905, 9906, 9912	20,000	20,000	8,000	11,000	16,500
9907, 9908, 9909, 9910, 9911	25,000	25,000	8,000	11,000	16,500

The R.P.M. speeds shown in charts on pages 21, 22, and 23 are the most desirable for the types of materials shown. However, the optimum speeds will be affected by tool pressure, tool feed direction, type of wood and moisture content.

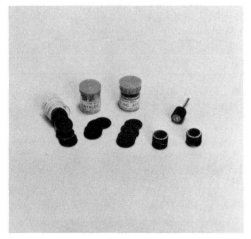

Sanding accessories include sanding drums in two abrasive grades and discs in three to cover most needs.

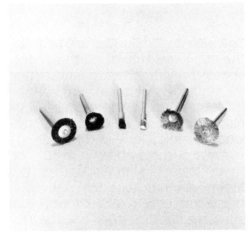

Wire and bristle brushes for rust removal and polishing chores.

Steel saws, Nos. 400 and 406, and emery cutting wheels, No. 409, cut or slot wood, plastic and metal.

All cutting is done with the sides of the cutters, not the bottoms or tips, which cut very poorly.

Cutting wheels. These are thin discs of emery used for slicing, cutting off and similar operations. Use them for cutting off frozen bolt heads and nuts, or to reslot a screw head which has become so damaged that the screwdriver won't work in it. Fine for cutting BX cable, small rods, tubing, cable and cutting rectangular holes in sheet metal.

Steel saws. There are two tiny steel saw accessories, one .005-in. thick, and the other .023-in. thick. You can use them to cut or slot wood, fiber glass, plastics, and soft metals.

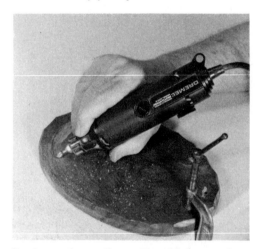

Basic carving action with a high speed cutter is side-to-side movement. Do not push cutter away from you.

High speed cutters

The high speed cutters are perhaps the most versatile of all the accessories. They range from ball shapes to cones to circular cutters like thick miniature saw blades. They can be used on hardwood or softwood, plastics, and soft metals.

Always remember as you use these that it is the speed of the Moto-Tool that does the work. Use these cutters with a light touch, and allow the cutting edges and the very high speeds to do the work. Do not apply much pressure as you work. It isn't necessary.

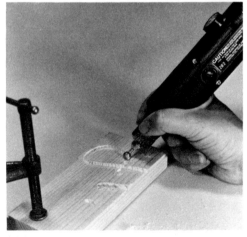

When carving, rest the heel of the hand on the table as a pivot point and guide tool with your fingers.

The most common use of these cutters is carving in wood. Their basic job is to remove material. Each cutter type will remove material in a different amount and shape. Your first task in selecting the cutter to use is to decide the shape you want to cut.

The best way to learn to use these cutters is to try them. Find a block of soft wood for a practice session. Clamp this to your work table. Fit a cutter (perhaps a No. 100 or a No. 114) into your Moto-Tool and turn the tool on at high speed.

Before you begin, realize that cutting is done with the sides of the cutter. Material is cut away as the spinning side of the cutter comes in contact with it. The end or bottom of the cutter cuts very poorly, and when you try to cut with it, the cutter will jump and chatter.

Now gently contact the wood with the cutter, getting the feel of the way it bites into the wood and tries to move away from it. Press down very lightly. If you are using either of the suggested cutters you will make a semicircular depression. Keeping very light pressure on for control, tilt the cutter so that the side contacts the wood, and guide it to the left. Cutters cut best when moved in a direction that opposes cutter rotation. It will remove material in its path and make a groove in the wood. Try moving in different directions and cutting with the cutter at different angles. You soon discover how to control the direction and depth of the cut, and the amount of material removed.

Most carving is done in a side-to-side stroking motion, with most material being removed during the stroke which opposes the rotation of the cutter. You also can stroke toward you. Do not push the cutter away from you and into the wood, because the center point of the cutter does little or no cutting and cannot clear itself of chips.

When carving, the heel of the hand rests on the table or workbench and serves as a pivot point. The tool is guided by the fingers.

You'll note that the cutter tends to move with the grain of the wood and to move in a curve if you don't control it. If you gently but firmly guide the Moto-Tool, you'll slice cleanly through the grain and can guide it where you want it to go. This is the first lesson to learn: how to guide the cutter with your fingers to cut the shape you want, firmly resisting its tendency to curve and follow the wood grain. Note that downward pressure on the tool is slight, but firm guiding is necessary.

As you begin to feel the way the cutter works, you can start carving simple practice shapes. Use the Moto-Tool like a paint brush, moving it back and forth to create shapes.

Note. If you hear the Moto-Tool start to slow down as you work, you know that you are bearing down too much. You aren't letting the high speed of the tool do the cutting. With a little practice, you will discover the right amount of pressure to apply.

The different sizes and shapes of high speed cutters are designed to enable you to make different types of cuts, and to work on different shapes. Some are for making rounded shapes; some are for cutting fine lines, such as the lines in a carved feather; others are for detail work — the kind you might encounter in carving the eyes in a horse's head.

Once you have gained the feel of cutting with a cutter, the best way to learn the use of each cutter is to "make chips" — that is, do a few hours of whittling on scrap wood. Try each cutter you have. Carve a simple flower into a board and use the different cutters to rough out and then finish the shapes. The more chips you make, the more you will learn about how cutters work.

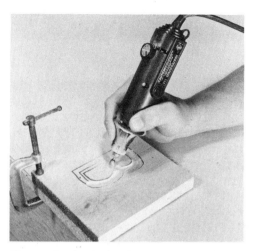

Use a simple design in scrap wood for control practice and to learn the cutting action of each cutter.

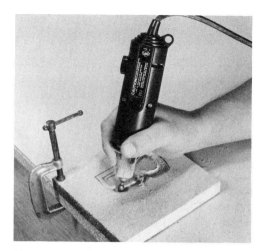

Here, to square up the side of the carving, the side of the cutter is worked against the vertical edge.

Use the smaller cutters for smaller work, and larger one for big work. After a bit, you will recognize the kind of work each cutter does best.

To deepen a cut as you carve in these practice sessions, don't bear down hard on the tool. Instead, make one pass, allowing the tool to cut at its own speed, with very light pressure from your hand. Then make a second and third pass. Each pass will remove more material and deepen the cut.

All of the high speed cutters can be used freehand, in the same way that an artist uses a paint brush. It will take a bit of practice to get to the point where you can cut exactly what you want freehand. You must hold the Moto-Tool firmly without applying excessive pressure to the cutter. The mastering of this seeming paradox requires practice. But you will acquire the knack in a short time if you stay with it. All at once, you will discover that you know how to do it, and that the tool is doing exactly what you want.

Here are some comments on the cutters, to help you in your selection:

Nos. 121 and 124. Flame shaped with cutting edges up and over the rounded tops, these cutters are used in an almost horizontal position. This assures that the greatest cutting area contacts the wood and material removal is fast. Keep your touch light.

Nos. 131 and 134. Pear shaped cutters with the cutting end larger than the arbor end. These cutters remove stock in a hurry, even with a very light touch.

Nos. 189, 190, 191, and 192. These ball-shaped burrs can be used to shape fine detail in wood carving, make small depressions, even hollow out the inside of a carved or turned wooden shape. The four are the same shape, but differ in size.

Nos. 193, 194, and 196. These are straight sided cutters with flat bottoms, and can be used to finish the side of a groove started with a round shaped cutter. With them you can make square-shouldered grooves and cuts. Remember that the cutting surfaces are *the sides* of these cutters, not the bottom.

No. 117. This has a round end but is wider at the top, so it can be used to blend from curved shape into a straight sided shape. This is a large cutter, with a lot of cutting edge, so be careful. Do not apply pressure. Let the cutter do the work.

No. 178. This looks like a flattened diamond. It has cutting edges on both the pointed end of the diamond and on the flatter top end.

This cutter is ideal for fast removal of material by using a stroking motion toward you or side-to-side stroking motion.

Nos. 118 and 125. Use these for removing small amounts of material and for carving fine detail. They give you good control for delicate cuts.

Nos. 197, 198, and 199. These look like small circular saws, and can be used to make narrow slits when the Moto-Tool is moved at right angles to the line of the cut (that is, when they are literally used like little saw blades.) Be very careful to keep these cutters straight in the grooves they are cutting. If you turn them even slightly, they will suddenly grab and the tool will jump from the groove. You could lose control of it.

Tungsten carbide cutters

Tungsten carbide cutters are hard and can be used to engrave and carve metal, make metal castings smooth, and shape details on ceramics. Carbide cutters can also be used to carve in alabaster and other soft stone. And they can be used for such difficult jobs as fitting ceramic tile around plumbing and wall switch boxes in the kitchen and bathroom. The speed of the Moto-Tool and the hardness of these cutters combine to give you a cutting power on extremely hard surfaces that few other tools can provide. All tungsten carbide cutters use the 1/8-inch collet.

One special use of tungsten cutters is on plastics with fiber glass or mineral fillers. In these materials, the filler is mixed with the plastic before casting. The fillers are very abrasive and may ruin other cutters, but tungsten cutters will work. Do not, however, use these cutters on unfilled plastics.

You should always wear safety glasses when using the Moto-Tool, but when doing work with tungsten carbide cutters, it is a good idea also to wear a face mask or shield. This full face protection prevents particles of metal or glass from becoming embedded in the skin of your face.

Caution: Never use a tungsten carbide cutter for drilling and never use it to enlarge a hole that is not already 50 percent larger in diameter than the cutter. The tooth form of a carbide cutter will cause it to grab and fracture in this kind of use, possibly creating a hazard.

A rundown of the tungsten carbide cutters:

Nos. 9901, 9902, 9903, and 9904. These all have the appearance of round files if you look at them closely, and are used much in the same manner as a file, but with power. These little rotating files will quickly remove flash from castings, smooth the rough edges of metal items such as copper pipe, and even dull the edges of freshly cut glass. The sharp edges of the 9901 and 9902 are also great for doing line work when creating a picture or design on glass.

Nos. 9905 and 9906. These are rounded cutters for carving designs in metal and other hard materials. They will stay sharp for a long time, even when used frequently.

Nos. 9907, 9908, and 9909. These cutters are ideal for carving metal. No. 9907 could be used to engrave your tools for identification. You can write your name on saw blades, both hand and circular, and on the hard steel of hammer heads, wood and lathe chisels.

No. 9910, 9911, and 9912. Number 9910 acts like a tapered round file, enabling you to work into depressions and to reach some interior surfaces. Just be sure the area in which you work is at least half again as large as the cutter. Number 9911 is much like the dentist's burr, with which you can cut into surfaces and then work down inside of the cut. Number 9912 has a flat bottom, and is ideal for making sharp corners in recesses created by round cutters. Use the round cutter to cut the recess to nearly the desired depth, then use No. 9912 to cut the sides of the recess, squaring them at the bottom.

Held at the proper angle, No. 9912 also will produce very fine lines, such as the outlines of feathers in a bird's wing, in wood or metal carving and engravings in glass and ceramics.

Small engraving cutters

These are very fine accessories for engraving fine lines, and require the use of the 3/32-in. collet. A glance will show you that these cutters have very small heads, and we recommend that you purchase a magnifying lamp or clamp-on magnifying device to use with them. That way, you can see just what the cutters are doing and can improve the accuracy of your work. Because you work so close to engraving work, be sure to wear safety glasses when using these cutters.

Nos. 105, 106 and 107. These have tiny ball ends, with No. 105 being the smallest and No. 107 being the largest. They are excellent as are all of the small engraving cutters, for carving very fine detail. Practice will teach you which of this series of cutters is best for each type of cut.

Nos. 108, 109 and 110. These cutters have flat ends and side flutes. Keep in mind that only the side flutes cut. The cutters are wider at the bottom than at the top, and thus can be used for undercutting, where the bottom of the slot or the shape is wider than the top, or for tiny fine line detailing.

Nos. 111, 112, and 113. Good for cleaning out and shaping deep, narrow grooves and similar work, these cutters are straight sided with relatively long cutting flutes.

When it comes to selecting a cutter, individual tastes vary. Much depends on the type of work, the type of material, your style of carving, and how much pressure you use. Three experts, asked to select the right cutter for a job, might choose three different cutters, and each would end up with a fine piece of work. Thus it is difficult to make specific recommendations on the type of work each cutter can do.

The best way to select a cutter is to select one that works in the material you are cutting and one that is the best size (small cutters for fine work and big cutters for large work), and then try two or three similarly shaped cutters in that category. You will quickly learn which cuts best for you.

Aluminum oxide wheel points

Aluminum oxide wheel points are miniature grinding wheels made in 27 different shapes, which means that there is a size or shape for virtually every possible grinding application. All require a 1/8-inch collet. They are excellent for sharpening any tool blade, for removing flash from metal castings, smoothing welded joints, grinding off rivets, and for any job that requires grinding. They can be used on any metal and are used to sharpen small drills, milling cutters, router bits and other tools made of high speed steel. Also good for restoring a screwdriver blade that has been damaged. Just grind it back to the proper shape.

Removing rust is one of the jobs these points do very well. Because of the variety available, they can be used on very complex shapes. If you have ever despaired of removing rust from small grooves and complicated castings, you'll find these points are the solution to your problem. If you use touch-up paint on your car, use one of these cutters to clean all rust from the spot first. Apply an undercoat to the bright metal, and then the final finish.

A face mask as well as safety goggles should be worn when using these points to protect your skin and eyes from flying bits of metal and grit.

In use, aluminum oxide wheel points wear and change shape somewhat. This tends to make them chatter at high speeds in the Moto-Tool and will cause roughness on the surface you are grinding. You can reshape any abrasive wheel by holding it lightly against a dressing stone (Part No. 415) for a few seconds at high speed. This returns the point to true roundness by removing any high spots, and also removes any glazing that might have occurred from grinding soft metals such as aluminum or lead. These materials tend to clog the pores of abrasive wheels, which then lose much of their abrasive quality. A treatment with the dressing stone makes them abrasive once more.

If you need an abrasive wheel point of a special shape for a particular job, and none of the available points will do, you can use the dressing stone to make it. Just reshape a wheel point you have which is close to the needed shape.

It is important that accessories in the Moto-Tool always run in a balanced condition. For this reason, it is a good idea to dress any abrasive wheel for a few seconds right after installing it in the Moto-Tool and before you begin work. This provides extra assurance of balanced running.

In addition to the 27 different shapes of aluminum oxide wheel points, there are a dozen plain shaped aluminum oxide wheels. These are plain round wheels in diameters ranging from 3/16 to 1 inch, and in thickness from 1/8 to 1/2 inch.

These plain wheel points are used like miniature grinding wheels wherever flat surfaces or edges are to be smoothed, deburred or shaped.

Silicon carbide grinding points

Silicon carbide grinding points are very hard, and have been designed for use on extremely hard materials such as glass, ceramics and stone. There are a dozen shapes available and all require 1/8-inch collets. They can be used to shape minor gemstones, carve pottery, remove excess hardened glaze from ceramics and engrave on glass. Plan to use them on any extremely hard material, where other abrasives won't work, for smoothing, cutting, and shaping.

Polishing accessories

There are three types of polishing accessories available. Polishing Point No. 427 and Polishing Wheel No. 425 belong to the first group. They are impregnated with fine emery and are ideal for polishing metals to a smooth finish.

No. 427 is 1/4 inch in diameter and 7/8 inch long, and is used with mandrel No. 424.

No. 425, the polishing wheel, is 1/8 inch thick and 7/8 inch in diameter, and is used with mandrel No. 402. You will remember that the reason for the use of mandrels is that they are permanent shafts which do not have to be replaced when the head becomes worn, and so keep the cost of replacement low.

Both the point and the wheel can be shaped to keep them in balance by holding them against a dressing stone — just as was described for the aluminum oxide wheel points.

Cloth and felt polishing accessories, which you can charge with polishing compound (Part No. 421), are the second type of polishing accessory.

No. 423. The cloth polishing wheel is 1 inch in diameter, and is used with mandrel No. 402. Use it for polishing all types of metals and plastics. It is especially good on jewelry and fine silver. You can buff with the wheel itself, or use it with the polishing compound. Polish a scratched watch crystal with this wheel and polishing compound and the scratches will disappear. Remember that polishing is done at slower speeds so the wheel will not wear too rapidly. Polishing plastics at too high a speed can create enough heat from friction to ruin the surface.

Nos. 414, 422, and 429. These are accessories made of felt. No. 422 is a bullet-shaped felt tip that is 3/8 inch in diameter, used with mandrel No. 401. It is excellent for polishing

in corners and hard-to-get-at places. You can use it alone or charged with polishing compound. Nos. 414 and 429 are felt wheels, also used with mandrel No. 401. No. 414 is 1/2 inch in diameter; No. 429 is 1 inch in diameter. You can use these for polishing open areas on metal and plastic items.

Always remember when polishing valuable gold, sterling silver and plated items that you want to remove accumulated dirt and oxidization, but not the precious metal. For this reason, be cautious about polishing with any abrasive material. The Dremel polishing compound is "jeweler's rouge," used by jewelers for polishing, and will not harm precious metals. The compound can be used with either cloth or felt accessories. Just touch the compound lightly to the revolving accessory to charge it with polish.

The third type of polishing accessories are the rubber polishing wheels, Nos. 201, 202 and 203. These require 3/32-inch collets. The chief function of the rubber accessories is to make an area very smooth. After polishing with these, complete the work by burnishing with the cloth polishing wheel. This will remove the swirl marks left by the rubber polisher and give the

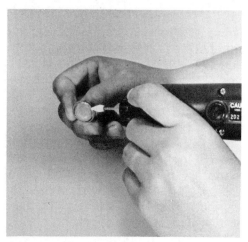

Rubber polishing tips bring a high burnish to precious and non-precious metals, gemstones and ceramics.

The cloth polishing wheel is good on jewelry and fine silverware. Use it with polishing compound.

work a very high luster.

The rubber polishing wheels come in sets of three and do not require polishing compound when used. No. 201 is colored blue for identification, and is intended for general polishing on most metals and stones. No. 202, colored tan, is for polishing precious metals, non-metal surfaces, ceramics, and stones. No. 203 is a set of six wheels, three each of No. 201 and No. 202.

Sanding accessories

For sanding, you can use either a small drum sander or sanding discs in the Moto-Tool. With them you can sand wood, fiber glass, and metal. (After grinding a metal surface smooth, you might want to finish the task by sanding the area lightly, followed by a polish with one of the polishing accessories.)

The drum sander (No. 407) is a neat little accessory which requires a 1/8-inch collet. The sanding bands on the drum can be replaced as needed. Bands come in coarse grit (No. 408) and fine grit (No. 432) and are easily slipped off and on the tiny drum.

The drum is expanded or contracted by adjusting the screwhead at the end of the flat side of the drum. To remove and replace a band, contract the drum. When the new band is in place, expand it.

Use the coarse band for rough shaping and first sanding of wood and fiber glass. Follow it by sanding to a smooth finish with the fine band.

You'll find these drums handy for sanding flat, beveled, and curved surfaces and inside surfaces that are hard to reach by other methods. They work on wood, fiber glass and plastics.

You also can do some shaping of wood pieces with the drum sander. It removes stock at a slower rate than a cutter, and thus gives better

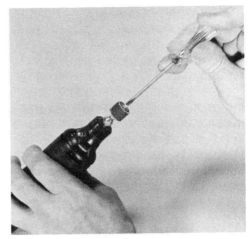

To replace a band on the drum sander, loosen the screw to contract the drum, and slide the old band off.

Slide the new sanding band on and then expand the drum by tightening the screw once again.

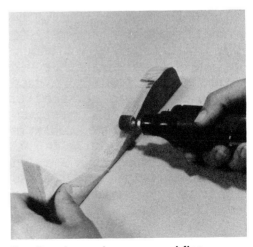

Sanding drums, in coarse and fine grits, are handy for sanding beveled, curved and hard-to-reach surfaces.

control when necessary.

The sanding discs, used with mandrel No. 402, are 3/4 inch in diameter and come in coarse (No. 411); medium (No. 412); and fine (No. 413). They are great for sanding when you make miniatures and ship, train or car models. The sanding is done with the face of the wheel. Very little pressure is required to use these discs. Just touch the face of the wheel to the work.

Wire and bristle brushes

Two kinds of brush accessories, wire and bristle, are available for the Moto-Tool, with three shapes of each kind.

Wire brushes are handy for removing rust and corrosion from anything, including shop and garden tools, doorknobs, knob plates, automobile parts, and electrical contacts. You can clean any surface to a bright and shiny finish by wire brushing it. (For such items as door knobs, brass lamp parts, etc., you can keep the part shiny by coating it with clear lacquer after polishing (with the wire brush.) Wire brushes can also be used to create an artistic effect on coarse grained wood objects.

These wire brushes must not be used at speeds in excess of 15,000 RPM. This means that you should not use them in constant-speed models of the Moto-Tool, which operate at a constant speed of 25,000 to 30,000 RPM, unless you control the speed by the addition of one of the Dremel speed control accessories. On the manually operated speed control No. 219, use a setting of 3 or lower. In the variable speed Moto-Tool models, you can use these brushes at settings of 5-1/2 and lower.

A glance at the pictures of the three brush shapes is all that is needed to tell you which type you should use. No. 428 is a wheel, with the brush action around the edge. No. 442 is a bowl-shaped brush that provides a scrubbing action on the surface. No. 443 is a straight-wire brush for getting into tight corners.

Don't use the wire brush accessories on delicate pieces such as silverware or antiques. For these, use the gentler bristle brushes, which come in the same shapes. Because the bristles are soft and flexible, these brushes can be used at the full 30,000 RPM if you choose.

You can use polishing compound with bristle brush accessories to polish in places where the felt or cloth buffs don't work well.

A word of advice: Before working with any valuable piece of jewelry, practice using these brushes. Get to know how they work, how long they should be held against the work for polishing, and how they work on paint, enamel and other coated surfaces. Then you will be able to judge the best way of using them to clean or polish your jewelry without damaging it.

The cutting wheel

Every homeowner and mechanic occasionally finds the need to cut off a bolt heat, reslot a damaged screw head, or cut a piece of metal rod. These are some of the jobs which can be performed by cutting wheel No. 409, which requires mandrel No. 402. This is a thin emery wheel designed for slicing, cutting off and similar operations. You can cut the metal of BX cable with it, for example, or trim a metal counter edge, or even cut conduit or a downspout. It is great for cutting openings of any shape in sheet metal.

It also can be used for delicate woodworking — making doll furniture, for example, or making the parts for a model ship, or cutting model railroad rails.

The cutting wheel is one of those accessories where it is especially important to remember that with the Moto-Tool, you only guide the cutter, and let the speed of the tool do the work. To cut with this, gently touch the cutter to the surface to be cut — and watch the cutter do its thing. Don't apply much pressure because the wheel isn't made to be pressed. The tiniest pressure is all that is needed at high speeds to cut even hardened steel parts.

Always use the circumference of the No. 409 wheel for cutting, and never use the side of this wheel for sanding or grinding. It is relatively brittle and will fracture if side-loaded.

As has been said several times before, always wear safety glasses when using the Moto-Tool — regardless of which accessory you are using.

If you have ever tried to remove your auto license plates, you know how difficult it can be to take off a bolt that is rusted and frozen to a nut. The answer is: Don't try to remove it. Use the cutting wheel to cut off the head of the bolt. It is easy and doesn't take long. You'll have the new plates on, held in place by new bolts (hopefully nylon) in a jiffy.

The steel saw

The cutting wheel described above works for almost any kind of cutting job, but a better accessory for woodworking is the steel saw. This miniature circular saw blade comes with its own arbor, and will cut wood, fiber glass, plastics, and soft metals such as aluminum. Use it for cutting or slotting.

Be extremely careful when using these steel saw blades. They will bind if not kept perfectly straight in the kerf or groove, and will jump from the groove. Unless you have good control at this time, the blade can run across the work, across your hand, and even up your arm, causing severe injury.

Always clamp any work before cutting it with a saw. *Never* attempt to hold the work with one hand and the saw in the other. Use both hands to hold the Moto-Tool, one to guide the tool and the other to steady and control it.

Steel saws come in two styles. No. 406 is .005 inch thick, and No. 400 is .023 inch thick. Use the thicker saw for cutting heavier material.

The only non-Dremel accessories recommended for use with the Moto-Tool are Number Drills.

Non-Dremel accessories

All Dremel accessories use either the 1/8- or 3/32-inch collet. The two other collets, 1/16- and 1/32-inch, are for use with number drills which require collets of these sizes (see table on pages 8 & 51). We do not recommend non-Dremel accessories except for number drills.

Using the accessories

You have seen the range of accessories for the Moto-Tool, and have a good idea of the broad scope of work you can do by using them. There are three important aspects to getting the best out of the Moto-Tool.

1. Select the right accessory for the job at hand. Until you have acquired personal familiarity, read the description of the accessories whenever you undertake a job you haven't done before. Check the list for the material the accessory works best in, the type of work it was designed to do. For example, cutters designed for wood or soft metals would do a poor job on tempered metal — and the cutter would be damaged in the attempt.

If the accessory does not come out after loosening the chuck cap, tap it gently on the bench top or side.

When using all accessories, always wear goggles to protect your eyes from flying grit and metal.

2. Work with any accessory on scrap material before using it for the first time on a project. As a rule, five minutes spent in familiarization is all that is necessary, and it can make a great difference in the quality of your work.

3. Learn how to use the great speed advantage of the Moto-Tool. Let the tool and its accessory do the work. Learn to guide the tool without forcing it. This, too, is a matter of practice with each accessory, and doesn't take long.

4. Always wear safety glasses when working with the Moto-Tool. Never make an exception to this

rule because in the great majority of cases, the accessories throw material as they cut or grind. Even a tiny speck of this material can cause eye injury. In addition, always wear a breathing mask when doing any work that creates dust or fine particles you might inhale.

Service and maintenance

All the information you need for regular care and maintenance of your Moto-Tool has been gathered into Chapter Ten. Read it before going to work with the tool for the first time.

The sticking collet

Occasionally an accessory will stick in a collet, so that when you loosen the cap and attempt to remove the accessory, it refuses to come out. Note that when this happens, pulling harder on the accessory will only make the problem worse, and cause the accessory to fit tighter into the collet.

The most common cause of a sticking collet is tightening the cap too much when inserting the collet.

The cap should be snug and tight enough to hold the accessory, but not extremely tight. A second cause of the problem is foreign matter in the collet.

The problem can be avoided by not tightening the cap too much, and by keeping the collet clean.

The correct procedure to follow to remove a sticking collet is:

1. Using the wrench, loosen the cap. Pull gently on the accessory.

2. If the accessory doesn't come out easily, gently tap the end of the accessory against the edge of your workbench or a similar surface. You will feel a slight click as the accessory goes in. You should then be able to take it out of the collet.

3. Occasionally a collet remains sticky even after the tapping procedure. If this happens, remove the cap entirely and lift the collet and accessory out.

4. Soak the collet and accessory in a penetrating oil or rust remover. This should allow you to remove the accessory.

Remember that you cannot forcibly pull the accessory from the collet, because as you pull, you pull the accessory tighter into the taper on the collet.

When tapping the end of the accessory against the bench, do it with care, especially if you have a grinding wheel accessory mounted in the collet. You could crack the wheel. The crack can be slight and you may not see it. But the next time you use the accessory, it may fly apart as soon as it comes up to speed.

If a collet ever does jam, don't hammer on the Moto-Tool and don't pry with a screwdriver in an attempt to remove it.

Because the Moto-Tool is so precisely made, there is very little tolerance between the collet and the hollow in the motor shaft into which it is inserted. Thus even a minute speck of rust can cause problems.

To avoid the possibility of a jammed collet, follow these points:

1. Store your Moto-Tool in a dry area, not in an excessively humid place.

2. Always remove accessories and collets before putting the tool away.

3. Examine collets for evidence of rust or of collected dirt before inserting them into the tool. Keep them clean at all times.

4. Always use the proper sized collet for each accessory. Never force a large accessory arbor into a small collet.

5. If you suspect a collet has been bent or damaged (from use, from a fall, etc.), replace it. Using it may create several problems, none of which you want.

6. If you suspect the arbor or shaft of an accessory has been bent, discard the accessory.

7. Arbors should slide easily into collets. Collets should lock and open easily. When you find resistance to either action, look for rust, dirt or signs of damage. It is best to discard suspected parts unless you can identify the problem (such as accumulated dirt) and clear it up.

8. Do not use any lubricant containing Teflon on the collet or accessories. The Teflon coating will make the accessory arbor too slippery, and the collet will not grip it properly.

Typical examples of what you can do with the Dremel Moto-Tool

No. 105
Engraving, carving, routing in wood, metal, plastic

No. 106
Engraving, carving, routing in wood, metal, plastic

No. 107
Engraving, carving, routing in wood, metal, plastic

No. 108
Engraving, carving in plastic, wood, metal

No. 115
Shaping, grooving, flats in wood, metal, plastic

No. 118
Carving, tapered holes in wood, metal, plastic

No. 125
Carving, tapered holes, shaping in wood, metal, plastic

No. 193
Inletting, grooving, carving in wood, metal, plastic

No. 194
Inletting, grooving, carving in wood, metal, plastic

No. 196
Removal, grooving, flats in wood, metal, plastic

No. 199
Slotting, grooving in wood, metal, plastic

No. 932
Grinding, sharpening, deburring in metal, plastic

No. 952
Grinding, sharpening, deburring in metal, plastic

No. 953
Grinding, sharpening, deburring in metal, plastic

No. 997
Grinding, sharpening, deburring in metal, plastic

No. 8193
Grinding, sharpening, deburring in metal, plastic

No. 83322
Working on hardened steel, ceramics & other hard materials

No. 84922
Working on hardened steel, ceramics & other hard materials

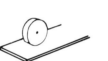

No. 85422
Working on hardened steel, ceramics & other hard materials

No. 414
Polishing metal, plastics

No. 422
Polishing in metal, plastics

No. 423
Polishing in metal, plastics

No. 425
For polishing metals, ceramics, semi-precious stones.

No. 429
Polishing soft metals, plastic

No. 460
Polishing metal, ceramics, semi-precious stones in hard-to-reach areas

No. 407
Sanding, shaping in wood, plastics

No. 408
Sanding, shaping in wood, plastic coarse grit

No. 432
Sanding, shaping in wood, plastic fine grit

No. 428
Rust removal, polishing in metal, hardwoods

No. 442
Rust removal, polishing, scraping metal & hardwood

No. 443
Rust removal, cleaning corners in metal, hardwood

No. 406
Cutting woods, plastics, fiber glass

No. 409
For slicing, cutting-off of metals

QUICK FIXES

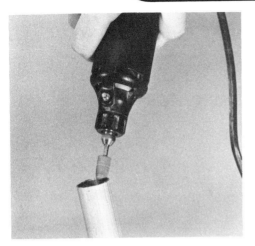

A.

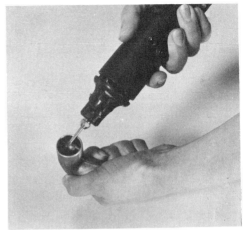

C.

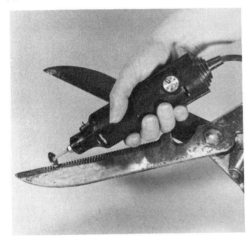

B.

D.

A. After cutting conduit or other thin-walled pipe, watch out for sharp edges and burrs. They can cut you and damage electrical wire you insert. Use Moto-Tool and abrasive accessory to quickly grind both inner and outer edges smooth.

B. Take rust and dirt off of tools with serrated edges by a quick brushing with the wire brush accessory. Keep speed of Moto-Tool below 15,000 rpm and always wear safety goggles when using wire brush accessories.

C. When preparing to sweat solder copper pipe joints, get the joints clean beforehand with a wire brush treatment.

This ensures more uniform soldered joints. Clean all parts which contact solder.

D. Using latex paint? Make this "lunch break" bucket. Filled with water, it keeps brushes soft when you have to leave for lunch and don't have time to wash them. Stiff section of coat hanger wire through holes in brushes supports them in the water. Use a 1/8-inch bit in the Moto-Tool and drill brushes slightly above ferrule. Same bucket can be used for varnish and oil paint jobs if filled with mineral spirits. It can keep brushes soft over night.

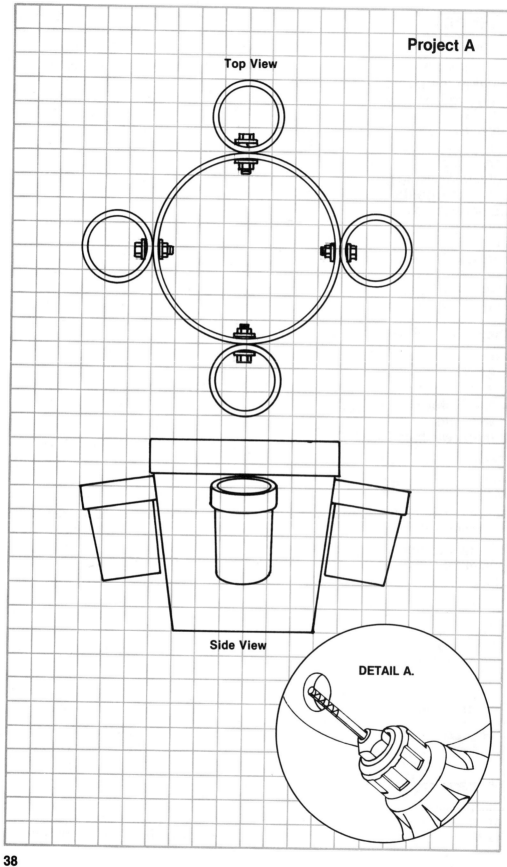

Top View

Project A

Side View

DETAIL A.

Project 1

FLOWER POT IDEAS

. . . .Clay and terra cotta pots provide the basic materials for a group of imaginative projects.

Technical tip: These projects are based on the Moto-Tool's ability to carve holes in clay and ceramic pots. Use silicon grinding points to carve through the wall of the pot. Do not use points as drills, but as grinders. Once an opening is made in the pot, switch to a tungsten carbide cutter such as the 9901. Use the sides of the cutter (See Detail A) to gradually widen the opening to the required dimensions.

Project A — Satellite Pots

Materials:
1 8-in. clay flower pot
4 2-1/2-in. clay flower pots
4 1/4-in. stove bolts 1-1/2-in. long, with nuts
8 metal washers for stove bolts

Tools:
Adjustable wrench
Moto-Tool
Silicon grinding points
Tungsten carbide cutter (9901)

This design makes an interesting and different planter for the patio or porch. In it, four 2-1/2-in. pots, held in place by 1/4-inch stove bolts and nuts, hang from an 8 in. pot, as shown in Plan A. Locate positions of small pots and grind hole for each bolt. Attach small pots with stove bolts, inserting metal washers under bolt heads and nuts. See Detail B. Don't overtighten bolts or you may crack the pots.

Project B — Tiered Pots

Materials:
2-in. clay flower pot
4-in. clay flower pot
6-in. clay flower pot
3/8-in. threaded rod, 26 in. long
4 nuts for 3/8-in. rod
6 metal washers for 3/8-in. rod
6 rubber garden hose washers
Eyebolt
Extended nut to fit 3/8-in. rod

Tools:
Adjustable wrench
Moto-Tool
Silicon grinding points
Tungsten carbide cutter (9901)

These tiered pots would make a great home for trailing plants. Review Plan B, then begin construction by grinding 2 new drain holes in bottom of each pot, between existing drain hole and sides. Next, insert

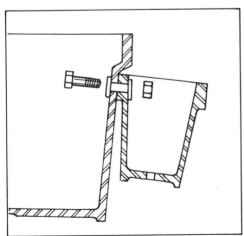

DETAIL B. Small pots are hung on larger pot like this, with stove bolt and washers.

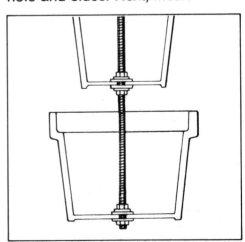

DETAIL C. Tiered pots are secured to threaded rod with assembly of metal and rubber washers and nuts.

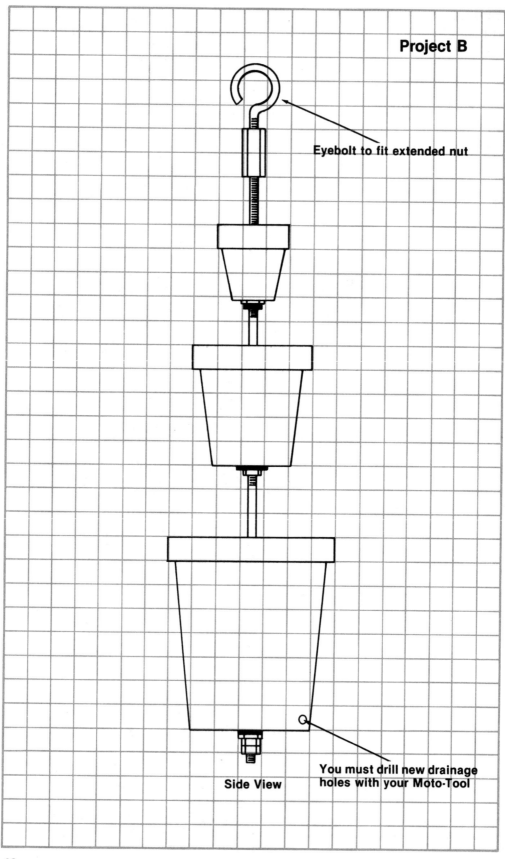

Project B

Eyebolt to fit extended nut

You must drill new drainage holes with your Moto-Tool

Side View

26-inch threaded rod through original drain holes and secure each with nuts and washers, as shown in Detail C. Follow this procedure: Thread nut on from top of rod to position of first pot. Slip metal washer, then rubber washer up from bottom of rod, then slide pot into position. Slide rubber washer, then metal washer up under pot. Now thread nut up from bottom of rod and tighten against washers until pot is securely held. Follow same procedure for each pot. After installing bottom pot thread on second nut to act as lock nut. Thread extended nut on top of rod and screw eyebolt into it as a hanger.

Project C — Bird House

Materials:
Clay pot, 4 to 6 in. in diameter
Clay saucer large enough to cover
 pot
3/8-in threaded rod
3 nuts for 3/8-in. rod
3 metal washers
Extended nut
Eyebolt or threaded hook
1/4-in. dowel, 3 in. long

Tools:
Moto-Tool and grinding accessories
Adjustable wrench

Here we have a weatherproof clay house, strictly for the birds. The size depends on the species you want to attract. As seen in Detail D, the saucer serves as the roof. Grind a 3/8-inch hole in the center of the saucer. Make the door by grinding a 1 to 1-1/2-inch hole in the side of the pot. Beneath the door, grind a 1/4-inch hole and press fit a dowel into it for a perch. Assembly is with threaded rod and bolts, like the tiered pots.

Project D — Patio Light

Materials:
6-in. clay flower pot
8-in. clay saucer

Tools:
Moto-Tool and grinding accessories

Bring soft candlelight to your porch or patio with this unique lamp. Grind a series of geometric designs in the side of a clay pot, carving through the clay with a silicon grinding point, then finishing up with a tungsten carbide cutter. Light comes from plumber's candle, fastened to the saucer with drops of hot wax.

DETAIL D. Bird house is suspended on hanger made of threaded rod through top and bottom, with hook on top.

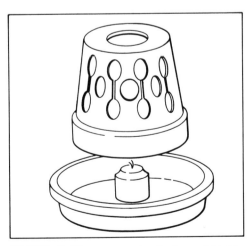

DETAIL E. Clay saucer is of clay pot lamp. Enlarge drain hole for ventilation using carbide cutter.

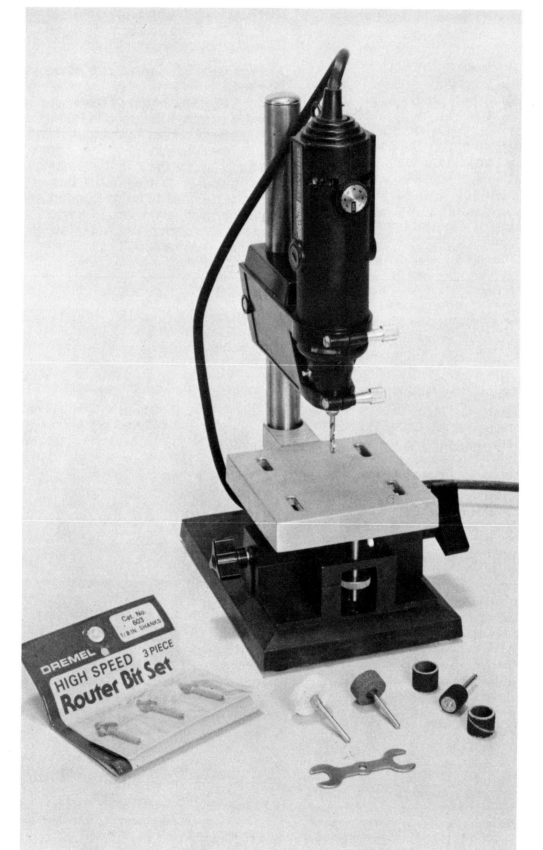

CHAPTER TWO

The Moto-Tool Drill Press

When you need accurate drilling, repeated drilling operations, countersinking, grooving, sanding and even routing, this drill press attachment with the Moto-Tool is ready.

No tool can bore holes in wood or other materials more quickly, conveniently or accurately than a drill press. This is just as true of the Moto-Tool Drill Press as it is for the larger shop models.

The conventional shop model drill press, for those who have never seen one, is a machine designed for drilling holes, though it can do a number of other jobs as well. It consists of four major parts: a head made up of a motor, chuck and operating mechanisms; a post or column on which the head is mounted; a base in which the post or column is anchored; and a table, mounted beneath the head, on which the work is placed.

To drill a hole in a workpiece with a shop model drill press, the operator fits a drill bit into the chuck. Then he positions the work on the table beneath the head. Now he turns the handle at the side of the drill press head, which lowers the chuck and drill bit to the work. When the drill bit contacts the work it starts boring. After the hole has been drilled, the chuck and bit are returned to their upper position.

Drilling with a drill press is very accurate, since you can place and clamp the work precisely, and since the drill mechanically contacts the work in the identical path each time. Other controls make it possible to set the depth of each hole. With the drill press, you can drill a series of holes, placed exactly where you want them, to the same depth without guesswork.

The drill press permits work other than drilling, too. By replacing the drill bit with a drum sander, for example, the drill press becomes a sanding machine. You can sand and shape wood by placing the work on the table and holding it against the spinning drum. Router bits can be installed, also. With these, the work to be routed or shaped is guided against the bit, which cuts the desired shape. You can carve edges on work, for example, cut recesses, or groove with it. In addition, the drill press can be used for some grinding and polishing operations. In all cases, the drill press motor remains stationary, while the work is moved up to the spinning accessory. The operator's hands are free to manipulate the workpiece.

Dremel engineers adapted the concept of the drill press to the Moto-Tool in developing the Moto-Tool Drill Press Attachment. This attachment is for use with Moto-Tool Models 245, 250, 260, 270, 280, 350,

370, and 380. The Moto-Tool simply is clamped into the drill press attachment and is converted into a compact drill press. With it, you are ready for drilling, routing, grooving, sanding, grinding, polishing and countersinking. (Note that to use a Model 260 Moto-Tool in the drill press, an adapter sleeve is required. The sleeve, Part No. 550090, is slipped over the front end of the Moto-Tool until it snaps in place. Then the tool can be clamped into the drill press attachment.)

Set up

To clamp the Moto-Tool into the drill press attachment, first loosen the two knurled knobs located on the front of the upper assembly. Now seat the Moto-Tool, chuck end down, in the clamp and turn these knobs finger tight. When you are mounting the Moto-Tool, be sure that the chuck lock pin of the Moto-Tool doesn't face the back, where it might accidentally contact the column. Position it so that it is at the side or front. If you are mounting a variable speed model in the drill press attachment, place the Moto-Tool so that the variable speed dial faces to the front. This automatically places the chuck lock pin in the proper position.

There is one major difference between the compact Moto-Tool Drill Press and full-size conventional drill presses. In the Moto-Tool, the motor is stationary on the post, and the work is brought up to the drill by raising the table, which is done by turning the table lifting knob. In industry, some small drill presses, called micros and used for precision work, operate in the same manner. If you are accustomed to standard drill press operation, where the spindle is lowered instead of the table being raised, this method will take a few minutes to get used to,

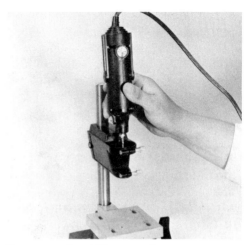

To set up the drill press, first loosen the knurled knobs, then place the tool in the attachment.

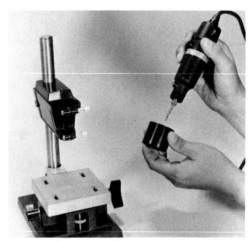

To use Moto-Tool Model 260 in the drill press attachment, you must have adapter sleeve No. 550090.

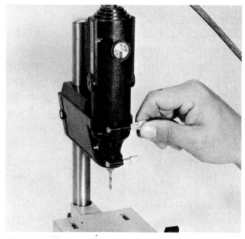

With the Moto-Tool in the drill press attachment, turn the knurled knobs on the front finger tight.

but it is an effective method and permits very accurate work.

When you first set up the Dremel drill press, spend a few minutes checking the various controls. These are:

1. The Column Lock. The knob on the right side of the column is the column lock. The head, holding the Moto-Tool, slides up and down the column, and should be locked in place after you have positioned it where you want it. A couple of turns of the column lock, until it is finger tight, are all that are needed.

2. The Column. The head slides up and down on the column. The fit on the column is fairly tight, and the head doesn't slide easily. To move the head up or down, first loosen the column lock, then move the head from side to side a little as you push either up or down.

3. The Table Lift. This is the black knob at the right side of the drill press base. As you turn it, the table moves up or down. The full travel of the table is 1 inch from its lowest to highest position. This means that the maximum drilling depth of the press is 1 inch, though this can be increased to 2 inches by drilling from both sides of the work.

4. The Table Lock. The smaller black knob at the left side of the table is the table lock. This is used for locking the table into position for operations other than drilling, such as sanding or grinding, in which the table must be stationary. Once the table has been raised or lowered to the desired position, turn the table lock knob finger tight to secure the table in that position.

5. The Table Stop. The knurled adjusting nut located in the front of the base is the table height stop. You adjust it to determine how far the table will rise, which, in turn, determines how deep a hole will be drilled. You can adjust the movement of the table from zero to the full 1 inch. To make the adjustment,

The column lock secures the Moto-Tool after it has been adjusted to the correct height on the column.

Turning the table lift knob raises the table, carrying the workpiece to the spinning bit for drilling.

Table lock, on left side of the tool base, is used to lock the table for routing and shaping operations.

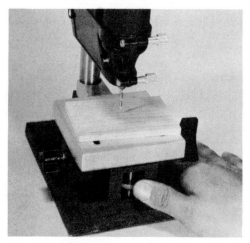

The table stop adjusting nut is set to determine how far the table can rise when the lift knob is turned.

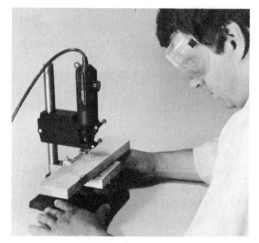

Never work on drill press without safety glasses. Contact lenses or regular glasses are not protection.

spin the knob until the table is at the height you want for your work. Spinning from left to right moves the table down, and from right to left moves the table up. When you turn the table lift knob after making this adjustment, the table will go no higher than the height you set.

6. *Table Slots.* Four slots have been cut in the table. The purpose of these slots is to allow you to bolt work fences and hold-down clamps in place. These slots are designed to be used with a No. 10 (3/16) carriage bolt. The bolt should be installed from the bottom and the slot width will engage the squared portion at the head of the bolt and prevent it from turning when the nut is tightened.

Safety

There is a tendency when working on the drill press to lean close to look at the workpiece during an operation. The cutters throw a lot of material and so there is an eye hazard as you work. Never do any work on the drill press unless you are wearing safety glasses. Incidentally, if you wear contact lenses, keep in mind that these offer absolutely no protection against flying objects. Wear safety glasses *and* your contacts.

Basic operation

These are the basic steps to perform a drilling operation on the drill press.

1. Adjust the height of the table according to the thickness of the work piece and the depth of the hole to be drilled.

2. Adjust the height of the drill press, taking the same factors into consideration.

3. Position the work on the table.

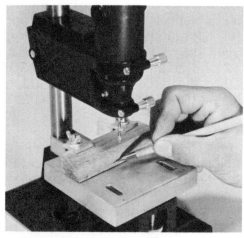

To drill a hole that does not go through the workpiece, first mark the intended hole depth on the side.

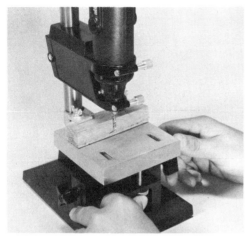

Next, place the workpiece behind the drill bit and adjust the table height so the bit matches your mark.

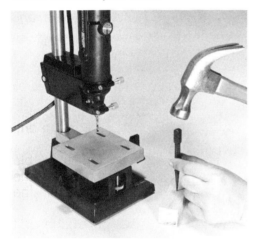

Before drilling any workpiece, punch an identification at the drilling spot to serve as guide in placing the bit.

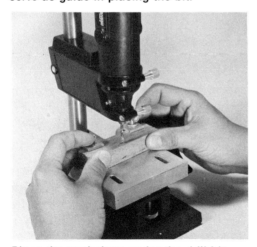

Place the workpiece under the drill bit, positioning the bit directly over the spot marked for drilling.

In drill press operation, it is customary to mark the point at which drilling is to take place by tapping a mark with a pointed tool such as an awl or a small nailset for wood or a center punch for metal. Use this mark to place the work directly under the drill.

4. Clamp the work in place or use guides that are secured.

5. Turn the Moto-Tool on at full speed for most work, or at a lower speed for drilling in plastics and some metals. See the speed charts in Chapter One for details.

6. Slowly turn the table lifting knob, raising the work to the drill. If

To drill the hole, slowly raise the table by turning the lifting knob. Lower it after the hole is finished.

you are drilling a deep hole, run the bit in and out of the hole several times to allow the bit to clear itself of chips as you drill deeper. Continue to turn the knob until the table is fully raised, then turn it back down again. The hole has now been drilled.

Figuring the height. First, measure the thickness of the workpiece. Then consider the hole depth. You may want to drill only to a certain depth, or drill all the way through the piece. If a certain depth is required, mark that depth with a pencil on the side of the workpiece as a reminder.

To set the drill press for the depth you want, first move the table to the full down position. Then turn the table stop adjustment to its full up position. That is, turn the knurled knob left to right until the knob is at the top of its screw.

Next adjust the height of the drill head so that the point of the drill bit is just above the top surface of the work, but not quite touching it.

Place the workpiece just behind or in front of the drill bit, so the bit can bypass it. Apply pressure to the table lifting knob (which will not move at this time) and turn the knurled table stop adjustment nut from right to left. As you do this, the table will slowly rise, (providing you keep a slight pressure on the table lift knob.) As the table rises, the tip of the drill bit will move down the side of the workpiece, and show you how deep into the work it will drill. When the bit reaches the depth you want the hole to be, stop turning the knurled adjustment nut and return the table to its full down position by turning the table lifting knob. For changing adjustments, the knurled knob will change depth 1/32 of an inch for each revolution. The knob can be marked with a pencil for reference for exact changes in depth setting.

You are now ready to drill. Clamp the work in position under the drill bit. Turn the tool on, and slowly turn the table lift knob. The work will rise into the drill bit, and drilling will begin. Continue to turn the table lift knob until it has raised the table as far as it can go. Now turn it back down again, and remove the work from the table. The hole has been drilled to the desired depth.

Drilling through the workpiece. Drill press operators, when drilling completely through a workpiece, place a pad of wood under the piece. You should follow the same procedure when drilling through wood or metal on the Moto-Tool drill

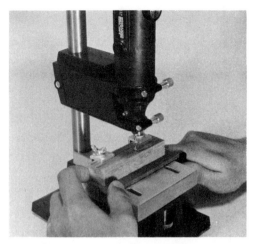

To drill a hole through a workpiece, you must place a pad, here 1/8-inch hardboard, under the work.

press. There are two reasons. First, when the drill bit breaks through the bottom of the workpiece, it sometimes causes splintering around the edge of the hole. If, instead of breaking through, the drill continues on into a wooden pad, the hole remains clean and unsplintered. The second reason is that the drill bit would come in contact with the surface of the table unless a pad had been placed underneath the work piece.

The pad can be any convenient thickness, starting at 1/8 inch, and should be as large or larger than the workpiece.

Changing accessories

Accessories can be changed without removing the Moto-Tool from the drill press clamp. However, since the tool is so easy to take out of the clamp, we recommend that you do so for changing accessories. There is much less chance that you will mount an accessory incorrectly, so that it runs out of balance, if you can see what you are doing during the exchange. In changing accessories with the tool in the mounting, you are working in the blind.

Work clamps

The four slots in the work table permit you to install your own work clamps, jigs and fences. A good way to attach any of these is to use No. 10 carriage bolts threaded up through the slots from the bottom, with wing nuts threaded on them from the top. You can make any clamp or fence to fit over these. The wing nuts make adjustment and replacement of any fixture easy. Carriage bolts have smooth heads with a square section just under the head. The square section fits up into the slot so that the bolt does not

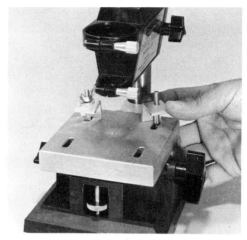

Hole is drilled in the top leg of the angle. Cut the back leg of the angle to make clamp for smaller work.

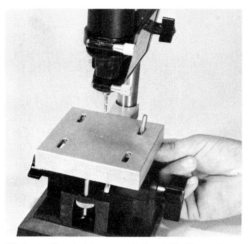

Slots in the table permit installation of clamps and fences. Use No. 10 carriage bolts with wing nuts.

Make a fence out of aluminum angle but mount it on the table with one leg to the front, as shown here.

Make the clamp by sawing 3/4 x 3/4-inch aluminum angle and drilling for the bolts, as shown here.

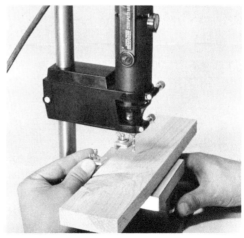

Work to be drilled should either be clamped or held by hand against column or a stop to prevent rotation.

turn as you tighten the wing nut. The length of the carriage bolt used is determined by the design and size of the clamp or fence.

You will find that short lengths of aluminum angle, which can be purchased at most hardware stores, make excellent clamps and fences. Drill a hole in one leg (side) of the angle for the bolt to go through. By making a slot rather than a hole in the angle, you can make it possible to adjust the fixture over a wider area on the table.

Work to be drilled should always be clamped in place, to assure accuracy and also to prevent the work from being rotated by the drill.

Drill bits to use

The largest drill bit which can be used in the Moto-Tool drill press is one with a 1/8-inch shank or arbor. Any smaller bit can be used as long as it is matched to the size of the collet. There are four collets available (See Chapter One) for the Moto-Tool, ranging in size from 1/8-inch down to 1/32-inch.

Drills in the smaller sizes, 1/8-inch and under, are described in several ways — by fractions or by numbers. Fractional drills are available in increments of 1/64-inch. Number drills are available in decimal sizes. Hardware stores with large tool sections and machine tool supply houses usually carry a good selection of Number Drills. Some hobby shops also sell fractional and decimal bits in small sizes.

We have included a chart of drills in this chapter, and the easiest way to understand drill sizes and their designations is to refer to the chart. The chart also shows the collet which should be used with each drill size.

Those drill bits designated by fractions in the chart are the most commonly used. Those in between

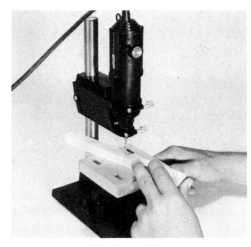

This shows how longer pieces are held against column during drilling to prevent rotation of work.

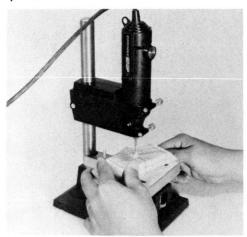

Fence or bolt can be used as stops against which to hold short pieces during drilling to prevent rotation.

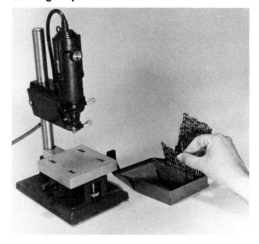

You can purchase Numbered Drills in sets, and those below 1/8 inch in size can be used with the Moto-Tool.

Chart of Drill sizes, showing Dremel collet for use with each size.

Collet No.	Drill No.	Decimal Equivalent
480	1/8″	.1250
	No. 31	.1200
	No. 32	.1160
	No. 33	.1130
	No. 34	.1110
	No. 35	.1100
	7/64″	.1094
	No. 36	.1069
	No. 37	.1040
	No. 38	.1015
	No. 39	.0995
	No. 40	.0980
	No. 41	.0960
481	No. 39	.0995
	No. 40	.0980
	No. 41	.0960
	3/32″	.0937
	No. 42	.0935
	No. 43	.0890
	No. 44	.0860
	No. 45	.0820
	No. 46	.0810
	No. 47	.0785
	5/64″	.0781
	No. 48	.0760
	No. 49	.0730
	No. 50	.0700
	No. 51	.0670
482	No. 50	.0700
	No. 51	.0670
	No. 52	.0635
	1/16″	.0625
	No. 53	.0595
	No. 54	.0550
	No. 55	.0520
	3/64″	.0469
	No. 56	.0465
	No. 57	.0430
	No. 58	.0420
	No. 59	.0410
	No. 60	.0400
483	3/64″	.0469
	No. 56	.0465
	No. 57	.0430
	No. 58	.0420
	No. 59	.0410
	No. 60	.0400
	No. 61	.0390
	No. 62	.0380
	No. 63	.0370
	No. 64	.0360
	No. 65	.0350
	No. 66	.0330
	No. 67	.0320
	No. 68	.0310
	No. 69	.02925
	No. 70	.0280
	No. 71	.0260
	No. 72	.0250
	No. 73	.0240
	No. 74	.0225
	No. 75	.0210
	No. 76	.0200
	No. 77	.0180
	No. 78	.0160
	No. 79	.0145
	No. 80	.0135

the fractional drills designated by numbers are less commonly used and therefore harder to find. When you buy drill bits in pre-assembled sets you usually get only the fractional drills. However, for working with models, miniatures, jewelry, etc., you may find a need for the Number Drills. These are usually bought individually, but some sets are available.

Marking the work

You want to be certain that you drill the hole exactly where it is needed. The easiest way to place the drill in the right place is to mark the spot on the work with a slight indentation before putting it on the drill table. For wood, the indentation may be made with a nailset, an awl, an ice pick or simply with an appropriate-sized nail. For metal, a center punch, available at most hardware stores, is commonly used.

After placing the work on the table and lowering the drill press head as needed, raise the table so that the work is just under the drill bit. Now carefully align the drill bit and the drill mark on the work, then clamp the work before drilling. A drop of oil at the tip of the bit will facilitate the drilling of ferrous metals.

Sanding on the drill press

Sanding and shaping on the drill press is done by installing one of the sanding drum accessories in the Moto-Tool.

To prepare for sanding work, you should make a wood or hardboard pad for the table. The pad can range in thickness from 1/8 to 1/4-inch. The reason for the pad is that the small screw on the sanding drum contacts the table and holds the drum a small fraction of an inch above the table level. Any work rest-

To use the drum sander, you need a table pad. Make it out of 1/8-inch hardboard the same size as the table.

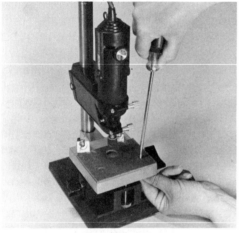

Countersink the screws below the pad surface. The center hole is larger in diameter than the sanding drum.

Use the fence to guide the workpiece when sanding edges smooth. This work is very difficult without a fence.

ing on the table that is pressed against the drum will show a slight lip as a result.

See the accompanying photographs and pattern for making the table pad, which is cut so that the bottom edge of the sanding drum can extend slightly below the surface, thus eliminating the lip and permitting an even sanding job. This same pad can be used for drilling, routing and other operations on the drill press, so you might choose to bolt it in place.

Once the drill press head has been adjusted so that the drum sander is in position in the cutout on the table, lock the table by turning the table lock control at the left side of the base.

The drill press normally performs two kinds of sanding operations: smoothing and shaping.

Smoothing edges. A metal or wooden guide such as the one shown in the accompanying photograph is used when smoothing edges. This guide is called a fence, and it should be used for straight edges since it is very difficult to make a perfectly straight smooth edge by making a freehand pass. Clamp the fence to the drill press table, adjusting its position so that the edge of the work, as it rests

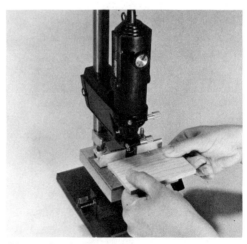

Clamp the fence so the work barely contacts the sanding drum, which then takes a light bite as the work passes.

against the fence, barely contacts the sanding drum. You want to take a very light "bite" with the drum as the work is passed across it. If it is necessary to remove more than just a slight amount of material in this process, make several passes and remove only a small amount of stock each time.

Shaping with the sanding drum. Shaping is a matter of removing material. Perhaps you want to make a square corner round, or shape the inside of a cutout. For the most part, shaping operations are done freehand and must be done with care since the sanding drum can remove material quite fast.

It is a good idea to mark the area to be removed with a pencil, giving yourself a guideline to follow during the operation. Practice a little with the drum in the drill press to get the feel of how fast material is removed (the amount will vary with the hardness of the workpiece) and how to control the workpiece in order to make small accurate cuts.

Sanding on the drill press is one of those situations in which the high speed of the Moto-Tool is important. Allow the speed to do the work. Don't apply much pressure with your fingers. If you take shallow cuts without pressure, you will find that you can remove a lot of stock quickly and accurately — in wood, plastic, and soft metal — and end up with a smooth surface. If pressure is required the sanding band is worn out and should be replaced.

Burning wood. If you press a wood workpiece too hard against the sanding drum, the sandpaper may overheat and burn the wood. Another cause for burning is attempting to sand with a worn drum band from which all the grit is gone. In this case, you are simply getting friction and no abrasive action, and the drum band should be changed.

Routing on the drill press

Routing to cut edges in a workpiece, make small wood joints, and to cut grooves also can be done on the drill press. If you do much routing, you should have the Moto-Tool routing attachment, which will be described in Chapter Three, but routing on the drill press is satisfactory for many common routing tasks.

You should be familiar with the router accessories, described in Chapter One. These are inserted in the Moto-Tool chuck for routing on

For most shaping operations on the drill press, the work is done freehand against the sanding drum.

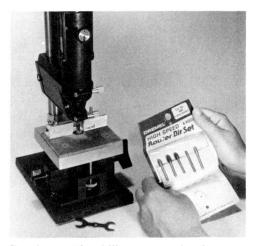

Routing on the drill press can be done by using Dremel router bits and feeding the workpiece to them.

the drill press. Each accessory was designed to make a different kind of cut, and you should practice a few minutes with each to familiarize yourself with them. You can then select the one that will do the job at hand best.

To use router bits for cutting edges in the drill press, first install a fence to guide the workpiece. A length of aluminum angle attached to the table by carriage bolts makes an excellent fence. See photo. The fence should be located behind the cutter or at one side, but not in front of the cutter. Never set the work up so that you must reach across the cutter while working.

The routing or cutting pattern should be sketched lightly as a guide on the workpiece. The drill press should be positioned with the router bit slightly above the table top. Then move the table upward with the workpiece next to the bit until you see that the bit will make a cut of the desired depth.

Turn the Moto-Tool on at full speed for most work, slower for work in plastics. Then, guiding the workpiece against the fence, move it against the cutter. The cut should be against the rotation of the bit — that is, from left to right. See paragraph below. Generally speaking, it is best to make cuts of about 1/8-inch depth or less on each pass. If a deeper cut is required, make several passes.

To cut recesses and other cuts in the field of the workpiece, do not use a fence. Place the work on the table so that the bit will enter the workpiece at the point where you want the cut to begin. Turn the router on and hold the work firmly with your left hand. Gently raise the table until the bit enters the workpiece to the depth you want. Then hold the workpiece with both hands and guide it through the cut you want. When the cut is completed, hold the work with the left hand

To make this internal recess, place the work below the router bit, turn the tool on, and raise the table.

while you lower the table with the right.

To hold the workpiece for this type of cutting, keep most of hand below table so it will bump the table if you slip — not the router bit. Guide the work with your fingers. Keep your fingers a safe distance from the spinning cutter at all times. Do not attempt to shape pieces that will bring your fingers close to the cutter during the operation.

Be prepared for a sudden jerk if the cutter grabs, which it might if it hits a knot in the wood or if you move the work too slow or too fast. Keep your fingers at least 2 inches from the cutter at all times to avoid injury in the event of grabbing or a kickback.

Direction of the work. It is important to remember that the Moto-Tool turns to the right, clockwise when viewed from above. This is the correct rotation for standard drill bits. When using routing bits, this means that the work must be fed from the left to the right, against the rotation of the cutters, for smooth, work. Let the high speed of the Moto-Tool do the work.

Grooving and edging. If you want to cut grooves or shape an edge, it is best to install a fence to guide the work. It is very difficult to make a perfectly straight groove without a guide. With the guide, the groove can be perfect.

You can straighten the edge of a piece of stock using a straight-edge router cutter, using the fence as a guide and taking a light cut. This setup makes a beautiful cut in hardwoods. In softwoods, you may find that the wood has a tendency to "fuzz" as it becomes smooth. There are two possible cures for this fuzzing. First, try reversing the stock end for end, which will permit planing or edging with the grain rather than against it. If this still does not produce a smooth surface, then put

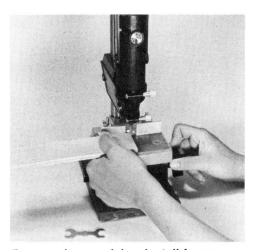

For grooving or edging, install fence as guide. Here table height is set before beginning to cut rabbet.

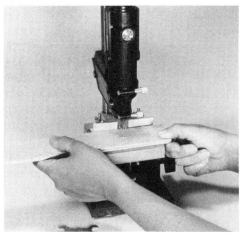

A rabbet is cut in the edge of the board. The opposite edge of another board is cut to make a rabbet joint.

the drum sander in the collet and take a light sanding cut with it, being careful not to disturb the straight edge of the cut you made earlier.

Rabbets. A rabbet is a notch cut in the edge of a piece of stock. An important use of the rabbet is in joining two pieces of wood. If you glued the two pieces together, edge to edge, you would have a butt joint. If you cut a rabbet in each piece and then fitted them together, you would have a rabbet joint, which is much stronger because it provides more gluing surfaces.

As a matter of fact, any woodworking joint that can be made with a full-size drill press can be made with the Moto-Tool drill press and the proper accessories. The only difference is in the size of the work. Thus, you could make miniature furniture with true furniture joinery, and you also can make some joints for full-sized furniture.

Grinding and polishing

You can mount grinding and polishing accessories in the drill press in the same manner as sanding drums. That is, use the table pad, adjust the

Use sanding drums for sharpening. Fence controls blade angle. Grind only relief, not cutting edge.

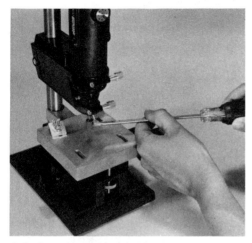

Grinding tip of damaged screwdriver to restore straight edge to blade. Left hand guides work.

This is the stone base for a statuette being polished to a high luster with the cloth wheel.

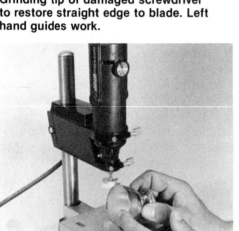

Cloth polishing wheel in drill press can serve as polishing tool if you don't have Moto-Tool Holder.

height of the drill press head so that the accessory fits into the cutout in the table pad, and lock the table at working height.

For either grinding or polishing, rest the work on the table and slide it up to the spinning accessory. Touch the work lightly against the accessory, and continue with light touches until the work is finished. Heavy pressure on the workpiece should not be used.

The use of other accessories

Most of the Moto-Tool accessories can be useful in the drill press. Wire brushes, for example, do an excellent polishing job in the press, and the work is faster and more accurate than when the job is done freehand. Just remember that wire brushes should not be used at speeds exceeding 15,000 RPM.

Circular saw accessories can be used in the drill press to cut narrow slots in the side of a workpiece. Be especially careful when using a saw, however. The saw is in a horizontal position and partially hidden from view as it cuts. As you approach the end of the workpiece, the saw will emerge through the end. If you are holding the piece by the end, the saw could cut your finger.

The Moto-Tool drill press will do many jobs, and the more you use it, the more you will find to do on it.

QUICK FIXES

A.

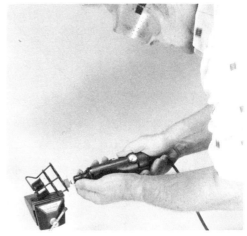

B.

C.

D.

A. One reason you might have trouble rethreading a pipe after a plumbing repair is the accumulated dirt, rust and pipe joint compound in the pipe threads. Use the wire brush in the Moto-Tool or Flex Tool to clean them out. Also, if pipe is large enough to permit it, clean threads inside fitting into which pipe threads.

B. Going to spray paint a small item like this? Get rid of all rust beforehand by grinding with an abrasive accessory. Operator wears safety goggles to keep flying bits of abrasive and rust from his eyes. He also uses a two-handed grip for good control of the tool. Select the abrasive grinding point shape that best suits the job.

C. Fine silver pieces like this which have tarnished can be cleaned with silver polish, but that is sometimes a long job, especially if an orante design such as this is involved. Use the cloth polishing wheel in the Moto-Tool to clean the high spots on the design and also for cleaning flat areas.

D. The point felt polishing accessory can complete the silver cleaning job by getting down into the crevices. Dremel Polishing Compound can be used in conjunction with any of the polishing points or wheels without damaging the silver.

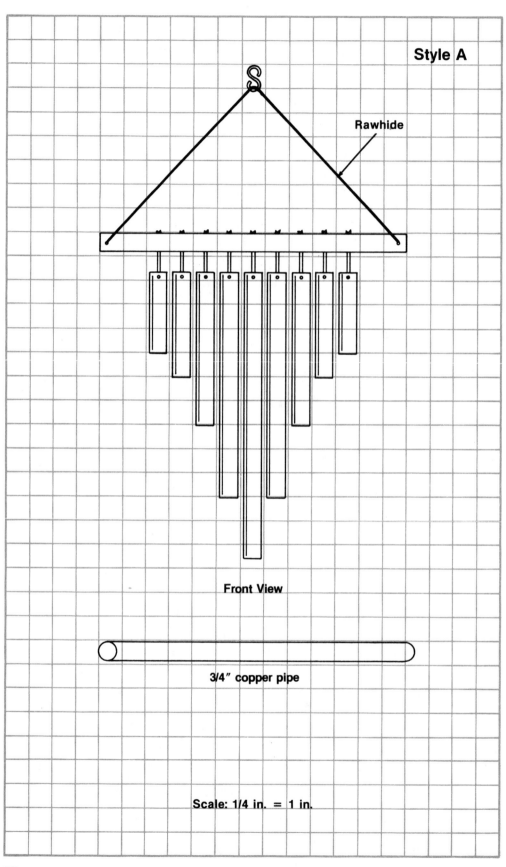

Style A

Rawhide

Front View

3/4" copper pipe

Scale: 1/4 in. = 1 in.

Project 2

COPPER WIND CHIME
There is no more pleasant sound than the melodic tinkling of a wind chime in an evening breeze. Here are plans for two made of copper. Take your choice.

Style A — Cathedral Chimes

Materials:
3/4-in. rigid copper pipe
1/8-in. rawhide lacing
1/8-in. wood dowels
S hook

Tools:
Moto-Tool Drill Press
Saw blade accessory No. 406
1/8-in. drill bit

Our Cathedral Chimes consist of 9 copper chime pipes suspended from a copper crosspipe. The crosspipe is 14-in. long. Chime pipe lenghts are seen on Plan A. Before beginning, make V-block jig (See Detail A). Use it on drill press when drilling 1/8-in. holes in pipes. Refer to Plan A for hole locations. Note holes near each end of crosspipe for the rawhide hanger. Holes go through both sides of pipes. Cut chime pipes and drill 1/8-in. holes near top of each, again using

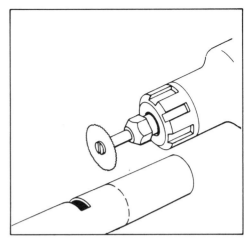

DETAIL B. To cut pipe, use No. 406 saw in Moto-Tool. Clamp pipe and hold Moto-Tool in two-handed grip.

V-block jig. When cutting pipe, clamp it to bench. Use saw accessory No. 406 in Moto-Tool, holding tool with both hands during cutting. Use aluminum oxide point in Moto-Tool to remove burrs and make pipe ends and holes smooth. Cut 9 pieces of 1/8-in. dowel, each 1-in. long, and press into holes in chime pipes. Tie rawhide laces around these dowels (See Detail C) and run up through holes in crosspipe, securing by big knots on top. Add rawhide with S hook, as shown, for hanging.

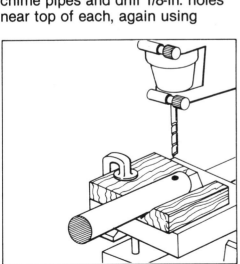

DETAIL A. Make this V-block jig to hold pipe while drilling. Clamp jig to drill press table.

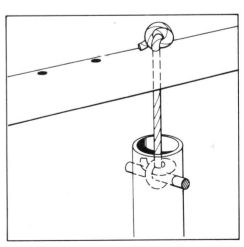

DETAIL C. Press fit a 1-inch length of 1/8-in. dowel in pipe, then tie rawhide around it as shown here.

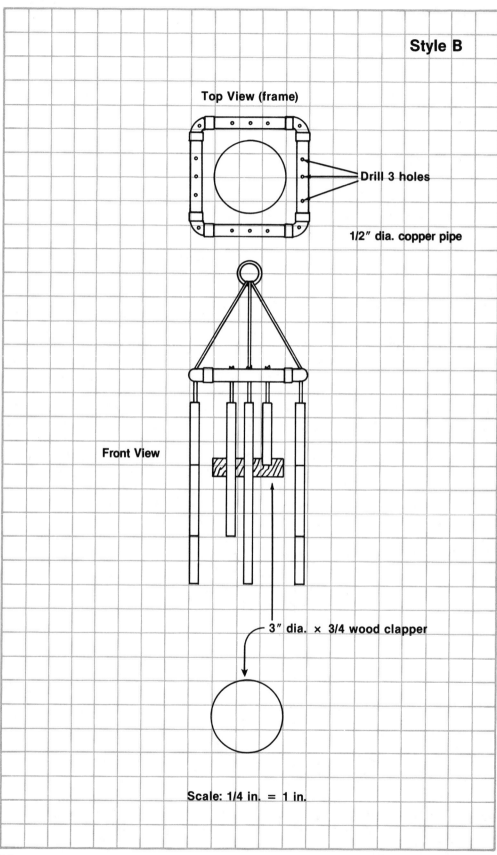

Style B

Top View (frame)

Drill 3 holes

1/2″ dia. copper pipe

Front View

3″ dia. × 3/4 wood clapper

Scale: 1/4 in. = 1 in.

Style B: Mandarin Chimes

Materials:
1/2-in. rigid copper pipe
1/2-in. 90-degree copper elbow
 fittings (4)
1/8-in. rawhide lacing
Redwood, 3/4 × 3-in.

The Mandarin Chimes offer a hint of Chinese decor. Make square top section of 4-in. pieces of 1/2-in. copper pipe joined by 90-degree elbows (See Detail D). Use drill press (with a hardboard pad under work) to drill twelve 1/8-in. holes in this frame (3 on a side), plus one at each corner. Plan A shows locations of holes and length of chime pipes. Cut 12 chime pipes as shown, and drill 1/8-in. hole near top of each, using V-block jig. Attach rawhide hangers to each, using dowels as was done in Style A. Make redwood clapper 3-in. in diameter to hang inside of chimes as shown in Detail E. Allow the copper to assume an aged look, or polish it, using polishing compound and a bristle brush in the Moto-Tool. After polishing, coat each tube with lacquer.

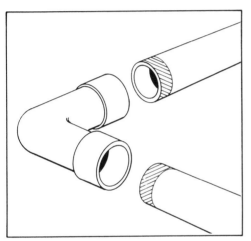

DETAIL D. Pipe elbows form the corners of the square top of the Mandarin Chimes.

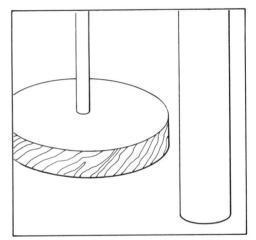

DETAIL E. Cut 3-in. circle of redwood and suspend on rawhide or a long dowel to serve as a clapper.

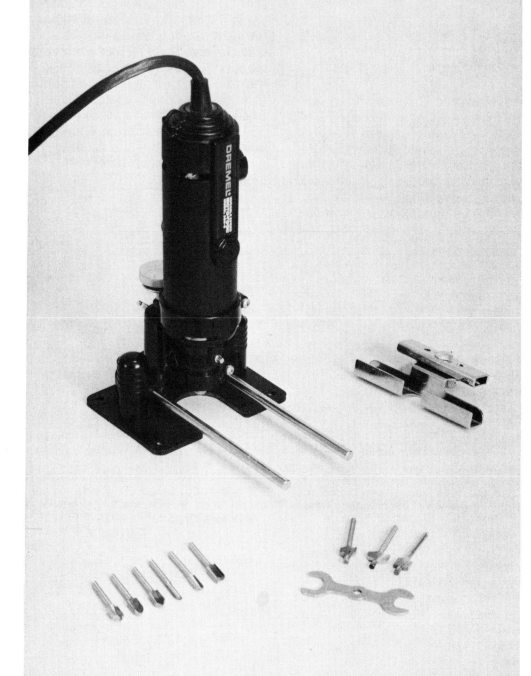

CHAPTER THREE

The Moto-Tool Router

The router is one of the most useful tools in woodworking.
With it, you progress from simple sawing and drilling into shaping
and machine carving of wood.

Basically, a router is a high-speed motor, mounted vertically so that the cutter in its chuck enters and cuts the wood workpiece directly below it. Some of the jobs a router will do are to carve decorative shapes in edges, cut recesses in surfaces, and cut internal grooves and channels of different sizes and shapes.

The Moto-Tool Router consists of a Moto-Tool, used as the power component, fitted to the Router Attachment. Though compact in size, this router can be just as precise and accurate as a full-sized model. It enables you to make cove edges, cut rabbets and dadoes, and make a variety of wood joints. Also, you can cut slots and veins, and rout out or recess areas on a surface so that inlays can be set In. It Is the ideal tool for cutting recesses for door and cabinet hinges to the exact shape and depth needed.

Making furniture? You can cut flutes in furniture legs with the router. Making a carving board? Rout a tree-shaped design in the center of the board to carry the juices to a collecting trough which you rout out at one end. Need a nameplate for your desk? Rout the letters out of a wood or plastic piece of the proper size.

The router is fun to use, and is a tool that encourages work. After learning to use it, you are likely to start trying to invent projects so that you can rout more often.

Setting up the tool

To install the Moto-Tool in the router attachment, first loosen the screws on the split ring clamps on the attachment. Next, loosen the wing nut on the height adjustment of the attachment. Turn the depth adjusting knob so that the upper or movable split ring is as high as it can go.

Insert the Moto-Tool, collet vertically down, in the holder, making

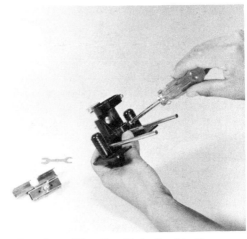

When installing the Moto-Tool in the router attachment, first loosen the screws on the split ring clamps.

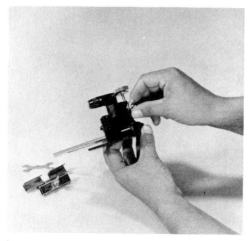

Loosen the wing nut on the depth adjustment of the accessory. This unlocks the depth adjustment.

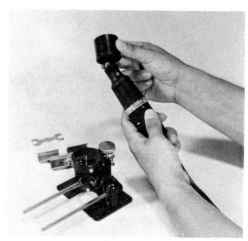

For the Moto-Tool Model 260, a sleeve is required to allow it to fit the router attachment.

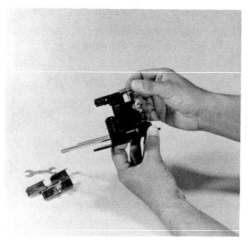

Next, turn the depth-of-cut adjustment knob until the upper ring is as high as it will go. Don't force.

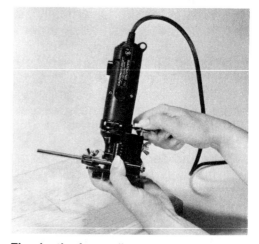

The depth-of-cut adjustment lowers the cutter 1/32-inch for each full turn of the knurled wheel.

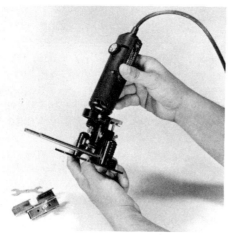

With the collet pointing down, insert the Moto-Tool so that it rests in the base of the lower split ring.

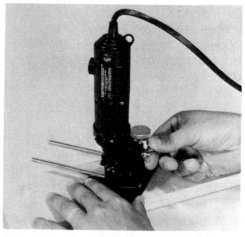

After the cutter depth has been set, it is locked in place by turning this wing nut finger tight.

sure that it rests on the base of the lower split ring. (If you have a Model 260 Moto-Tool, a sleeve is required to allow it to fit in the router attachment. The groove inside the top of the sleeve snaps over the ridge just below the nameplate of the Moto-Tool. Align the split in the sleeve on the Moto-Tool with the split in the top split ring of the router attachment.)

Once the Moto-Tool is in place, tighten the screws on the split ring clamps. The router is now ready for use.

Grips on either side of the router base permit you to hold and guide it. Practice controlling the cut.

Router controls

Grips. Two grips, one on either side of the base, permit you to hold and guide the router. If you have never used a router before, your first few minutes with this one should be spent in getting the feel of guiding the tool by holding these grips.

Depth-of-cut adjustment. The depth of the router's cut can be adjusted from 0 up to 5/16 inch. The depth is adjusted by turning the knurled depth adjustment wheel on the attachment. The cutter is lowered 1/32 inch by each full turn of the wheel. A calibrated scale on the side of the router housing gives a visual measurement of the depth of cut.

Depth adjustment lock. The depth adjustment wheel should be locked after adjustment, so that it holds tight while you work. The wing nut on the depth adjustment is turned finger tight to lock it.

Edge Guide. The edge guide permits you to make straight cuts easily. Two guide rods protrude from the attachment, and the edge guide is clamped over these. Fit the locator notches in the edge guide over the guide rods, then tighten the wing nut to lock the guide in place.

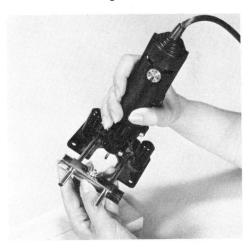

The edge guide, extended out from the router on rods, permits you to make perfectly straight cuts.

Edge guide is shipped upside-down on router. When this is corrected, the wing nut and bolt must be reversed again to get everything in the correct position. Additional clearance is gained by turning guide around not by turning it upside-down.

To set the edge guide, measure the distance from the edge of the workpiece to point where the cut is to be made. Then loosen the locking nut on the edge guide and move the guide until it is this same distance from the cutter. For accuracy, measure from the edge of the workpiece

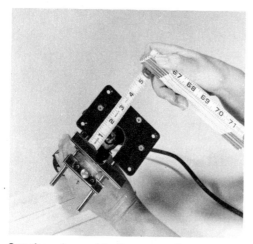

Set the edge guide the same distance from the cutter as the distance from the workpiece edge to the edge of the cut.

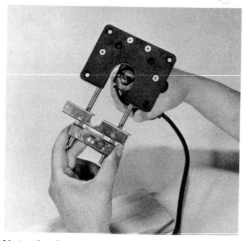

Note the four holes at the corners of the router base. These permit it to be mounted in a shaper table.

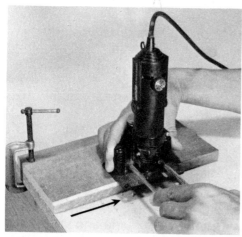

When shaping an edge that is toward you, move the router along the workpiece from left to right.

to the edge of the intended cut nearest the edge of the workpiece. Then set the edge guide by measuring the same distance from the face of the edge guide to the cutting edge of the cutter.

Cutters. Router cutters are mounted in the collet in the same way as other cutters. See Chapter One. The cutter shank is inserted into the collet as deep as it will go, and then the chuck cap is tightened with the wrench. The cutting part of the router bit extends only about 1/2 inch below the chuck cap when properly installed. Always unplug the electrical plug of the tool before changing cutters.

Use as a shaper. You will find four holes drilled in the base of the attachment. These permit the router to be mounted in a table so that it can be used as a miniature shaper. We will go into this use later in the chapter, where we will show you how to build a compact shaper table.

Using the router

If you have never used a router before, or if you have used only a big one, collect some scrap wood and practice routing with the pieces clamped to your workbench. If you have used a full-sized router, you will have to become accustomed to the smaller size, lighter weight and easier handling of the Moto-Tool Router. You should get the feel of guiding the router by the hand grips.

Direction of work. The Moto-Tool turns in a clockwise direction when viewed from above, as was explained in the chapter on the drill press. This should be kept in mind when operating the router. You want to move the router so that the cutting edges are advanced into the wood. This means that if you are:

1. Shaping the edge of a workpiece with the edge toward you, move the router from left to right.

2. Shaping the edge of a work-

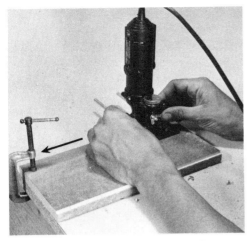

Shaping an edge on the far side of a board, move the router along the workpiece from right to left.

To set depth of cut, loosen the wing nut on the router back and then turn the large knurled adjusting knob.

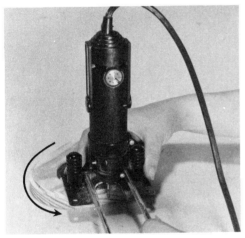

When shaping the outer edge of an oval or circular workpiece, move the router counterclockwise.

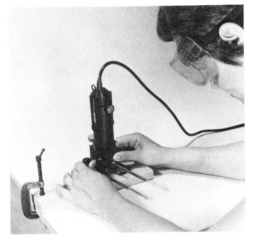

Safe router operations call for safety goggles, and the use of both hands to guide the tool.

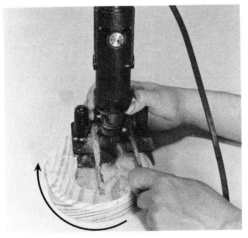

If shaping the inner edge of an oval or circular workpiece, move the router around the work clockwise.

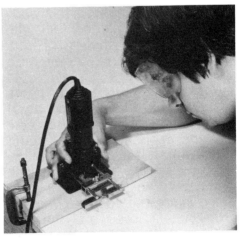

In the beginning, practice on scrap wood and learn to make precise cuts right where you want them.

piece with the edge away from you, move the router from right to left.

3. If you are shaping the outer edge of a circular or oval piece of work, move the router around the work in a counterclockwise direction.

4. If shaping the inner edge of a circular or oval workpiece, move the router around the work in a clockwise direction.

Setting the depth of cut. To set the depth of cut, loosen the wing nut at the back of the router, and turn the large knurled adjusting knob until the cutter extends the required depth. The cutter moves 1/32 inch for each complete turn of the adjusting wheel. Check the depth adjustment gauge located on the left side of the router. It is marked in 1/16 inch graduations, which means that the indicator will move one full mark for each two turns of the depth adjustment wheel. Tighten the locking screw after adjusting the depth, then check the depth reading again. Sometimes the depth changes slightly as the locking screw is tightened. Reset the depth if necessary.

Beginning the cut. Turn the router on at full speed. Grasp the handles or posts on each side of the router base firmly. For more accurate work, you will find it best to rest the heels of your hands on the workpiece while guiding the tool with your fingers. The friction of your hand will keep the router from moving out of line.

When making any kind of a cut, the router should be turned on at full speed *before* the cutter contacts the wood. If the cutter starts to turn while it is in contact with the workpiece, you may get a sharp kick of the tool and lose control of it, risking injury and possible damage to the cutter. Because of the high speed on the Moto-Tool, the kick is minimized when the cutter is spinning as it contacts the workpiece.

Using the edge guide, you cut a shape along the edge of a workpiece. Use for wood joints and decorative edges.

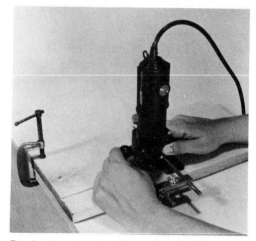

Beginning at one edge, you can cut grooves or channels across the workpiece. Use the edge guide.

Blind cut is made when you lower cutter into wood surface and begin cutting. Here, area to be routed is marked.

Router safety

As you will discover quickly, the router throws a lot of material as it cuts. It is imperative that you wear safety glasses to protect your eyes.

Always pull the electrical plug on the router when changing bits. If the Moto-Tool should start accidentally as you are doing this, you could be badly cut.

When a router bit becomes dull, have it sharpened by a professional or install a new bit. When a bit becomes gummed or clogged, clean it before further use.

Always be certain that the workpiece is firmly secured by clamps before working on it. Otherwise it might be thrown by the spinning bit, especially if the bit should hit a knot in the wood.

Never attempt to hold the workpiece with one hand while holding the router with the other. Clamp the work and hold the router with both hands.

Keep your eyes and your attention on the work in front of you. If there is a distraction in the room, stop work until it subsides.

Speed of the cut

Never force a cut with the router. Let the speed of the Moto-Tool and the sharp edges of the router bit do the work. In hardwood or grainy softwood, you will have to move more slowly than in grain-free softwood. In either case, you will find that the router cuts smoothly and easily at the proper speed.

If you force the router into a cut, especially in hardwood, the bit will take bigger bites, making a rougher finish. You may also slow the motor down by forcing the cut. Combined with the bigger bites, this slow speed can cause splintering and gouging instead of smooth cutting.

The proper feed is a matter of experience. The hardness or graini-

ness of the wood, the depth of cut being used, and the bit size all enter in to determing the proper feed. The larger the bit and the deeper the cut, the slower the router should move in the work. Wood that is knotty, pitchy or damp will cut slower.

It is also possible to permit the router to cut too slowly. If you hold it back from its normal cut — something you might do, for example, if you were concentrating on cutting an intricate shape and were very concerned about following a guideline — you permit the router bit to spin in place without cutting. This produces friction and heat, and you may then get burning or glazing on the workpiece. If the bit gets too hot, it will lose its temper or hardness and will be ruined.

The proper feeding speed is not difficult to ascertain. The secret is to let the tool do the work. It tends to work at the right cutting speed. Don't force it, and don't hold it back. Learn to guide it with a minimum pressure.

Concentrate in the beginning on learning to control the router to make precise cuts just where you want them. Learn to judge how fast the tool cuts, and how it tends to move slightly in the direction of its rotation. By applying light, even pressure, you can offset the slight feel of torque and guide the router along the cutting line.

Working with the router

Essentially, there are four types of work the router will do:

1. Edge cuts. Using an edge cut, you cut a shape along the edge of a workpiece. The edge guide is always used for this type of work so that your cut is perfectly straight. Edge cuts make a decorative edge (for example, the edge of a plaque or a shelf board) on the workpiece.

You also use edge cuts to make certain wood joints. You can make several cuts with different cutters to make unusual decorative edges.

2. Cut recesses, grooves and channels which start at an edge. Using this type of cut, you begin at an edge and cut into the field of the workpiece. If you were making a small wall rack with shelves, for example, you would cut grooves across each of the side panels in which the ends of the shelves would fit. The grooves would be just wide enough to receive the shelves, and when assembled, the shelves would be well supported.

In cutting a recess for a cabinet hinge, you would begin at the edge and, using a freehand side to side motion, cut into the field making cuts not quite the full width of the recess. Continue making successive cuts into the field until the recess is routed out. Then outline the recess with a final blind cut around its perimeter. Because the cutter is always at the same depth, your recess will have a smooth and uniform depth.

3. Blind cuts. When you lower the cutter into the surface of a workpiece instead of starting at an edge, you make a "blind cut." Blind cuts are for routing out internal recesses and grooves. You might rout an internal recess, for example, to inlay of another species of wood into it. To make an inlaid chess board, you might make 64 such recesses.

When making blind cuts, keep the maximum depth of the cut to 1/8-inch. This will assure longer life for the cutting bit and less strain on the Moto-Tool. If you want to cut deeper, make several passes.

4. Freehand routing. All of the above cuts involve the use of a guide to produce straight cuts. You can also make freehand cuts. If, for example, you wanted to carve your signature into a surface, perhaps to make a nameplate, you could pencil

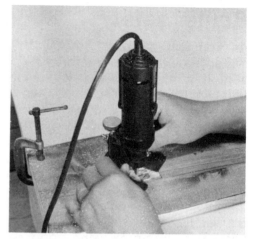

Observing the guide pattern drawn on the workpiece, router is moved back and forth across indicated area.

Blind recess has been cut within marked area on workpiece. Cuts like this should be no more than 1/8 inch deep.

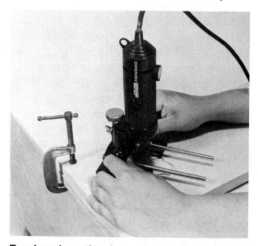

Freehand routing is routing without the use of a fence or other guide. Sketch design on the wood first.

the signature on the surface and then cut a groove along the pencil line. In wood carving, you could use the router to cut away large areas of wood around the area to be carved. Then you could switch to the high speed cutters in the Moto-Tool to carve the design you want in the remaining wood.

Recessing

To make recess, first lightly pencil a guideline on the workpiece surface showing the outer dimensions of the cut. Then set the depth of the cutter, and begin freehand cutting at the top of the marked area, just inside the guide line. When you have routed out the field of the recess, clamp a guide across the work to steer the router as you dress the edges of the recess. Cut to the guideline.

For slots and small recesses, it is better to use the guide from the beginning, and do no freehand cutting.

If the recess is to be deeper than 1/8 inch — perhaps 1/4 inch — make the first cut with the depth set at 1/8 inch. When the entire recess has been routed out, go back and, with the cutter depth set at 1/4 inch, repeat the entire recessing process.

The maximum depth to which you can cut is 5/16 inch.

One caution to observe when cutting any type of fairly large recess (but not larger in dimension than the base of the tool): Make the first cut of the recess, then move the router *away* from it for the second and successive cuts. The reason is that the router base rests on the workpiece surface. As long as you are moving *away* from the first cut when making a recess, the router will have solid surface beneath it. If, however, you move the router toward the cut, and make the second and successive cuts beyond the first cut, the router will not be firmly based.

If the recess is large or larger than the base of the router, you cannot make a second cut to increase its depth.

Fences and guides

The edge guide, as noted before, serves to guide the router in making straight cuts. The edge guide rides along the edge of the workpiece and therefore can only serve when that edge is perfectly straight. In addition, the edge guide permits cuts no more than 2-1/2 inches in its normal position, up to 4-1/8 inches by

For routing a groove or recess in the field of a workpiece, use a straight-edge guide clamped in place.

For guided cuts that are more than 4-1/8 inches from an edge, use a straightedge guide clamped to the work.

removing the edge guide, turning 180 degrees and replacing.

There will be times when you want to make guided cuts more than 4-1/8 inches from the edge. To do this, you must improvise a *straightedge guide.* A straightedge guide is nothing more than a perfectly straight piece of wood or metal clamped to the workpiece with C-clamps or other clamping device.

Position the straightedge guide so that when the back of the router rests against it, the router cutter bit is located where you want to cut. Remember to calculate the width of the cutter bit in making this placement. It is generally best to draw any guideline to indicate the edge of the cut.

Now turn the router on at full speed and place it against the clamped straightedge guide. Hold it firmly against the guide as you move it along the guideline and make the cut.

If it is necessary to make successive cuts, loosen the clamps and move the straightedge before beginning the second cut, and move it for each cut thereafter.

A box guide can be useful if you must cut the same internal groove or recess over and over again, as you would in recessing the 64 squares on a chess board. A box guide is simply a frame of wood, like an empty picture frame, made so that the router is guided by the four interior sides. You must make each box guide to the specific measurements of the job at hand, but the time is well spent because of the resulting accuracy and speed of cutting.

A pattern guide is just the opposite of a box guide. That is, the router is guided by the outside of the pattern, whereas with the box, it is guided by the inside faces.

Let's assume for a minute that you want to cut rectangular reces-

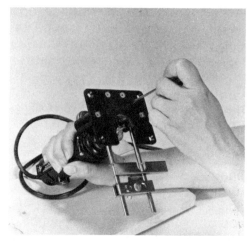

If it is necessary to remove edge guide rods, loosen the two Phillips screws in bottom of baseplate.

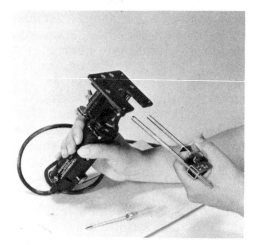

With the screws in the bottom of the baseplate loosened, pull straight out on the edge guide to remove it.

A box guide is a frame much like a picture frame surrounding the router to guide it, as shown.

ses in a number of square wood workpieces. The idea of the pattern guide is to cut a rectangle against which the router is guided to make the first outline cut of the rectangular recess. With that cut made, you then rout out all the material inside of it, and you have your recess.

The important thing in making the pattern guide is to make it small enough so when the base of the router rides against the pattern edge, the cutter is positioned where you want it. Pattern guides below approximately 2 inches on a side are not practical because they do not provide enough guiding surface.

To plan the pattern, measure the distance from the cutting edge of the cutter bit to the back of the base plate of the router. Then make a full-sized drawing of the cut you wish to make. On this drawing, make a smaller outline drawing located as far inside of the full-sized drawing as the distance from the cutter edge to the router back plate. Use this small drawing as a pattern to cut the pattern guide from 1/8-inch hardboard.

Place the pattern guide on the workpiece and clamp it down. Turn the router on and place the back of the plate firmly against this guide. Lower the cutter into the work and, cutting in a counterclockwise direction, make the cut. Be sure to hold the router against the pattern guide piece during the entire cut.

If you plan to remove the center material inside the outline, then use a box guide, described earlier, instead of the pattern guide.

Router bits

Nine high speed router bits are available for use with the Moto-Tool router. All have 1/8-inch shanks. Router bits available for full-sized routers generally have larger shanks. Do not attempt to use any of these bits in the Moto-Tool router.

It is important to use the proper-sized accessories in Moto-Tool collets, as was noted in Chapter One, for safe operation and to avoid damage to the collet.

Straight bits. Three straight bits are available. These are Nos. 650, 652, and 654, which are, respectively, 1/8, 3/16, and 1/4-inch bits. These measuremets indicate the width of the cut each bit will make. Straight bits are flat on the bottom for cutting square grooves, rabbets and dadoes, and for leveling recessed areas.

Veining bits. Two veining bits are available. These are Nos. 610 (1/4 inch) and 632 (1/4 inch). A veining bit is designed for decorative grooving, carving, lettering, and making small coves and other shapes. No. 610 cuts a vein with a V-bottom. No. 632 cuts a vein with a round bottom.

V-groove bit. One V-groove bit is available, No. 640, and is a "corner round bit" for cutting quarter diameter shapes or chamfered edges and for various types of decorative carving.

Piloted bits. Three piloted router bits are available. These are Nos. 612, 613, and 614. No. 612 is a 3/32-inch beading bit. No. 613 is a 3/16-inch cove bit. And No. 614 is a 1/8-inch rabbet bit. These bits all have 1/8-inch pilots. Refer to the accompanying drawings to see the shapes and dimensions cut by each bit.

A *piloted* bit is one which has an extension of the shaft below the cutter blade. This small extension is a pilot for guiding the bit along an edge. Thus a piloted cove bit will cut a cove shape along the edge of a workpiece without the need for any other kind of guide. The pilot itself rests against the bottom part of the edge and automatically limits the depth of cut. Piloted bits are intended specifically for decorative cutting of edges.

No. 612 is a beading bit. It is used

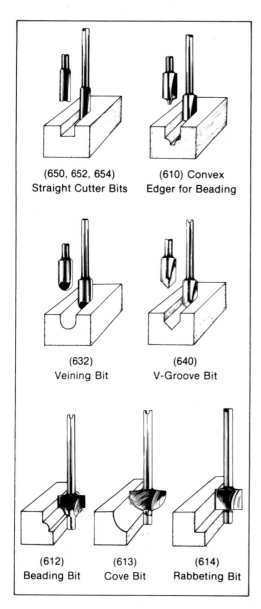

(650, 652, 654)
Straight Cutter Bits

(610) Convex
Edger for Beading

(632)
Veining Bit

(640)
V-Groove Bit

(612)
Beading Bit

(613)
Cove Bit

(614)
Rabbeting Bit

to round the top edge of a workpiece.

No. 613 is a cove bit. It is used to cut a cove or concave shape in the edge of the workpiece.

No. 614 is a rabbet bit, designed specifically for rabbeting. A rabbet is a square cut, and in the case of this bit, is a cut 1/8 inch deep and 1/8 inch in from the edge of the workpiece. This can be used as a type of decorative edging. You also can make rabbet joints with it for joining two pieces of 1/4-inch stock together. Cut the rabbet on the top side of one piece and on the bottom side of the other. The two pieces can then be glued together with the shaped edges fitting into each other. A rabbet joint is much stronger than a butt joint where the two pieces are simply glued edge to edge.

Sharpening bits. Dremel router bits are made of high speed tool steel and will retain their sharpness for long periods of cutting. But they will eventually become dull through use or through cutting in extremely hard materials. Then they should be sharpened.

Sharpening of router bits is a specialized art. You should have your bits sharpened by a professional.

There are a number of ways to protect router bits and retain their sharpness. One sure way to ruin the sharp edge of a router bit is to get it hot. A bit can become heated by being forced to cut too fast in hard work, or by being restrained so that it cuts too slowly, thus spinning and creating friction. To avoid both problems, allow the cutter to work at the optimum speed for the material in which you are working.

While you always start a blind cut by lowering the bit to the surface of the work and allowing it to cut into the work, you should do this no more than absolutely necessary. This practice can subject the cutter to high temperatures and cause it to overheat, especially in very hard materials.

Another way to protect your router bits is to remove any paint, varnish or dried glue from the workpiece before routing. These materials are very abrasive and will quickly dull cutters. Also, avoid using router bits in hardboard, particle board and other manmade wood products. The resins and binders in these products are extremely tough on any kind of cutting tools, including the carbide tipped variety.

The router as a shaper

A shaper is a cutting tool used in furniture making and other wood shaping arts. It will cut molding and form various decorative shapes on the edges of work. It can be used to accurately cut many wood joints.

The shaper is, in a sense, the opposite of a router. You hold the router and move it to the workpiece. The shaper is a stationary machine mounted in a table, and you move the workpiece to it. To convert a router to a shaper, then, you need to make a table and mount the router in it. The router is mounted upside down in the table, so that the cutter extends up through the table top.

In this chapter, you will find plans for constructing two shaper tables. One is simple in design and quick to build. The other is fancier and includes drawers for storage. Either design is an interesting project and would extend the use of your Moto-Tool router.

Using the shaper

There are some precautions to take when using the shaper. First, never work with very narrow pieces. After shaping, use the Dremel Table Saw

to cut the molding to the width you want.

Keep in mind that when you turn the router upside down in the shaper table, the rotation of the tool is reversed. The work now should be fed from right to left so that you work against the rotation of the shaper cutter.

When selecting stock for use in the shaper, be sure it is free of splits, checks and knots. The fast spinning router bit will hurl a knot quite a distance and the workpiece may be ruined at the knot location.

Always wear safety glasses when using either the router or the

See sketch for details. Remove router base plate by taking out screws.

The box guide must be fairly large and is made specifically for the particular routing job at hand.

PROJECT. A cutout the shape of the router base is made in the hardboard under-top of the shaper table.

Versatile Shaper Table
With Drawers for Storage

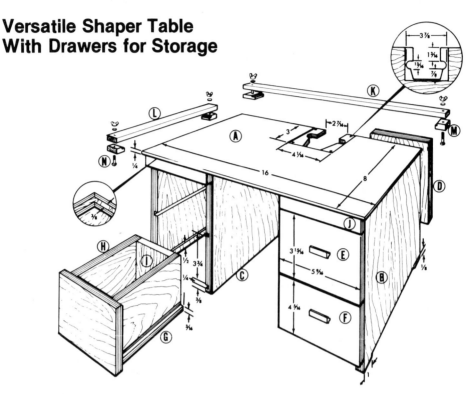

MATERIALS IN ORDER OF ASSEMBLY

A. Table top made of 16 × 8 × 1/4-in. plywood, topped
   by 16 × 8 × 1/8-in. hardboard.
B. Two outside pieces 6-3/4 × 9-1/2 × 1/2. Start drawer
   guides 1/2 from bottom.
C. Two inside pieces 6-3/4 × 9-3/8 × 1/2. Start drawer
   guides 1/2 from bottom.
D. Two backs 4-5/8 × 9-3/8 × 1/2.
E. Two upper drawer fronts 5-9/16 × 3-15/16 × 1/2.
F. Two lower drawer fronts 5-9/16 × 4-5/16 × 1/2.
G. Four drawer bottoms 5 × 6-1/8 × 1/2. Route a
   3/16 × 3/16 lip on bottom edge.
H. Eight drawer sides 6-3/16 × 3-7/16 × 1/2.
I. Four drawer backs 3-9/16 × 3-7/16 × 1/2.
J. Two front supports 5-9/16 × 1 × 1/2.
K. One guide 18″ × 1-3/4 × 3/4.
L. One guide 10″ × 1-3/4 × 3/4.
M. Four table guide clamps 1-1/2 × 1-3/4 × 3/4 notch
   to fit table top.
N. Four bolts 1-3/4 × 3/16 with washers and wing nuts.

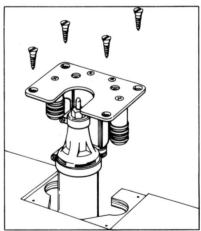

This is a deluxe shaper table, complete with drawers for storage of Moto-Tool accessories and other small parts and two guide assemblies. The Moto-Tool router fits into the cutout on the top, as shown. Note that the base of the router does not need to be removed before installation in the table.

Four small flathead woodscrews (not listed in materials list) hold router in place.

The table top consists of two parts, a 1/4-in. plywood piece, 16 × 8-inches, topped by 16 × 8-inch 1/8-inch hardboard. The cutout shown in the top detail drawing is made in the plywood top to support the Moto-Tool router. A cutout in the hardboard into which the router base fits is 3 × 4-1/4-inches.

shaper. Because the work is so fascinating, you will find yourself leaning quite close to the work watching the cutters shape the wood. Sawdust and shavings will be flying in all directions — and into your eyes if they are not protected by safety glasses.

When you feed work into the shaper, the cutter blade often is hidden by the workpiece. This creates a situation which could be dangerous. To protect yourself, *never permit your fingers to come within 4 inches of the cutter.* Use a pusher stick (see photo) for pushing work past the cutter. The

pusher stick will protect against accidental movement of your fingers too close to the cutter.

If you use your hand to push or guide a workpiece (beyond 4 inches), always anchor the heel of that hand against the table and use the fingers to push or guide the work. Any slip then will be no more than a finer length.

The shaper can be used in the making of jewel boxes from fine wood, clock cases, and other small cabinetry jobs where good wood joints are important to the project. You could make miniature moldings for doll houses, carve your

PROJECT. The router with its base plate removed fits into the cutout on the shaper table's under-top.

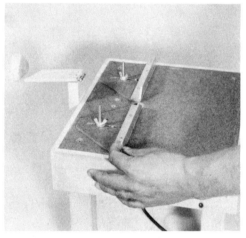

PROJECT. Right fence is placed back a little to guide work before cut. Left fence is forward, to guide work after cut.

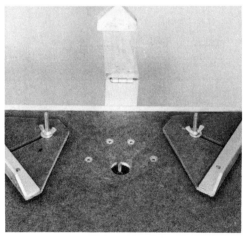

PROJECT. Four screws through top of the shaper table holder router in place. Use flathead machine screws.

The right fence, set back, guides the work before the cut. The left fence is set to guide work after the cut.

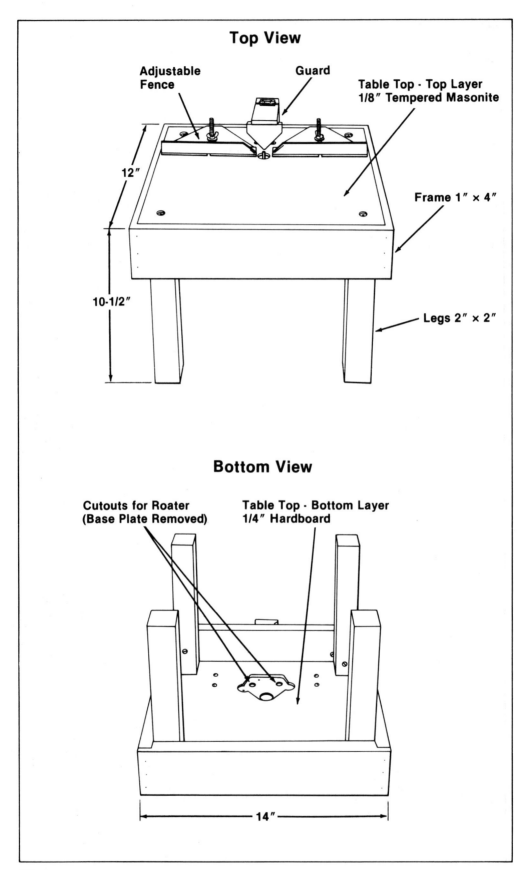

Top View

Adjustable Fence

Guard

Table Top - Top Layer 1/8″ Tempered Masonite

12″

10-1/2″

Frame 1″ × 4″

Legs 2″ × 2″

Bottom View

Cutouts for Roater (Base Plate Removed)

Table Top - Bottom Layer 1/4″ Hardboard

14″

own picture frames, and make distinctive moldings for cabinet doors.

The combination of the router and the shaper brings you a range of woodworking capabilities and yet demands little space.

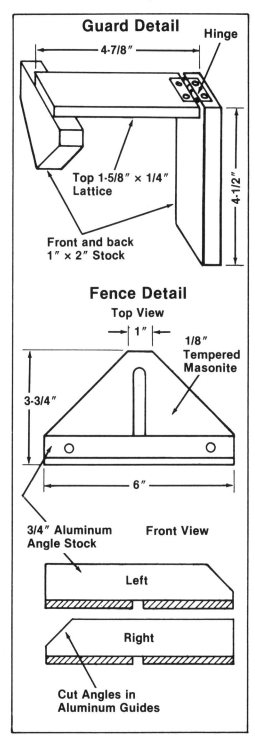

Guard Detail

Hinge

4-7/8"

4-1/2"

Top 1-5/8" × 1/4" Lattice

Front and back 1" × 2" Stock

Fence Detail

Top View

1"

1/8" Tempered Masonite

3-3/4"

6"

3/4" Aluminum Angle Stock

Front View

Left

Right

Cut Angles in Aluminum Guides

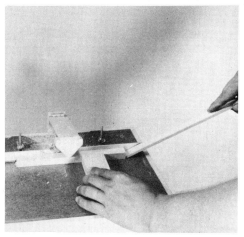

PROJECT. Always use a push stick to push work into the cutter. Never let fingers closer than 4 inches from cutter.

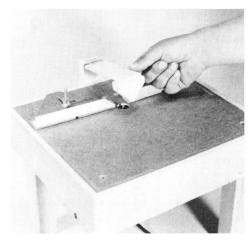

Guard attached to back of table is hinged for lifting, stays down during work.

With the router upside down in the shaper table, work should be fed from right to left across it.

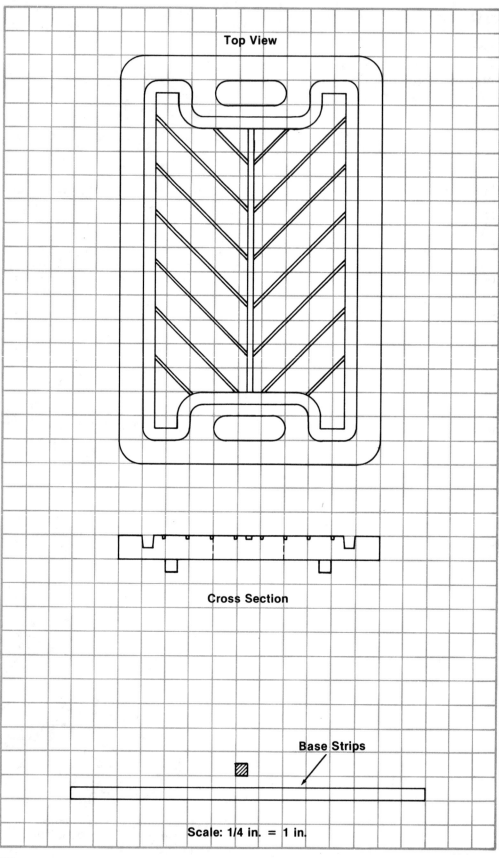

Top View

Cross Section

Base Strips

Scale: 1/4 in. = 1 in.

Project 3

CARVING MEAT TRAY
You'll be proud to carve the roast at the dinner table on this beautiful tray.

Materials:
1 × 2 hardwood of your choice
2 1/2 × 1/2 × 14 hardwood strips
Finish nails
Waterproof glue

Tools:
Moto-Shop Scroll Saw
Dremel Table Saw, Disc/Belt Sander
Moto-Tool with router attachment
Router bits No. 610, 632, 654 and 640
C-clamps and bar clamps
Straightedge

Begin by gluing hardwood stock with waterproof glue, clamping as shown, in Detail A, to make block slightly larger than finished size (11 × 7-in.). Be sure wood is aligned and surface is flat. After glue sets, trim block to finished size on table saw. Next, pencil in location of cutouts for handgrips at each end. Use Moto-Shop Scroll Saw to make these cutouts, as described in Detail B. Shape rounded corners on the disc sander, and sand top and bottom surfaces smooth. Refer to Plan A and draw gravy trough and

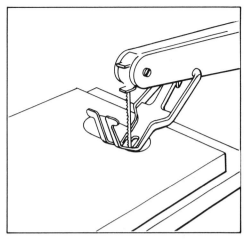

DETAIL B. To make handles, drill hole in waste area, feed saw blade through it, then make internal cut.

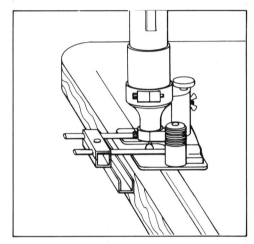

DETAIL C. Edge guide of router attachment controls routing of gravy trough or channel on tray.

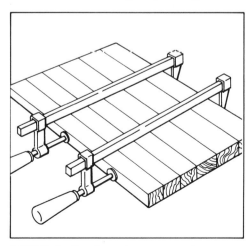

DETAIL A. Use bar clamps to hold hardwood pieces as glue dries. Use waterproof glue to permit washing.

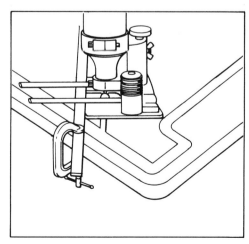

DETAIL D. For cutting "tree" troughs, clamp straightedge guide to tray. Move guide to rout each branch.

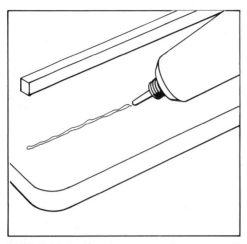

DETAIL E. Apply glue on tray bottom and attach 1/2 × 1/2 bottom strips by gluing and finish nailing.

"tree" design on top surface. Trough is 1/2-in. wide. Rout inner and outer edges of this trough using Moto-Tool with router attachment, edge guide, and No. 632 router bit (See Detail C). Then rout out material between with router bit No. 654. Round off top and bottom edges of tray using bit No. 610. Now rout "tree" pattern, making each branch 1/4-in. wide. Remove edge guide from router. Use router bit No. 640 and clamp straightedge guide, as shown in Detail D, across surface, moving it for each cut. After tree has been routed out, complete tray by sanding thoroughly. Glue and nail with finish nails the 1/2 × 1/2-in. strips on bottom as supports. Leave the tray unfinished or make an oil finish by rubbing surface with mineral oil and wiping clean.

QUICK FIXES

A.

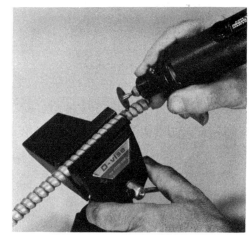

B.

C.

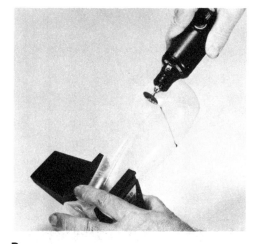

D.

A. Big augur bits can be restored after becoming dull or suffering damaged cutting edges. Use an abrasive wheel small enough to hone the edge, but don't change the shape or angle of the edge as you grind.

B. BX armored cable for electrical installations can be cut using the No. 409 emery wheel. Just cut across one link in the cable, then twist. Be careful to cut just the surface and not into the insulated wires inside.

C. When installing an electrical switch or wall outlet, trim the corners and edges of the cutout in the wallboard with an emery cutting wheel. Entire cutout can be made with the wheel, but job is done better with a hole saw.

D. The bottoms of plastic bottles in which detergents and other produces come make excellent throwaway containers for paints, thinners, solvents and other materials which are poured from a can before application. Rinse the plastic bottle first, then clamp it in the D-Vise by its handle. Use the No. 409 emery wheel in the Moto-Tool to cut around the circumference.

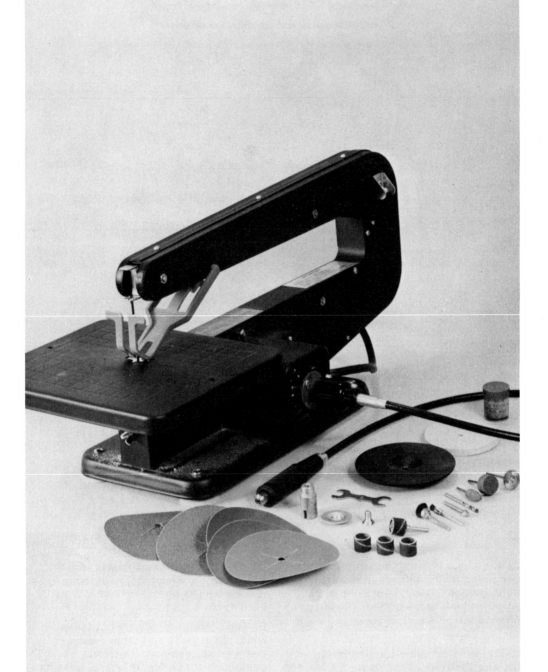

CHAPTER FOUR

The Moto-Shop

A multi-purpose workshop, the Moto-Shop provides a scroll saw, a disc sander, and the flexible shaft attachment which enables you to do accurate work in places that are difficult to reach.

The Moto-Shop is a complete workshop that will fit on a kitchen table. It combines a fast cutting, accurate scroll saw, a disc sander, and a flexible shaft tool that uses the same cutters and accessories as the Moto-Tool. The basic unit is the scroll saw, but by connecting different attachments to the power takeoff, the unit is converted to a sander, a buffing wheel, and a flexible shaft machine. With this combination you can saw, drill, polish, sharpen, sand, buff, carve, engrave and perform other operations.

With the hand gripping top arm of the saw, depress the blade holder on top of the arm and remove the saw blade.

Setting up the tool

The Moto-Shop is packed with the saw table unattached. Assembly consists of attaching the saw table to the body of the machine. The accessories — the sanding disc, buffing wheel, and flexible shaft — are designed for use from the power takeoff on the right side of the tool.

Attaching the saw table. Take the Moto-Shop from its box and place it on a table or workbench. Perform the following steps to attach the saw table:

1. With the hand gripping the top arm of the saw, remove the saw blade by pushing down on the top blade holder with the thumb. With

Remove the top wing nut of the table slide bracket, leaving the bolt in, and loosen the bottom wing nut.

the blade holder depressed, lift the blade out of the slot in which it rests at the top. Then lower the blade slightly and move it forward to detach it from the lower blade holder.

2. The table slide bracket extends upward from the base and has two wing nuts on it. Loosen the bottom wing nut and slide the table slide bracket upward about 1-1/2 inches. Retighten the wing nut.

3. Remove the top wing nut and its washer. Leave the bolt in position.

4. Locate the quadrant on the bottom of the saw table. Note that it has a curved slot in it.

5. Attach the saw table to the table slide bracket by inserting the bolt on the bracket through the curved slot in the quadrant. Be sure that the extruded boss at the top of the table slide bracket enters the hole in the quadrant. Place the washer on the outside of the bracket and tighten the wing nut over it.

6. Loosen the bottom wing nut and allow the slide bracket to drop all the way down to its original position. Retighten the wing nut.

7. Now replace the saw blade. Always be sure, when mounting a blade in the saw, that the teeth are pointing *downward*. For most cutting, they also should face the front, but they can be faced to the left or right if desired.

Insert the bottom of the blade into the lower blade holder by sliding the blade through the slot in the holder. Then push the blade holder down and insert the top pins of the blade into the upper blade holder. The blade is now ready for cutting.

Note: The unit will not operate without a blade mounted in the holders. When sanding or using the Flex-Shaft, a blade, preferably the No. 8030, should be installed. 8030, should be installed.

8. Locate the blade guard and note that it has pivot pins on the inside of the back of each arm. Insert

Attach the saw table to the table slide bracket by inserting the top bolt through the quadrant slot.

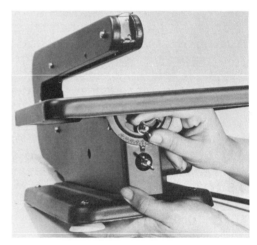

Now put the wing nut and its washer back on the bolt, and tighten it to secure the saw table in place.

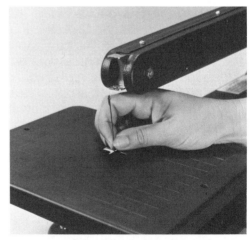

To replace the saw blade, insert the bottom end of the blade in the lower blade holder beneath the table.

Saw teeth must face down. Depress the blade holder on the arm and insert blade pins into the blade holder.

Insert the pivot pins inside of the back of each arm on the blade guard into the holes on the saw arm.

Lay the Moto-Shop on its right side and lubricate the connecting link bearing through the hole.

the left pivot pin in the hole on the left side of the top arm. Pull the arms of the blade guard apart slightly and snap the other pivot pin into the matching hole on the right side of the top arm. The scroll saw is now ready for work.

The Moto-Shop motor

The motor of the Moto-Shop runs on standard 110/120-volt household current, and operates at 3,450 RPM. The motor has two sealed bearings that never need lubrication. It is characteristic of the shaded pole motor to run a little warm, but this does not affect overall performance, so don't be concerned about it.

While the shaded pole motor itself never needs lubrication, it is necessary to place a few drops of ordinary non-detergent motor oil SAE 10, 20, or 30 on the connecting link bearing. This is done by laying the Moto-Shop on its right side and locating the hole on the left side of the frame opposite the motor housing. Insert the oil can in this hole and place several drops on the bearing.

Moto-Shop scroll saw

The Moto-Shop scroll saw will cut softwood up to 1-3/4 inches thick and hardwood up to 1/2 inch. It will cut aluminum up to 1/16 inch thick and copper to 18 gauge (3/64 inch thick).

The blade guard on the tool is one of the safest for this kind of saw. It not only keeps your fingers clear of the blade, but also acts as a hold down to keep the workpiece on the table. This helps prevent the blade from lifting the work and assures more accurate cutting.

While many scroll saws are designed so that cutting can be done with only one segment of the blade, the Moto-Shop has an adjustment which allows the table to be raised.

Thus, when one section of the blade becomes dull, you simply loosen the lower wing nut and raise the table slightly. This brings a new, unused section of the blade to the cutting area.

The short stroke of the saw blade, which makes this possible, also is a safety feature, since, because of the short stroke, even if contact is made with the blade, only minor damage at most would occur to the fingers.

For sawing work at an angle, the table can be tilted in either direction. Just loosen the top wing nut under the table and tip it to the desired angle. A calibrated scale on the quadrant under the table permits setting of angles.

With most scroll saws, you must turn the work when you want to saw the opposite angle on the other edge of a piece of work. (For example, if you were making a 45-degree miter cut at each end of the workpiece.) With the Moto-Shop saw, you simply tip the table in the opposite direction. By checking the scale on the quadrant, you can see that the angle is opposite and equal. If you cut a 45-degree angle at one end, you would tilt the table to set it for 45 degrees in the opposite direction. The cut across the other end of the work would be a reverse 45 degrees.

If you place the Moto-Shop on a smooth surface, the rubber suction cups at each corner will prevent it from sliding during use. If the work surface is rough — such as the surface of a well-used workbench — you may have to use a pad under it. A good one for the purpose is one sold for household kneeling. Another is the typical typewriter cushion. These pads will keep the Moto-Shop from moving in normal use.

The suction cups may be removed so that the Moto-Shop can be attached to a workbench. Use four

Move the table up or down to use sharper area of a blade after the part in use becomes dull.

For sawing the workpiece at an angle, the saw table can be tilted 45 degrees in either direction.

With the table tilted, feed the work into the saw to make an angled cut. Reverse the table for an opposite angle cut.

#10 round head or pan head wood-screws, 1-1/2 inches long, driven through the holes in the base and into the bench.

Cutting wood. Always feed wood workpieces into the blade of the scroll saw slowly and steadily. Do not force the wood into the blade or you may bend or break the blade. The rate of cutting depends to a large extent on the hardness of the workpiece and the sharpness of the blade. If the saw seems to be cutting slower than it should, you should suspect (1) a dull blade, or (2) a hard section of wood (perhaps a hidden knot).

If you find that the blade "wanders" when you are cutting, it is another indication that the blade is dull or that you are forcing the cut and causing the blade to bend or bow as it runs. First ease up on the pressure. If that doesn't improve the cutting action, then move the saw table up a little so as to use a new segment of the blade for cutting. If you have already used all segments of the blade, it is time for a new blade.

If all of the above do not correct the "wandering" problem, you may be applying side pressure to the blade as you cut. To check for this, release your grip on the workpiece slightly while you are cutting, and watch to see if it tries to nose slightly to the right or left. If it does, this indicates side pressure. Concentrate on feeding the workpiece straight into the teeth on the blade.

In order to cut wood more than 1-1/4 inches thick, the blade guard must be removed. To remove the guard, simply pull the pivot pins out of their holes in the top arm. When you have finished sawing the thick stock, be sure to re-install the guard.

The throat of the scroll saw — from the blade to the inside back of the bow — is 15 inches deep, allowing ample room for cutting boards and small panels. If you plan to

Always feed wood workpieces slowly, steadily, and straight into the saw blade. Do not force the cut.

Throat of the saw is 15 inches deep. Make a practice run to see if panels will turn in it before starting cut.

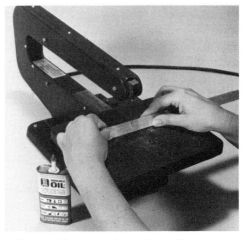

Before cutting metal, lubricate the saw blade with a light machine oil or rub it with a bar of parafin.

scroll inside cuts in a panel that approaches the limit of size of the throat, it is a good idea to remove the blade and make a practice run. That is, pretend you are cutting and move the panel as you would if the blade were in place. This will show you that you will (or will not) be able to turn the workpiece within the throat for the planned cuts.

Cutting metal. You can cut soft aluminum (the kind sold at your hardware store) up to 1/16-inch thick, and copper up to 18 gauge (3/64 inch thick). It is important when cutting metal to hold the work firmly on the table because there is

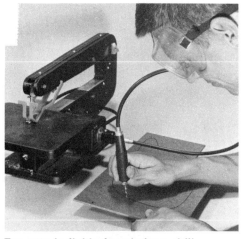

For cuts in field of workpiece, drill 2 adjacent holes with No. 150 drill (1/8-inch) in the waste area.

a tendency to buck as the saw sometimes grabs. Before cutting metal, lubricate the blade with machine or household oil or parafin. Coating the line to be cut with parafin or a crayon also helps. Feed the work slowly and with a steady pressure, but do not force the work into the blade. If you do, you will find it difficult to follow the line along which you are cutting and the blade may break. Metal is slower to cut than wood, so be prepared for it.

Inside cuts. Inside cuts are cuts that do not penetrate the edge made in the field of a workpiece. To make an inside cut, first drill two adjacent holes 1/8 inch in diameter and break the web between them (you can use the flexible shaft with High Speed Twist Drill No. 150, which is a 1/8-inch bit) in the waste area. Remove the blade from the saw, thread it through the hole in the workpiece, and then reinstall it.

Start the saw and make the inside cut, following your guidelines on the workpiece. When the cut is done, remove the saw blade again, pull it through the workpiece, and reinstall it on the saw.

Straight cuts. One of the great advantages of the scroll saw is its ability to make curved and reversed curve cuts, and to follow nearly any

Thread the saw blade through the hole you have drilled and reinstall it. Then begin cutting.

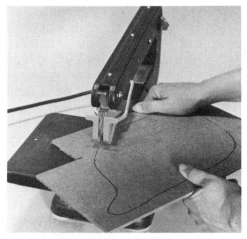

Guide work so that you cut along the guidelines on the workpiece. When the cut is finished, remove blade.

The blade can be mounted facing front, right or left. Here it is mounted facing to the right.

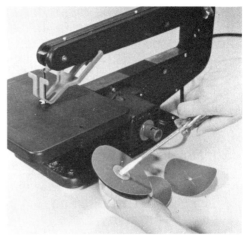

To mount sanding disc, insert screw through the washer, sanding disc and backing pad into the arbor and tighten.

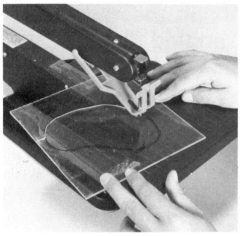

Some plastics melt at low heat. Experiment with each type to discover practical cutting speed.

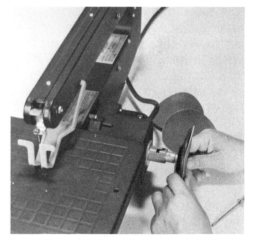

Insert the arbor into the power takeoff. Press on the disc slightly and rotate it until pin enters slot.

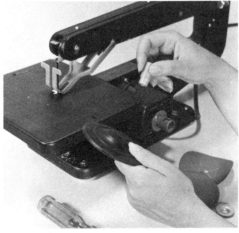

Sanding disc assembly consists of an arbor adapter, rubber backing pad and faceplate screw and washer.

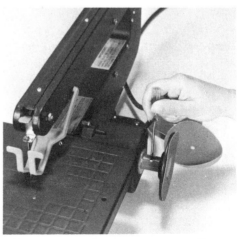

With the arbor all the way in, turn disc until you see the adapter set screw in the inside slot. Tighten it.

irregular guideline you might draw. You can, for example, make the intricate cuts necessary to create a jigsaw puzzle with interlocking pieces. (Jigsaw is another name for scroll saw, and the puzzle is named for the saw which made it possible.) Because the scroll saw cuts easily in all directions, it is difficult to make straight cuts with it.

If you look at the blade holder in the Moto-Tool, you will see that the blade can be mounted facing to the front or to the side. Slots in the holder accept the pins of the blade in either direction. For most cutting, the blade should be installed with the teeth facing to the front. The side slots make it possible to cut large scroll work. With the blade facing to the front, large pieces, when turned during scrolling, may hit the back of the frame. If this happens, release the blade and workpiece, and engage the blade in the appropriate side slot. Then continue to cut.

Cutting plastic. There are a number of different types of plastic materials on the market, and each reacts to heat in a slightly different way. The heat generated by the blade may melt some plastics quite quickly, so that the plastic material either fills the teeth on the blade and prevents cutting or fuses again behind the cut so that parts will not separate. Others will melt at higher temperatures and thus be easier to cut. So, while the Moto-Shop will cut all plastics, you will have to experiment with each to determine how fast it can be cut and how much pressure can be used.

The best way to cut plastic is to leave the protective paper on it, if it came covered that way. It also helps to lubricate the line to be cut by rubbing it with the corner of a block of parafin or a crayon.

Do not let melted plastic accumulate on the blade, as it may cause the blade to bind and break.

Blades for the scroll saw. Blades for use with the scroll saw include No. 8029, a fine tooth, and No. 8030, a coarse tooth. These come in packages of five. If you plan to do much sawing, it is good to have a supply of extra blades on hand.

The fine blade is for fine cuts in softer and/or thinner materials and for metal. The coarse blade cuts softer woods quite fast but with a rougher cut. It is good for hardwood cuts but not as good for metal as the fine blade. If you are not sure which one to use, try both to see which works best in any particular job.

Using the sanding disc

The round extension on the motor housing at the right side of the machine as you face it is the power takeoff for driving the sanding disc, flexible shaft and buffing wheel. These accessories are mounted on special adapters that fit into the power takeoff.

Note that whenever you operate an accessory on the power takeoff, the scroll saw blade must be in position on the saw. While the saw blade *must* be installed in order to

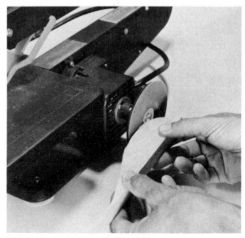

Hold the work in both hands and use the left or forward side of the disc for all disc sanding operations.

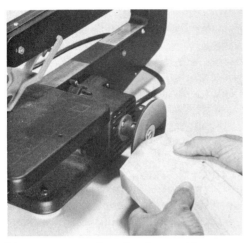

The coarse sanding disc is good for shaping on the disc sander because it removes material rapidly.

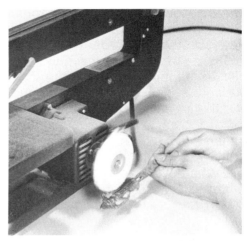

Do not buff against the face of the buffing wheel. Hold the item to be polished against the spinning edge.

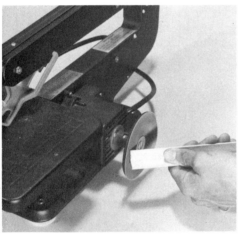

Discs quickly fill with metal and lose their abrasiveness when used to sand soft metals such as aluminum.

To attach the flexible shaft to the power takeoff, first turn Moto-Shop on.

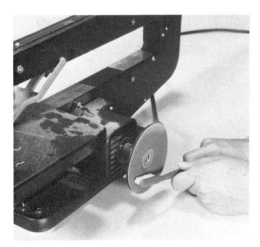

Sanding discs last longer if you brush out accumulations of dust. An old toothbrush works fine for this.

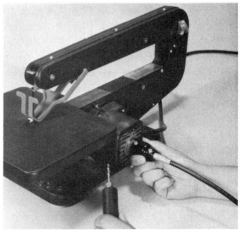

With Moto-Shop running, push nylon coupling as far into power takeoff as it will go. Then lock it by turning. Be sure hand piece is held in one hand.

use the power takeoff, you should never attempt to saw at the same time you use the power takeoff.

The sanding disc assembly consists of an arbor adapter, a washer, a screw, a rubber backing pad, and a sanding disc. To assemble the sanding disc, center a sanding disc against the rubber pad. Place the faceplate washer in the center of the sanding disk and then insert the arbor screw through the washer, sandpaper and rubber pad. Now thread the body of the arbor on the end of the screw protruding from the back of the rubber pad. Use a wide-bladed screwdriver to tighten the assembly.

Mounting the sanding disc assembly. To mount the sanding disc assembly on the power takeoff, first tilt the Moto-Shop and look down into the power takeoff. You will see a pin extending through the power takeoff shaft. (You don't have to tilt the Moto-Shop everytime you use the power takeoff. Just do it the first time to become familiar with the pin on the shaft.)

Insert the sanding disc arbor into the power takeoff with the slots on the arbor aligned with the pin in the power shaft. With slight pressure on the disc, rotate it slowly until you feel the pin enter the slot. When properly installed, the arbor slides all the way in; if you have not aligned the slots with the pin, the arbor will slide only part way in.

With the arbor all the way in, turn the sanding disc slowly until the adapter set screw comes into view in the inside slot. Tighten this set screw. (Note that the pin on the power shaft drives the accessory. The set screw does not, and is there to retain it during operation. Thus it need be only nominally tight).

When you turn the switch to ON, the sanding disc will spin at 3,450 RPM. To use the disc, hold the work in both hands and touch it against the spinning wheel. Sand only on

the forward side of the disk — that closest to you. If you have never used a sanding disc like this before, practice with some scrap wood to get the feel of how to touch the work to the disc, how to apply pressure to the workpiece, and how to turn the workpiece as you sand. The work is easy and a few minutes of practice is all that is needed.

Three different grades of sanding discs are available — coarse, medium, and fine. The coarse paper is a 60 grit and is excellent for shaping wood because it removes material rapidly. The general practice is to cut away material with the coarse

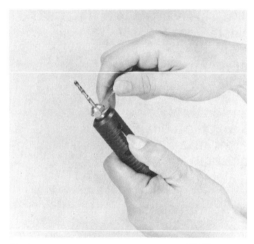

To insert accessory, turn saw off. Then depress chuck locking lever and turn chuck cap by hand until it locks.

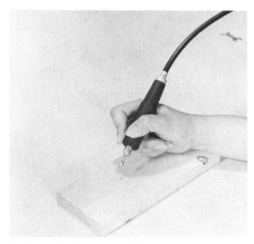

Hold shaft like a pencil between the thumb and forefinger. Control tip by moving the fingers, not the hand.

grit, and then use the finer discs to produce a smooth surface. The best results come when you use the three grades successively.

The medium grade (100 grit) is for minimum shaping, since it takes very little material, and for the first sanding of a piece. The fine grade (150 grit) is for final finishing of all woods. You can use these wheels, and especially the medium and fine wheels, on metal and plastics as well as wood. (Watch the heat build-up when working with plastics.)

When soft metals are used against these discs, they quickly fill with metal and lose their abrasiveness. Be sure to use all of the abrasive face of each disc so as not to waste any when sanding soft metals. And, if you have much of this type of sanding to do, have an ample supply of discs at hand.

The sanding discs will last longer and do a better job if you keep them free of accumulations of dust or other materials. Use an old toothbrush to clean away build-ups of material.

The buffing wheel. Attachment No. 4325 is a 3-inch buffing wheel made of multiple layers of cloth sewn together. It is fitted to the same arbor adapter as the sanding discs, and in the same manner.

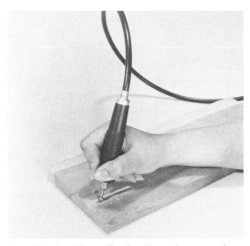

As with the Moto-Tool, allow the speed of the tool and sharpness of the cutter, not pressure, to do the work.

When the buffer is spinning, hold any wood, metal or plastic piece against its spinning edge to buff it to a shine. Do not buff against the face of the buffing wheel. A really good use of the buffing wheel is the buffing of work which has been coated with wax or polish. The buffer will bring it to a smooth, gleaming finish.

You also can use the buffer with Dremel No. 421 polishing compound for final finishing to a glassy smoothness. This technique can be used to repolish scratched watch crystals or plastic safety glasses.

The flexible shaft

The flexible shaft attachment for the Moto-Shop really makes this tool versatile. The flexible shaft is a 34-inch shaft which connects to the power takeoff. The other end of the shaft has a handpiece with a chuck and collet similar to the kind used in the Moto-Tool. The handpiece uses all the accessories and bits that the Moto-Tool does. For detailed information, see Chapter One.

There is a difference, however, between the Moto-Tool and the Moto-Shop flexible shaft. The Moto-Shop flexible shaft turns at 3,450 RPM. This means that although the flexible shaft can accommodate all the Moto-Tool accessories, the mode of operation must be slightly different because of the different speed.

The Moto-Flex Tool, which also has a flexible shaft attachment, operates at the speed of the Moto-Tool if you require this kind of speed for your work.

The flexible shaft will sand, cut, carve, drill, engrave and polish. The handpiece is a comfortable fit for the fingers and control of the tool is easy. Because of its shape, the handpiece can be worked in areas too restricted for other tools. This makes it particularly useful in the making of models and miniatures.

Setting up the flexible shaft. The method of attaching the flexible shaft to the power takeoff is slightly different than that for the other Moto-Shop accessories. Here are the steps:

1. Check the screw in the nylon coupling on the power-takeoff end of the flexible shaft. It should be screwed all the way in, and should not be removed or loosened.

2. Turn the Moto-Shop motor on.

3. Push the nylon coupling of the flexible shaft as far into the power takeoff as it will go.

4. To lock it in position, turn the nylon coupling of the flexible shaft counterclockwise while pushing it in.

5. To prevent the cable from becoming disconnected while the machine is running, grasp the handpiece (the end with the chuck) and twist the cable one half turn counterclockwise. (That is, to the left if the cable is held in your right hand.)

The handpiece. The chuck in the handpiece of the flexible shaft consists of a collet secured by a check cap, as in the Moto-Tool, and the chuck locking lever. The chuck locking lever has the same function as the locking pin of the Moto-Tool. It locks the shaft so the chuck cap can be tightened or loosened during a change of accessories.

Never try to operate the chuck lever while the flexible shaft is running.

The tool comes with a wrench to fit the chuck cap. To install an accessory in the chuck, depress the chuck locking lever and rotate the chuck cap by hand until the lock pins snaps into the depression in the shaft and prevents it from turning. You can feel this action when it happens, and the shaft will no longer turn.

Loosen the chuck cap with the chuck wrench. Remove the accessory in the chuck, and insert the shank of the new accessory as far as it will go into the collet. Keep the chuck locking lever depressed all during this operation. Now tighten the chuck cap gently and firmly but not excessively tight. Finally, release the chuck locking lever. This lever should never be pressed when the tool is running or when the flexible shaft is being engaged to the power takeoff. Damage can result.

Using the flexible shaft

Hold the flexible shaft like a pencil between your thumb and forefinger. Control the movement of the tip by moving your fingers rather than your whole hand — as you do when writing. This gives you more precise control over the work.

For best results, use the flexible shaft with a delicate touch. Press the tool lightly against the work. Do not apply heavy pressure. If you hear the motor begin to slow down, you know you are applying too much pressure. Simply relax a little and let the accessory in the chuck come back up to speed.

The best work is done when you allow the speed of the tool and the sharpness of the cutter do the work. If you press too hard or push the cutter into the work, you change the bite of the cutter and reduce its efficiency.

If you have been using the Moto-Tool and are familiar with the action of various cutters, you will have to practice a little with the same cutters, learning to use them effectively at the slower speed of the flexible shaft. Once again, this is a matter of feel. Many jobs, notably carving, will take longer with the flexible shaft. You may find that the larger cutters tend to chatter and cut roughly. This is due either to the slower speed and or the density of the material you are working on, or both. If this happens, it is best to switch to a smaller cutter.

If you have not used the Moto-Tool, you will learn to use the flexible shaft quickly and find it extremely convenient. Read the section of Chapter One dealing with the accessories and learn what they are used for.

The sanding drum and sanding discs are easy to use and perform top quality work. The wire brush and polishing accessories also work very well and because of the convenient size of the handpiece, are easy to use on small work such as jewelry. The engraving cutters and abrasive wheel points also are effective in the flexible shaft. The No. 409 cutting wheel will not work at this speed.

The high speed cutters depend to a large extent on speed to do their best work. They will work well in the flexible shaft on some materials, and not so well on others. In general, the smaller sized cutters will work for you. The high speed routers are less likely to do a smooth, controllable job.

For a hundred different jobs in small wood, metal and plastic work, the Moto-Shop is an ideal tool.

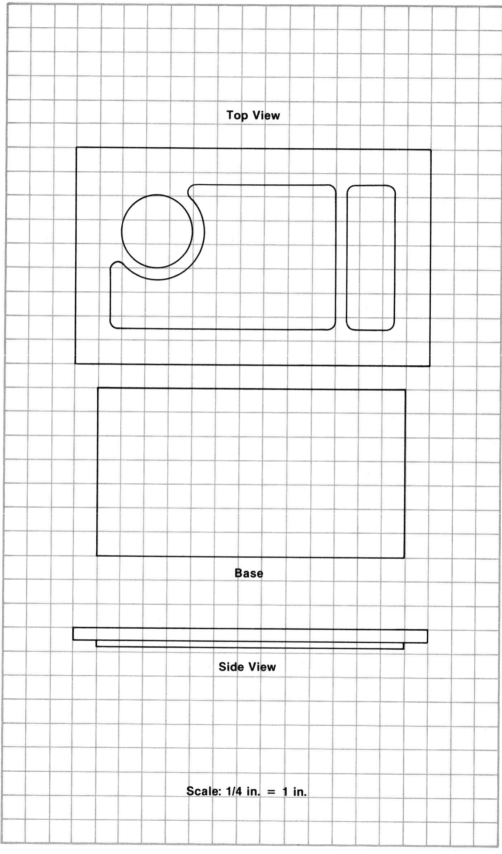

Top View

Base

Side View

Scale: 1/4 in. = 1 in.

Project 4

SANDWICH SERVING TRAY

For serving sandwiches and a beverage. It's pretty and practical.

Material:
1/2-in. birch plywood
1/4-in. tempered hardboard
Waterproof glue
Wood putty
Wire nails

Tools:
Dremel Table Saw
Moto-Shop Scroll Saw
Moto-Tool, with sanding drum
 accessory, Paint brush, Clamps

The tray consists of two parts, a frame and a base, which are shown on Plan A. Overall size of the finished tray is 9 × 15-inches. Begin project by transferring the pattern to the wood parts, drawing each line on the wood surface to serve as a cutting guide. Cut the outside dimensions on Dremel Table Saw, with a circular saw, using a fence guide to assure straight cuts. The three cutouts in the frame are inside cuts on the scroll saw. In each case, drill a starter hole in the waste area (See Detail A), feed the scroll saw blade up through the hole, and then make the cutout by following the guidelines. Next, sand the cutout edges, using the Moto-Tool with the drum sander accessory. See Detail B. (If you own the Disc/Belt Sander, this work could be done on it.) Sand all edges slightly round, or, for a nice extra touch, use the Moto-Tool and router attachment with Router Bit No. 610 to round all top edges. Attach the hardboard base, tempered side up, using waterproof glue and wire nails. See Detail C. After the glue has dried thoroughly, seal plywood with wood sealer, apply finish of your choice.

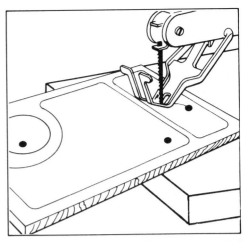

DETAIL A. To make inside cut on scroll saw, drill hole in waste and feed blade through it. Then cut on guidelines.

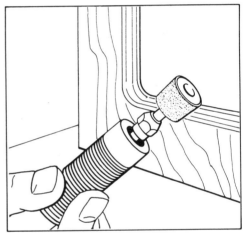

DETAIL B. Sanding drum on Moto-Tool or Moto-Flex tool is used to finish edges. Use coarse then fine grit.

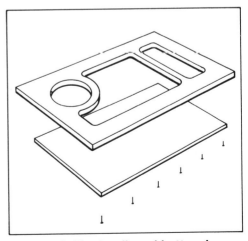

DETAIL C. The hardboard bottom is attached to the tray by waterproof glue and wire nails.

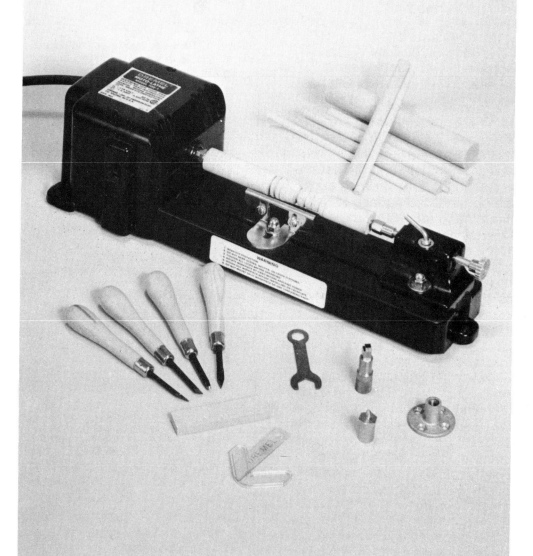

CHAPTER FIVE

The Moto-Lathe

You don't need a full-scale woodworking lathe to turn small parts. The Moto-Lathe turns stock up to 6 inches in length and 1-1/2 inches in diameter for making, duplicating and finishing small round items.

The lathe brings to your compact workshop the capability of making beautiful and intricate turnings in wood, metal, and plastic. With it you can produce items such as small chair spindles, candlestick holders, drawer knobs, model airplane propeller spinners, small cups and bowls, bases for chess men, and a variety of other carved round items.

In addition to shaping pieces on the lathe, you can use it for sanding, buffing, polishing and other finished operations.

The Moto-Lathe is a true wood lathe scaled down to compact size. It will make turnings in hardwood, softwood, plastics, and soft metals such as aluminum, copper, and brass. You can turn wood up to 6 inches long and 1-1/2 inches in diameter with it.

Many persons who might find a lathe useful in their shop and craft work have never had the opportunity to use one. The Moto-Lathe offers them a chance to add new dimensions to their work.

Lathe Safety

Follow the instructions for electrical safety given elsewhere throughout this book. Use properly grounded cords, extensions, and plugs in correctly grounded receptacles. Never work in a damp area or stand on a damp floor while operating the lathe.

Always wear safety goggles when using the lathe. Flying chips and dust can injure your eyes. Work in a well lighted area.

Always keep the tool rest, on which the chisels are held, close to the workpiece to avoid the possibility of the chisel slipping down between the work and the tool rest. When adjusting the tool rest for square stock to be turned, rotate the work by hand to make sure all corners clear all parts of the lathe before the motor is turned on.

Intricate turnings of small chair spindles, knobs, small cups and the like can be turned on the compact lathe.

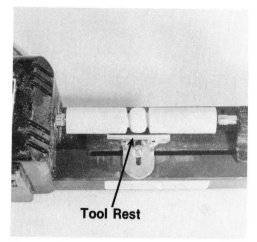

Tool Rest

The tool rest should be 1/4-inch or less from the workpiece. Be sure the corners of square pieces clear the rest.

To insert the three rubber feet, moisten the narrow tips and twist them into the holes in the base.

Always turn the lathe off when mounting or dismounting a workpiece. Unplug it when changing attachments and when performing any service on the lathe.

Do not use wood that contains knots or knot holes.

Never wear loose sleeves, jewelry, a necktie or anything else which could become entangled in the revolving workpiece. Do not reach over a revolving workpiece.

Setting up the lathe

Three rubber feet come in the lathe accessory kit. Moisten and twist them into place, inserting their pointed tips into the holes on the bottom of the lathe. They prevent the lathe from moving when normal pressure is applied to cutting tools.

If you find that the pressure you apply moves the lathe as you work, then you can anchor it to a piece of 1/2-inch plywood, 18 by 18 inches square or larger. Use three small carriage bolts. (You can rout out recesses on the bottom of the plywood for the nuts with the Moto-Tool.)

Wood screws could also be used and might be better because the torque of a screwdriver is less than that of a wrench and would reduce the chance of breaking a foot off of

the lathe. If you choose to use small carriage bolts be careful not to over tighten them, causing a lathe foot to break off.

Position the lathe on the board with the headstock assembly, which has the ON-OFF switch on it, at your left. Set the lathe so there is room in front of it to rest your hands on the board.

The lathe is now ready for use. But before you mount your first workpiece, you should learn something about the lathe and its parts.

Familiarizing yourself with the lathe

As you gain skill in lathe work, you possibly will begin looking through magazines and books for new projects and new ways to use the tool. For this reason, you should have an understanding of common lathe nomenclature. And before you begin working with the Moto-Lathe you should become familiar with its main parts and their adjustments.

The headstock. The headstock is the box with the ON-OFF switch on it at the left side of the lathe as you face it. It contains the motor, and has a projecting arbor called a *spindle* which causes the workpiece to turn. On the left end of the head-stock is the *spindle lock,* which is depressed to lock the spindle when you change attachments. *Drive centers* and *faceplates* are the attachments which connect the workpiece to the headstock spindle and cause the work to rotate. They thread onto the spindle.

The tailstock. The tailstock is the adjustable assembly at the right side of the lathe as you face it. It moves back and forth on the *lathe bed,* which is the base of the lathe extending from the headstock to the right end. In spindle turning, the workpiece fits between the headstock and tailstock, and the tailstock is moved back and forth as necessary to support the right end of the workpiece.

A slot runs the length of the lathe bed and the tailstock slides in this slot. To move the tailstock, loosen the locking nut on the lower front lip of the tailstock using the wrench which comes with the lathe. Slide the tailstock to the position you want and then lock it by tightening the lock nut.

In the tailstock you will find the *tailstock screw assembly,* which is adjusted by turning the knob on the right end of the tailstock. The tailstock screw is a long threaded rod which extends through the tailstock. On its left end is the *tailstock live center* which is lined up with the center of the headstock spindle. In spindle turning, the right end of the workpiece is held by the tailstock live center.

The tailstock screw is adjusted toward the headstock spindle by turning the knob clockwise, (away from you) and is adjusted away from the headstock spindle by turning it counterclockwise (toward you). For added support, the tailstock screw should not be adjusted outward from the tailstock any more than is necessary to hold the work. Once the tailstock center is

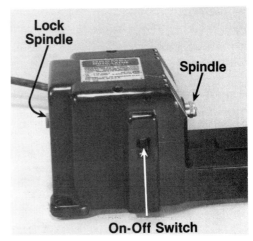

On the headstock are the ON-OFF switch (front); the spindle lock (left side); and the spindle (right).

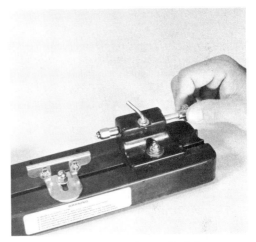

The tailstock screw, also called the adjustable ram, moves the live center to and from the workpiece.

After the tailstock screw has been adjusted, it is locked in place by turning the tailstock lock lever.

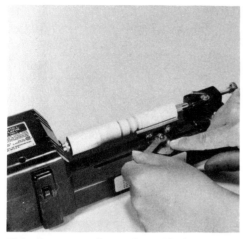

Chisels rest on the tool rest during work. The rest should be centered in front of the area to be worked.

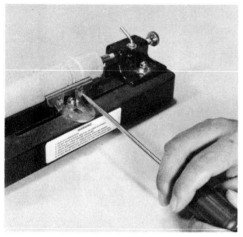

The height of the crossarm of the tool rest can be raised or lowered as needed after loosening screws.

Workpieces larger than 1/4 inch in diameter are turned by the spur center which is mounted on the spindle.

securely adjusted, lock the screw in place by turning the *tailstock lock lever* on top of the tailstock.

The tool rest. The tool rest is just what its name says, a place to rest the cutting chisels as you make lathe turnings. In most operations, the tool rest should be set 1/4 inch or less away from the work. The tool rest assembly is mounted with the rounded end of its base away from the workpiece. A bolt, which extends through the slot in the tool rest and the slot in the lathe bed, holds the tool rest in place. To move the tool rest, loosen this bolt, move the tool rest and retighten the bolt.

The tool rest height is factory set at the best height for most work. However, the crossarm of the tool rest may be raised or lowered, as needed. Simply loosen the two screws in the crossarm and move it to the desired height, then retighten the screws.

Centers. The centers, mentioned before, are threaded on the ends of the headstock spindle and tailstock screw and actually hold the workpiece.

There are four attachments for use on the headstock spindle of the Moto-Lathe. One is the *spur center,* used when you turn workpieces larger than 1/4 inch in diameter that are supported by the tailstock screw and center. Use the spur center for such long work as turning short tool handles, candlesticks, chair spindles, etc. It has a sharp point and spurs in the form of a cross on the end that contacts the work. The spurs fit into small slots or grooves you cut in the end of the workpiece (to be explained later), and the point fits into the center of the work. The spurs drive the workpiece.

A *face turning* is one where the work is supported only by an attachment on the headstock spindle. This allows you to cut into the face of the work as well as its outer circumference.

One attachment which can be used for a face turning is the *woodscrew drive center,* which has a threaded woodscrew on one end which holds the workpiece. The woodscrew center is screwed into the back of small, short workpieces on which you want to make face turnings, and then is threaded onto the headstock spindle.

If you were to make small wooden drawer knobs, for example, you would screw the woodscrew center into the back of the work and use your chisels to shape the outer contours of the drawer knob and also to turn decorative beads, coves, etc., on the front or face of the knobs.

A much more commonly used method of making face turnings is with the faceplate, which also threads onto the headstock spindle. The *faceplate* both holds and turns the work. The faceplate has four screw holes in it, through which it is screwed to the workpiece. The purpose of the faceplate is to enable you to make face turnings as described previously, but it is used for larger, longer workpieces than the woodscrew center will hold.

The *lathe chucker.* Workpieces smaller than 1/4-inch in diameter cannot be used with the spur center, because they are too small to engage the spurs. Nor can they be attached correctly to the faceplate or woodscrew drive center. The lathe chucker is a special holding device which enables you to work on round or square pieces ranging from 1/4-inch down to 1/16-inches.

The lathe chucker is made of brass and contains, in the end which faces the tail stock, a series of square brass tubes, one telescoping inside the other. The smallest of these has an inside

For small workpieces, use the threaded woodscrew drive center screwed into the back of the piece.

When work is to be done on the face of a turning, the workpiece is screwed to the faceplate.

For very small workpieces, use the brass lathe chucker, made up of tiny telescoping square tubes.

The lathe chucker mounts on the spindle. Select the tube which best holds the small work to be turned.

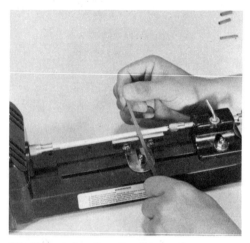

Small work is often flexible and may break under pressure. Small files allow you to cut without pressing hard.

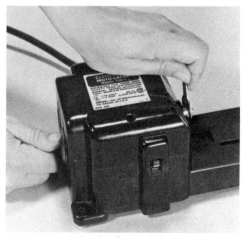

To remove a center from the spindle, first press the spindle lock (left), then use wrench to loosen the center.

measurement of 1/16 of an inch. To use the chucker, select the tube which will best hold the workpiece to be turned. This tube, and all larger tubes, are then inserted into the chucker, which has been threaded onto the headstock spindle. It might be necessary to flatten the sides of round or slightly oversized workpieces so they can enter the brass tube.

The other end of the work is supported by the tailstock. The chucker body contains a centering point which can be used for marking the center for the tailstock end of the workpiece. With the appropriately sized tubes in the chucker body to serve as guides, push the workpiece through the smallest tube until it touches the center point. A light pressure will cause an indentation in the center of the workpiece end. This center mark will be used in holding the work in the tailstock, as explained later.

Useful hints for using the chucker. Use hardwood for turnings as small as those accommodated by the lathe chucker. Softwoods may not take the pressure of the cutting tool and could crack. Needle files, which are very small files you can buy at your hardware store or home center, are recommended instead of chisels for very small turnings. You don't need much pressure on the file to make it cut. Draw the file across the workpiece as you cut with it. If held in one place, the file cannot clear itself of chips.

Whatever cutting tools you use, let the tool do the cutting. Use as little pressure as possible. Small pieces, and especially long pieces with small diameters, are quite flexible. If they bend under the pressure of the cutting tool, they may come off the centers and fly out of the lathe.

Each of these centers and the faceplate threads on to the headstock spindle. To put a center on or remove it from the headstock spindle, you first lock the shaft by depressing the *shaft lock* on the left end of the headstock. Keep this lock depressed as you use the wrench to loosen or tighten the center. Once the center is loosened, you can turn it off the spindle with your fingers.

The tailstock live center. The center on the tailstock screw is the tailstock live center. It has a pin or point in its center, and a circular "collar." The point must enter the workpiece at its center. The tiny collar also must enter and help support the workpiece.

Lubricating the tailstock center. Because the lathe turns at 3,450 rpm, the tailstock center tends to become quite warm as you work. Be careful when touching it. You can keep the heat at a minimum by lubricating the center with a drop of machine oil. Carefully wipe the center after oiling to prevent staining of the workpiece or splattering of oil.

Spindle and faceplate turnings

As mentioned briefly before, there are three basic types of turnings you can do on the Moto-Lathe.

1. *The spindle turning.* In this type of turning, used for long turnings such as chair spindles, tapered legs, tool handles, etc., the workpiece is held between the headstock and tailstock centers. The chisels cut on the outer circumferences of the work.

For work larger than 1/4 inch diameter, use the spur center. For work under 1/4 inch, use the lathe chucker.

2. *The faceplate turning.* This type of turning is used for making bowls and other shapes in which you want to contour the outer circumference as well as to hollow

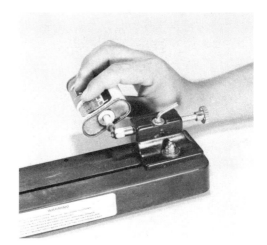

To avoid a buildup of heat on the tailstock center, occasionally put a drop of light machine oil on it.

A spindle turning is any turning supported between the headstock and tailstock, as shown here.

A face turning is supported only by the faceplate or woodscrew center, with the work face unobstructed.

When extra support is needed during cutting of outside surfaces of a face turning, tailstock is moved up.

Turnings on the woodscrew center typically are knoblike objects too small for mounting on the faceplate.

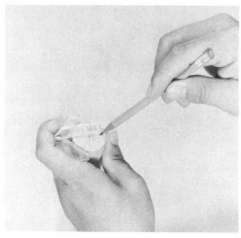

Dowels fit into the angle on the dowel center finder and the plastic arm provides an accurate diameter.

out or carve the face of the workpiece. The tailstock center is not ordinarily used to support the workpiece.

In some cases, however, where you want extra support, you can move the tailstock in to support the workpiece while you make cuts on the outer circumference surface of the work, and then move the tailstock back out of the way when you are ready to work on the face of the turning.

3. *The woodscrew center turning.* Small face turnings, typically knob-type objects too small to be mounted on the faceplate, are mounted on the woodscrew center. Cutting can be done on both the circumference and the face of the work.

Centering the work

To mount a spindle workpiece in the lathe, you first must locate and mark the center points at each end. The points in the headstock and tailstock centers should be as close to the true center of the workpiece as possible if it is to turn properly. However, it is seldom possible to locate the centers exactly and thus initially the work will vibrate somewhat.

The easiest way to be sure the work is closely centered is to draw two or more diameters across the end of round work, or draw two diagonal lines across square work.

Round work. The Moto-Lathe deluxe accessory kit contains a small plastic center finder for dowels. A machinist's combination square which contains a center head may also be used. With the Dremel center finder, fit a dowel into the angle of the device and you will see that the plastic arm of the finder automatically shows you the diameter of the dowel. Use this arm as a guide to draw lines across the ends of the work with a pencil. Draw the first line along the arm, then rotate the finder 90 degrees and draw a second line at a right angle to the first. When finished, you will have an "x" intersecting in the center of the dowel. To assure accuracy you may draw additional lines, each of which should cross the others at the center of the round workpiece. If the dowel is slightly out of round you will bracket the center in this way closely enough to spot the centerpoint by eye.

Use an awl, an ice pick, or even a small finishing nail to make a small hole at this point. With the center finder, mark the center of the opposite end of the workpiece and make another hole with your pointed tool. These holes are where the points of each of the centers (headstock and tailstock) are inserted.

Mark these lines carefully, and also carefully insert the center's point into the hole you have made. The spurs of the spur center must enter the wood of the workpiece so as to drive it. You must cut small slots or grooves along the diameters you have drawn, at right angles to each other, into which the spurs will fit.

Cut these slots with a backsaw or a hacksaw. Turn the workpiece on end and hold it in place with a vise. Cut the slots about 1/16-inch deep. When making these cuts, be sure the blade of the saw crosses the center point and that the slots are 90 degrees to each other.

Another way to cut these slots in soft materials is with the spur center itself, but be careful. You don't want to damage the center using it this way. Remove the spur center from the lathe and find a bolt that threads into it. Place the spurs of the spur center carefully on the end of the workpiece, so they exactly cross the center point you drew. Then tap on the bolt head to drive the spurs into the wood. A light tap should do. Do not use the

Make a small hole with an awl, an icepick or a finishing nail at the points where diameters intersect.

Use a backsaw or hacksaw to cut slots 1/16 inch deep at right angles to each other on the end of the workpiece.

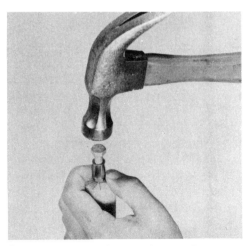

The spur center also can be used to cut spur slots. Always thread bolt into the center before hammering.

spur center for this purpose without inserting the bolt. If you tap directly on the spur center, you may damage its threads. The same procedure can be used to position the tailstock live center on the right end of a workpiece. Make sure both ends of the workpiece are deeply imprinted so the stock cannot suddenly fly out of the lathe and hit you in the eye or elsewhere. Never attempt to use the tailstock screw to squeeze the spur center into an ungrooved workpiece end. Doing so could damage your lathe.

If, for any reason, you wish to remove a workpiece from the lathe before it is completed, make a mark on the work and a corresponding mark on the headstock center so that you later can remount the work exactly as it was before. In this way, the work will be recentered accurately and will not tend to vibrate when remounted.

Square stock. If the corners of the end of the stock you are about to work on are truly square, you can mark the center of the workpiece by carefully drawing lines diagonally from corner to corner. The point at which these lines intersect is the center point. Mark the center with an awl or small nail.

If the corners of the end of the workpiece are not exactly at 90 degrees to each other, draw lines diagonally from corner to corner, as shown in the accompanying photographs. Unless the work is badly out of square, this will show you the approximate center. To check further, place the point of a compass or dividers at the point where the lines intersect and scribe a circle of the maximum size possible.

This will show you the maximum circumference you can get with the center at that point. By moving the center point from side to side or up and down, a somewhat larger circumference will be possible and the workpiece will vibrate less during the initial rounding and truing cuts.

With square stock as with round stock, you must cut small slots for the spur center. You may use the same techniques described under *round work,* cutting the spur slots with a backsaw or a hacksaw, or by using the spur center itself. With a saw, cut slots 1/16-inch deep diagonally from corner to corner on one end of the workpiece. Insert the spurs into these slots when mounting the work in the lathe. Also, tap the tailstock center impression in place at the center, using a wooden mallet or plastic faced hammer.

You can mount the workpiece in the lathe after it has been marked and prepared for centering and you have chosen the proper center for the job.

For spindle turning, loosen the lock lever on top of the tailstock and, by turning the knob towards you or counterclockwise, move the tailstock center back as far as it will go into the tailstock.

Now depress the shaft lock on the left side of the headstock and thread the spur center onto the headstock spindle. Turn it finger tight, then release the shaft lock.

Place the workpiece between the centers, fitting the point on the headstock center into the marked hole and the spurs on the headstock center into the pre-cut grooves on the workpiece.

Next, move the entire tailstock assembly to the left until the tailstock center touches the workpiece. Lock the tailstock in place. Then adjust the tailstock screw so that it firmly centers into the workpiece and its point enters the center hole in the right end of the workpiece. Do not extend the tailstock screw any farther out from the tailstock than is necessary.

The workpiece should be held between the two centers tightly

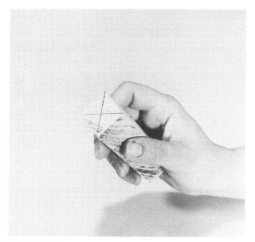

To find the center of square stock, just draw lines from corner to corner, and make hole where lines cross.

MOUNTING SPINDLE WORK. To mount spindle workpiece, first turn tailstock screw all the way back.

MOUNTING SPINDLE WORK. Next, move the tailstock to the left to touch the end of the workpiece.

MOUNTING SPINDLE WORK. Lock the tailstock in this position, using the wrench supplied with the lathe.

MOUNTING SPINDLE WORK. Now adjust the tailstock screw to fit snugly against the workpiece.

MOUNTING SPINDLE WORK. Finally, lock the tailstock screw in position by turning the lock lever.

enough so that it does not come off, but not so tightly that you cannot rotate it easily by hand.

An easy way to adjust the tailstock is with the lathe running and the work held between the centers. Turn the lathe on and tighten the tailstock adjustment knob until the lathe motor just begins to labor slightly. Then loosen the knob until the lathe begins to run freely. At this point, lock the tailstock lock lever.

The work should now rotate freely. Note that the workpiece will seldom initially run absolutely true. The work will be an approximate balance, however, if you have marked the ends correctly and fitted the workpiece between the centers properly.

To compensate for any slightly out-of-true turning, the workpiece you choose should be somewhat larger in diameter than the finished piece is intended to be. It is almost impossible to find the exact centers of both ends of either round or square stock, so this should be taken into consideration when selecting the wood to be used. When you start with round stock such as a dowel, the work will wobble somewhat if the centers are off even slightly. A light truing cut across the entire length will quickly bring the workpiece into round with the centers as the circumference reduces in size. On square work, your first step should be to turn the square until it is round along the length of the piece that is to be turned.

If the initial vibration is severe and you have little diameter to spare, you can correct the situation by relocating the center holes at each end of the workpiece.

Making a new center hole on the ends of the piece can present problems, since you already have a hole out of center. A quick repair can be made by drilling a small hole at the

site and filling it with a piece of round hardwood toothpick. You can then re-measure for the center hole and carefully place it in the center, where it must be. If you have selected a workpiece somewhat longer than you intend the finished turning to be, a simpler solution is to saw off a small portion of each end of the workpiece and then re-measure for the correct centers.

Mounting faceplate turnings

Workpieces to be turned as face turnings also should be carefully centered and secured on either the woodscrew drive center, for smaller work, or the faceplate, for bigger pieces.

The faceplate. For faceplate turning, the workpiece must be from 1-3/8 to 1-1/2-inches in diameter at the left end. Pieces that are smaller or larger than these dimensions cannot safely be turned using the faceplate.

The faceplate has four screw holes, and is mounted on wood workpieces by means of four wood screws or flathead sheet metal screws. The length of the screw

Note that the first 1/2 inch of all faceplate work should not be worked. Mark it with a pencil as a reminder.

may be determined by the thickness of the workpiece. A very thin piece may require shorter screws, but the longest screws practical should be used.

Depending on the length of screws you use, the first 1/2-inch or so of the workpiece measured out from the faceplate must not be worked deeply. The reason is that the screws holding the faceplate to the end of the workpiece are driven into this portion of it and a deep cut in this area would cut into the ends of the screws.

It is practical to support a workpiece up to a maximum of 1-1/2-inches in length on the faceplate. Since the area containing the screws cannot be cut into, only about one inch of the length can be deeply shaped. A workpiece longer than 1-1/2-inches would require tailstock support.

And you *can* shape longer workpieces, probably up to about 2 inches long, by moving the tailstock to support the turning while you rough the outside circumference to the approximate finish diameter. With the additional support of the tailstock, this is a safe cutting operation. The tailstock is then moved away and the end of the workpiece can be hollowed or

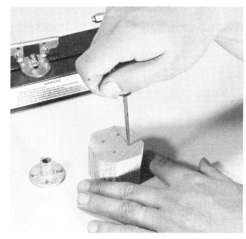

MOUNTING FACEPLATE WORK. Now use an awl or icepick to make starter holes at the marked positions.

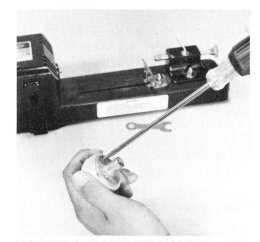

MOUNTING FACEPLATE WORK. Use 1/4 to 1/2 in. flathead woodscrews, driven into starter holes, to fasten faceplate to work.

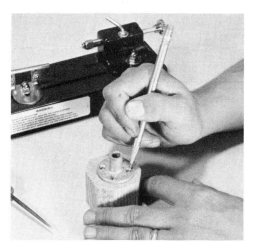

MOUNTING FACEPLATE WORK. Center the faceplate on the end of the work and mark screwholes with a pencil.

MOUNTING FACEPLATE WORK. Plastic such as this can be fastened to faceplate by drilling small pilot holes first.

shaped as required. Work very carefully on the face of an overlong faceplate turning, remembering that it doesn't have standard support. Cut gently with chisels in the end grain, and avoid cuts which require heavy hand pressure.

Faster stock removal can be had in removing the inside material of the face by using a Moto-Tool fitted with a high speed cutter in place of a chisel.

Mounting the faceplate. When possible, start with a workpiece that is round or nearly so. Owners of the Dremel Moto-Shop can scroll saw a square piece of wood into a circle. Or a circle can be scribed on the square and the corners of the wood can be cut off with a handsaw until a near-circle remains.

Place the workpiece on a table, left end up. Position the faceplate on the end of the workpiece, centered as nearly as possible. Hold the faceplate while you mark the screw positions with a pencil on the workpiece end through the four screw holes. Use an awl, ice pick or nail to make a small hole at each of these screw hole markings.

Fasten the faceplate to the workpiece by driving the four screws through the holes. Now mount the faceplate with the workpiece at-

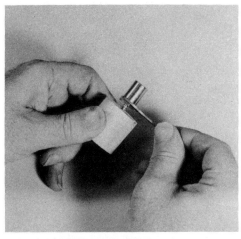

WOODSCREW MOUNTING. After finding the center and making hole, wrench turns woodscrew center into the work.

tached on the headstock spindle. You are then ready to begin turning.

Plastic faceplate turnings. The method of attaching the faceplate to the workpiece described in the previous paragraphs applies only to wood workpieces. Most plastics will accept sheet metal screws if a hole slightly smaller than the screw is drilled first. With some materials it may be necessary to attach the faceplate to the plastic workpiece with No. 6 x 32 machine screws. The holes must be drilled and tapped to receive these screws.

You can purchase a tap wrench and a tap of the right size for several dollars. Consult with your hardware store and buy machine screws, a matching tap, tap wrench, and a drill bit of the right size if you don't already have these items.

Drill the holes as marked on the end of the work. Then turn the tap into each hole. The tap cuts threads in the sides of the holes so that the screws can be threaded in.

The woodscrew center. As noted earlier, workpieces smaller than 1-3/8-inches in diameter are turned on the woodscrew center.

To attach the woodscrew center, mark the center of the work. For softwoods, make a small starter hole with an awl or ice pick at this center. Insert the woodscrew center into the hole and turn it tightly into the work. Then thread the center on the headstock spindle.

To avoid splitting hardwoods, a starter hole smaller than the screw on the center should first be drilled. Many plastic pieces can also be mounted on the woodscrew center if a hole smaller than the woodscrew is drilled first.

The lathe chisels

Four lathe chisels are made to shape work on the Moto-Lathe.

1. *No. 1001, 60-degree chisel.* This chisel is used for rounding

square stock, cutting deep V's and beads, undercutting, squaring shoulders and smoothing a reduced round piece.

2. *No. 1002, 30-degree chisel.* This chisel has the same uses as No. 1001, except that it cuts at a different angle. In cutting a deep V, for example, this chisel will cut sides that are not as steep, assuming both chisels are held at the same angle on the tool rest.

3. *No. 1003, parting tool.* This is used chiefly for sizing and parting (cut-off) cuts. It also can be used for starting deep shoulders, V's and for undercutting.

4. *No. 1004, round end chisel.* This chisel is used for rounding square stock, smoothing any concave curved surface, and is also used to create shallow coves and curves.

All of the chisels except the parting tool are used with their blades resting flat on the tool rest crossbar. The parting tool rests on its edge instead of its flat side. These four chisels will perform the great majority of lathe work you will want to do. However, chisels of other shapes, for easier cutting of special shapes, can be purchased in most hobby shops.

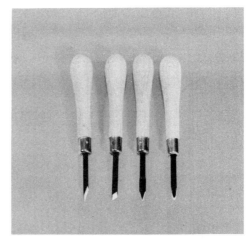

The four chisels are (l. to r.) the 60-degree, the 30-degree, the parting tool, and the round-nose.

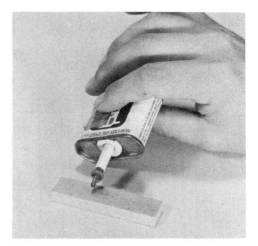

Stone should be oiled before use. Soak it in oil or apply a number of drops and rub them in with your finger.

Sharpening lathe chisels

A dull chisel is difficult to use and does poor quality work. As it gets dull, a chisel has a tendency to chatter, burn, and cut unevenly, and to gouge the work surface. It will no longer peel away good chips.

The lathe chisels supplied with the Moto-Lathe are made of hardened steel and have been ground sharp when you receive them. Before the first use, hone them a few strokes on an oilstone to give them the best edge.

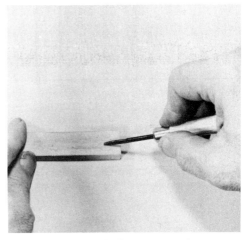

HONING CHISELS. To sharpen the parting tool, lay each side of blade on stone and push forward (here, to the left).

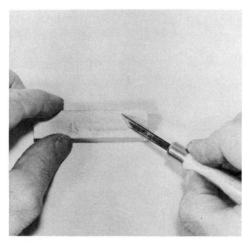

HONING CHISELS. 30- and 60-degree chisels are "sliced" along stone with blade flat (here, right to left).

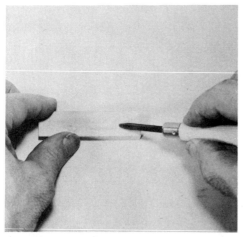

HONING CHISELS. Round-nose chisel is rotated as it moved right to left on stone so all edges are honed.

SHARPENING CHISELS. Disc-belt sander sharpens chisels. Use fine grit belt. Touch blade lightly and momentarily to belt.

The chisels will become dull in ordinary use. They will stay sharp longer when you work in softwoods than in hardwoods. To maintain the sharpness of your chisels, never allow them to overheat while cutting, as this destroys their temper and their ability to hold an edge. Also, never attempt to turn man-made materials such as hardboard or particle board. These are made with resin binders and are very hard on all cutting tools.

How often should you sharpen your lathe chisels? The best answer is, "Hone them frequently." Experienced lathe workers stop every 15 minutes or oftener to hone a chisel — depending on the material they are working with. There are several reasons for this:

1. A sharp chisel is easier to use and cuts better. The work is smoother, and the cuts more accurate. There is no point in waiting until the good edge is completely gone before honing.

2. By honing the chisel edge, the sharpness is retained. Honing is simply replacing the very fine cutting edge. If you cut for a very long time without sharpening a chisel, you make it necessary to take the time to do a sharpening job rather than a honing job. When a barber strops a shaving razor before each shave, he is honing, not sharpening, the blade. He keeps the fine edge on the blade for a long time by using this method.

An oilstone to sharpen your chisels is included in the Moto-Lathe accessory kit. To prepare this stone, first soak it in household oil and as you use it add a few drops of oil spread over the entire surface.

Look carefully at the drawings on this page to see the best way of using the oilstone. Always stroke the chisel *with the bevel flat on the oilstone* as if peeling a thin slice from the stone. Do not pull it back on the stone, but lift it and return for another stroke.

When stroking the round end chisel, roll it so the entire edge will contact the stone during each stroke.

In all cases, continue stroking, lessening your pressure with each stroke, until the edge is fine and sharp. If you hone frequently, you should be able to restore the edge to the chisel in half a dozen or so strokes.

Be extremely careful of sharpening woodworking chisels on an electric grinder. The chisel heats up very quickly on such a grinder, and the heat would remove the temper from the steel and ruin the tool.

If you have a Dremel belt sander, you can sharpen chisels that have been nicked or badly dulled by touching them against the turning sander belt. Just give the blade two or three quick touches, without touching the cutting edge. Grind only on the lower portion of the bevel. Finish the cutting edge entirely by honing. A chisel that requires extensive grinding can be kept cool by dousing it in water as you proceed.

You also can use the disc sander on the Moto-Shop for this purpose.

When using either the belt or the disc sander, use quick, deft touches against the abrasive surface. Do not hold the blade against the surface, as it will heat quickly.

There are two basic chisel actions performed on work in the lathe. One is called "scraping," although the chisel actually cuts. The other method is called "cutting."

A *scraping cut* is done with the chisel blade resting on the tool rest and with the chisel horizontal to the bench top. The cutting edge cuts straight into the workpiece surface. Used in this manner, the chisel cuts away thin shavings from the workpiece. The scraping cut is slow, but precise and easily controlled, and can be used for all lathe turning operations. It is the method a beginner should use.

A beginner should not merely push the chisel into the workpiece so the blade simply rubs against the work. Hold the chisel firmly in your hands, but don't keep your hands rigid. Move the chisel into the workpiece for a scraping cut using a slight rocking motion on the tool rest. You'll soon start to get the "feel" of when you are removing a good scraping wood chip.

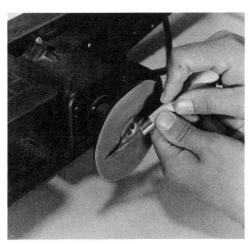

SHARPENING CHISELS. Do not hold chisels against disc sander for more than a few seconds or heat may build.

A scraping cut is made with the chisel blade parallel with the lathe base, going straight into the work.

All faces, inside diameters and combination approaches are shaped with the scraping method.

Scraping cuts dull the chisels faster, but are much easier to do and are less likely to damage the workpiece.

Cutting takes much more skill and practice and is done with the chisel blade tilted up and the handle lowered so the chisel edge cuts into the downward moving workpiece surface. Correctly done, it shears off shavings somewhat like peeling a potato. Workpieces can be reduced in diameter quickly by a cutting action. Cutting leaves a smoother surface when properly done, and will result in faster removal of unwanted stock.

Positioning the tool rest

The tool rest should be placed close to the workpiece — no more than 1/4-inch from it, and preferably closer. If the workpiece is longer than the tool rest, place the rest at the left end of the work at the bebinning, and move it to the right as the work progresses. Also, as the workpiece is reduced in diameter, the tool rest should be moved inward toward the work to maintain the 1/4-inch or less gap. A larger space between the workpiece and the tool rest may cause the chisel to "grab" and be thrown from your hands, or could result in a damaged workpiece.

The top of the tool rest crossbar should be parallel to the centerline of the workpiece and for most work either at the same height as the centerline or just below it. The position in which the crossbar is set as it comes from the factory usually works well and should be tried first. To reset the crossbar, loosen the two locking screws on the tool rest and move the crossbar off the rest to the desired position, then tighten the screws again.

When cutting on the faces of faceplate turnings, rotate the tool rest 90 degrees so that it is parallel to the face. Its height should be at or just below the center line of the work.

Holding the chisel

The chisel should be held with both hands. One hand should rest on the table top or edge of the lathe bed and hold the cutting end of the chisel down against the tool rest.

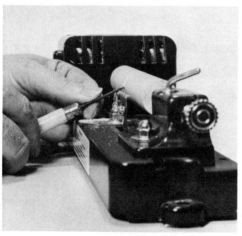

A cutting cut is made with the chisel at an upward angle and the blade turned slightly upward into the work.

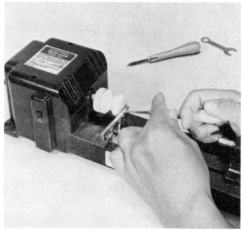

The tool rest is turned across the face of the workpiece, as shown, when you do work on the face.

The thumb or two fingers should rest on top of the tool to hold and guide it and to control the depth of the cut. The other hand should hold the wooden handle of the chisel. This hand does most of the moving when you create the various shapes on the workpiece.

To begin a cut, feed the chisel edge slowly into the workpiece to obtain the depth of cut required. Simultaneously, while maintaining this depth-of-cut, move the cutting edge to the right or left, as required.

When making a long cut, hold the blade of the chisel between your thumb and index finger. Allow the index finger to slide along the crossbar of the tool rest, using the rest as a guide. Support the wooden handle of the chisel with your other hand.

Direction of the work

Observe that the workpiece held between centers in the lathe turns toward you. That is, the surface on which you are working turns downward in front of you, traveling from the top down past the tool rest. This means that the surface travels into the cutting edge of the chisel as you hold it against the work-piece. This is true when you are turning a spindle and also when you are shaping the outer circumference of a workpiece held by the faceplate.

However, the face of a faceplate turning moves in *two* directions. The left side, nearest you, moves downward in the same manner as the surface of a spindle. But the right side, beyond the center of the workpiece, moves upward. Thus, when you work on the face of a faceplate turning, you must not work to the right of center or the chisel will tend to lift up and there will be no cutting action. The cutting edges of a lathe chisel are designed to work with the stock moving down against them.

Practice. No explanation can give you the insight that a few minutes of practice will. As previously described, mount a square workpiece in the lathe and turn it down to a cylinder, using the round end and 30 and 60 degree chisels. These cuts should be light, letting the chisel do the work without forcing it. As the work approaches cylindrical form, the chisels will seem to be cutting more smoothly. Once the workpiece is cylindrical, practice with each of the chisels. The round end and the 30 and 60 degree

Arrow shows direction of rotation of workpiece — downward toward you. Work only above center of the workpiece.

Arrow shows direction of rotation of face turning. Work only to the left of center and above centerline.

chisels are used with their flat sides resting on the tool rest crossbar. The parting tool, however, is held on edge. The round end chisel, with its bevel side down, will cut efficiently around most of its arced tip. The 30 and 60 degree chisels will cut with their point, with the entire cutting edge or with just the heel of the cutting edge. The parting tool cuts only at its point. When the chisels are cutting properly they will remove chips rapidly without chatter. For most cuts, the chisel should be cutting into the wood to a pre-determined depth while it also moves in a sideways direction. When properly used, the chisels will remove chips and leave a relatively smooth surface on the workpiece. For scraping cuts, the chisel is held horizontally. For a cutting action the blade is tilted upward and the handle downward, with the cutting edge meeting the workpiece above its centerline to permit the chips to peel off the work. The contours of the work are formed by holding the cutting end of the chisel on the tool rest while manipulating the handle to achieve the shapes desired.

As you work, you will discover that the position of the tool rest and the angle at which you hold the chisel are interdependent. That is, the best position for the tool rest is determined in part, at least, by the angle at which you hold the chisel. You should experiment a bit with chisel angles and tool rest positions to find which combination works best for you.

Generally, the tool rest will give better results if positioned a bit below the centerline for scraping cuts, and as high as it will go for cutting.

Do not set the level of the tool rest above the centerline of the workpiece, because then you will merely burnish the work.

When working with small diameter turnings, remember that your movements should be small. A sudden large cut could ruin the work.

Rounding square work

Frequently you will start with a square workpiece, with the object of making all or part of it round. This is called "roughing off." The first time you mount a square workpiece between centers and approach the turning piece with a chisel, you are likely to be a bit ap-

ROUNDING A SQUARE. Mount the square workpiece between centers. This piece is 1 x 1 inch walnut.

ROUNDING A SQUARE. Round center portion first. Use any chisel except parting tool.

prehensive. When the workpiece is turning, the speed makes it appear round — yet you know it is square and that you are not cutting into a smooth round surface.

There is no need for apprehension. A sharp chisel will cut those square edges surprisingly fast. Use the tip of the round end chisel for rough cutting and then use the 30 and 60-degree chisels with their entire cutting edges against the work to smooth off the cylinder.

Start at the center of the workpiece and work outward to the ends. Very gently move the chisel into the work until it is cutting about 1/16 of an inch deep. With the same motion, and with your forefinger against the edge of the tool rest to serve as a depth guide, slowly slide the chisel along the work, holding the same depth as you move. Let the chisel travel the full length of the area you want rounded, then go back and begin another pass. Continue to make passes like this until the square piece has been rounded.

Obviously, if the workpiece is longer than the tool rest, you will have to move the rest as you make these cuts. And, as the diameter of the workpiece is reduced, move the tool rest closer to the work to maintain a 1/4-inch gap or less.

The work of roughing off a large square can be hastened and the vibration lessened if you "chamfer," or bevel, the corners of the square before the work is mounted in the lathe. The work is thus an octagon instead of a square and is closer to being round. This work can be done on the table saw, the scroll saw, on a jointer and by various other means.

Tapering round work

When you want to taper a turning, turn the tool rest so that it is at the

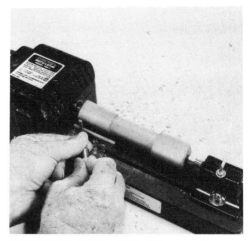

ROUNDING A SQUARE. After rounding center, move tool rest to next work area. It must be less than 1/4 inch from work.

ROUNDING A SQUARE. Move tool rest to the third work area and reduce it to same diameter as the rest of the piece.

ROUNDING A SQUARE. The walnut square is now rounded and ready to be made smooth by sanding.

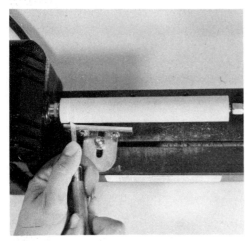

TAPERING. To begin, set tool rest at the angle of the desired taper, then cut with 30- or 60-degree chisel.

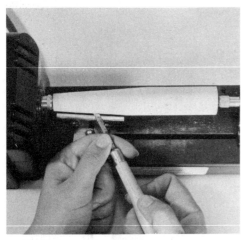

TAPERING. As cut progresses, move tool rest in closer to workpiece. Keep it at the desired angle.

TAPERING. This is finished taper. If taper is longer than tool rest, move rest, resetting at the angle of the taper.

angle of the taper you want to create. If the workpiece is no longer than the tool rest, this presents no problem. If the workpiece is longer than the tool rest, you will have to move the tool rest carefully to maintain the correct angle.

Intricate profiles

To turn a block of wood into an intricate turning, such as the delicately carved leg of a piece of miniature furniture, a template to guide your cutting is very helpful, especially if several duplicate pieces are to be made.

Begin by drawing an outline pattern on paper of one side (or half) of the turning you want to make. Then glue this drawing to a piece of light but stiff cardboard.

Draw lines across the template at the key points where the contour of the drawing changes. Cut out the profile of the template with scissors so the contours that remain are the reverse of the intended turning.

When the cylindrical workpiece has been reduced to the diameter of the largest part of the finished turning, hold your cardboard template next to the work and transfer each line from the template onto the workpiece with a pencil. These lines tell you where the contours will change on the turning, and thus indicate where to make cuts.

You can mark these lines with the work turning in the lathe or with the motor off. If you mark them while the work is turning, touch the pencil only lightly to the workpiece or you will quickly dull the pencil and make wide and inaccurate marks.

You will have to remark the piece occasionally as you cut away the pencil marks during the shaping operations. As the work progresses, periodically compare the turn-

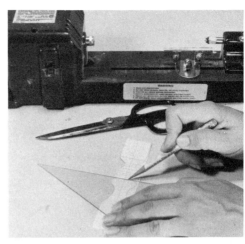

PATTERN CUT. Make a drawing on paper of the cut you intend to make. Drawing should be full size.

PATTERN CUT. Paste the paper pattern on light cardboard. Draw lines across it wherever diameter changes.

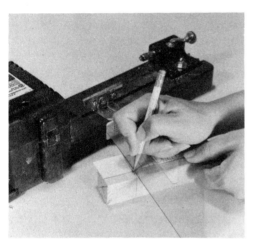

PATTERN CUT. Ends which will remain square should be marked on the workpiece, using pattern as guide.

PATTERN CUT. Use the parting tool to make sizing cuts at the marks denoting the beginning of the square parts.

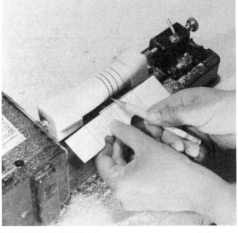

PATTERN CUT. Reduce the area between the shoulders to the largest diameter in your pattern.

PATTERN CUT. Use pattern as a guide to transfer lines to workpiece. Each line represents a diameter change.

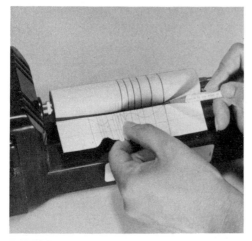

PATTERN CUT. Procedure is the same for round workpieces, except that no reduction of diameter is necessary.

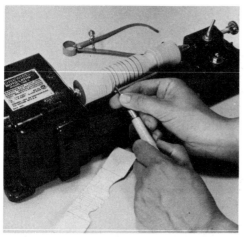

PATTERN CUT. Use the parting tool to make a sizing cut on each pencil line. Sizing cuts serve as guides.

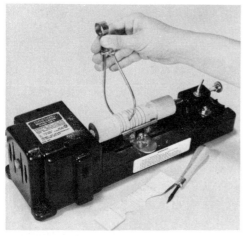

PATTERN CUT. Use calipers to check depth of each cut. Cuts are nearly as deep as finished surface will be.

ing to the template until the desired shapes are achieved. Templates can be used for faceplate as well as spindle turning.

Completing the work

Sizing cuts. Sizing cuts are grooves cut with the parting tool to the depth you wish to reduce part of the workpiece to. They are made with the parting tool held on edge for a scraping approach. These should be made at the appropriate pencil marks you transferred from your template to the work. Each groove should be cut almost to the depth you want on the finished piece, but not quite. You want to leave a little of the wood for the finishing operation.

A pair of outside calipers should be purchased for use when making sizing cuts and when reducing any segment of the workpiece to a predetermined size. These offer an excellent means of determining that you are making each sizing cut accurate in depth.

Use a ruler to set the calipers to an opening slightly larger than the finish diameter you want before you start cutting. Then, as you cut with the parting tool in one hand, hold the calipers in the groove with the other hand, holding them from above and behind the workpiece so as not to interfere with the cutting. Apply a slight rocking motion with the parting tool so chips are removed evenly. When the calipers just slip over the workpiece, you know the cut is the correct depth. Stop cutting.

If there is a section of a spindle workpiece to be left square, you start with a square block rather than a cylinder, and mark the parts that are to be left square on at least two sides of the workpiece with a pencil. As the work rotates, you will

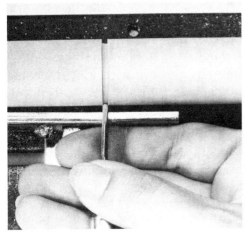

DEEP SIZING CUTS. Sizing cuts are made with parting tool. First cut should be no more than 1/8 inch deep.

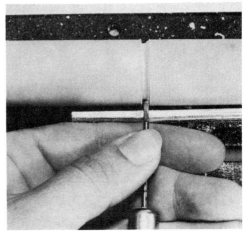

DEEP SIZING CUTS. To cut deeper than 1/8 inch, widen groove slightly by cutting a little off one shoulder.

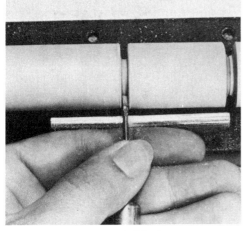

DEEP SIZING CUTS. With the cut widened, again use the parting tool to deepen the cut.

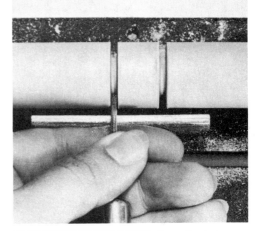

REDUCING DIAMETERS. To reduce a diameter, first make sizing cuts at both ends of area to be reduced.

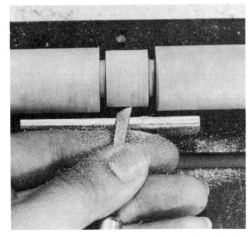

REDUCING DIAMETERS. Check depth of sizing cuts with caliper, then begin removing material between cuts.

REDUCING DIAMETERS. Diameter reduced. Use round-nose, 30- or 60-degree chisels to remove material.

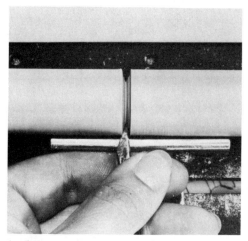

SHOULDER CUT. Using 30- or 60-degree chisels and cutting approach, form either square or slanted shoulder.

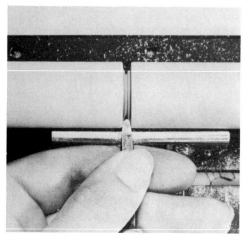

SHOULDER CUT. First cut should be no more than 1/8 inch deep. Widen adjacent area before cutting deeper.

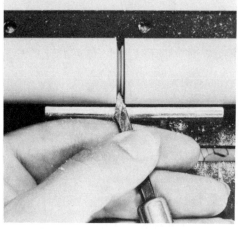

SHOULDER CUT. After widening, make second cut at side of shoulder. Widen area each time you cut deeper.

be able to see these lines, and know that you should not shape beyond them.

Once the workpiece is turning, use the parting tool to cut on the lines marking the edge of that part of the workpiece to be left square. These cuts provide a permanent mark for you. Now use the round end chisel and make the unmarked portion of the workpiece round, as described in the section on rounding square work. Then proceed all sizing cuts before turning your intended design on the cylinder.

When all the sizing cuts have been made to the correct depths, you are ready to use the 30 or 60-degree chisels or the round end chisel to complete the job. This means shaping the shoulders, cutting any V grooves, etc. Refer to your template and the sizing cuts for guidance in this work.

A *shoulder* is the side of a cut that separates a larger diameter from a smaller one, or separates a square section of a turning from a round portion. A shoulder can be square, angled, or rounded. The best way to cut a square shoulder is with the parting tool held on edge. Move the parting chisel gently into the work, using a slight vertical rocking motion to peel chips out.

The edge of the square shoulder can also be cut with the 60-degree chisel, held so that the chisel's edge is at a right angle to the centerline of the workpiece.

If the shoulder is to be more than 1/8-inch deep, stop at that depth and reduce the diameter of the workpiece adjacent to the shoulder. In other words, cut a valley alongside the original cut. Then continue to deepen the shoulder cut. This is good practice because when you make a deep cut, with wood on both sides of the chisel point, you force the chisel to cut both sides simultaneously. This invites over-heating of the point, and subsequent dulling. By cutting the "valley" beside the shoulder, you make it possible for the chisel to cut only one side, and thus reduce friction.

V grooves. V grooves are cut with the 30 or 60-degree chisels. For a narrow and fairly shallow V groove, move the point of the chisel straight into the work surface. To make a wider V groove, first make a slanted cut to one side, then a slanted cut on the other. Cut each side to a maximum 1/8-inch depth, then clean out the wood between these cuts. Continue in this manner until the cuts meet at the bottom to form a V groove of the desired width and depth.

Round-bottom grooves. For cutting round bottom grooves and long concave curves, use the round end chisel. Round bottom grooves are called "coves," and moving the round end chisel straight into the work surface will create a cove the size of the end of the chisel. To produce a wider cove, first make the chisel-sized cove, then move the chisel handle in an arc to the right and left. This fans the chisel back and forth in the workpiece and widens the cove.

Bead cuts. A bead is a raised, rounded portion of the design. To make bead cuts, begin by making sizing cuts with the parting chisel to create the sides of the bead. Then make pencil marks to indicate the center of the top of the bead. Use the 30- or 60-degree chisel to shape the beads to the desired contour.

Move the point of the chisel to the side of the bead. Then, using your fingers on the tool rest as a fulcrum, turn the chisel handle in a swinging motion as necessary to shape the curve of the bead. Repeat the process until both sides of the bead are formed.

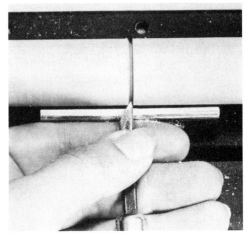

V CUT. To cut small V, use 30- or 60-degree chisel. Make one cut straight in to form left side.

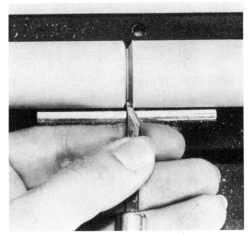

V CUT. Make a second cut adjacent to the first but at the opposite angle to form the right side of the V.

V CUT. The finished small V should be no deeper than 1/8 inch. Larger Vs require removal of material.

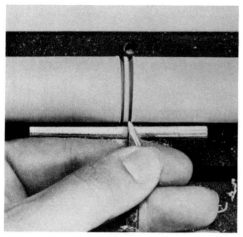

V CUT. Determine width of top of large V. Make a small V cut at each side, leaving material between cuts.

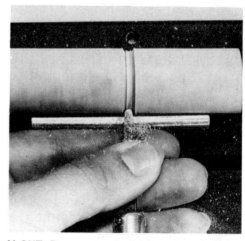

V CUT. Remove material between the small Vs, being careful not to disturb the outer sides.

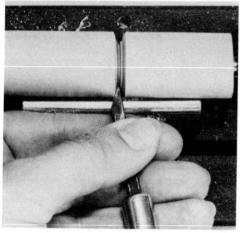

V CUT. Now make two more V cuts at the bottom of the groove, one to the left and one to the right.

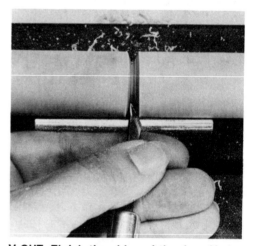

V CUT. Finish the sides of the deep V and make them join in a neat V at the bottom.

V CUT. The finished large V. The angle of the V determines which chisel is used in making cuts.

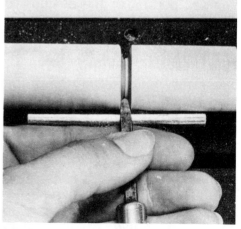

COVE CUT. The simplest cove cut is made using the round-nose chisel moved straight into the workpiece.

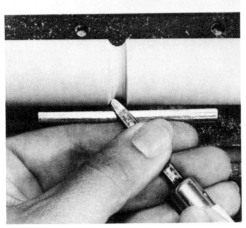

COVE CUT. Wider cove cuts are made by pivoting the chisel after first cove is cut. Here it is moved left.

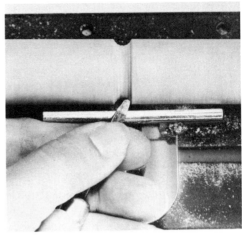

COVE CUT. Pivot the chisel on the tool rest, moving the handle to move the blade left or right, as needed.

COVE CUT. After the basic shape has been cut, pivot the chisel back and forth to make the cove smooth.

COVE CUT. A wide tapering cove is made in the same manner. Begin with a simple cove cut and widen gradually.

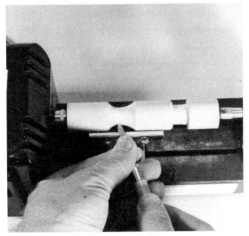

COVE CUT. With each sweep of chisel, widen and deepen cove. Chisel is pivoted and moved as required by the taper.

COVE CUT. The completed cove, ready for final finishing. When cutting, work carefully to get wanted taper.

MAKING A BEAD. Begin by making sizing cuts to the desired depth on both sides of the bead.

MAKING A BEAD. Use the caliper to assure that sizing cuts are almost to the depth of the finished bead.

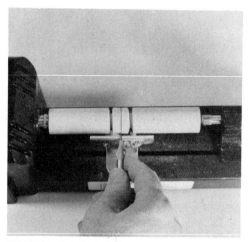

MAKING A BEAD. Mark the center of the bead by holding a pencil to the workpiece as it turns.

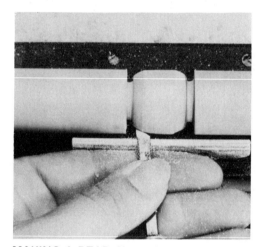

MAKING A BEAD. Use a 30- or 60-degree chisel to cut bead, beginning in the sizing cut.

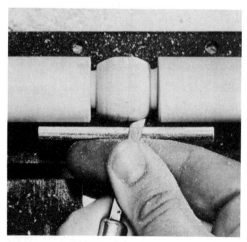

MAKING A BEAD. Work from the cut to the top of the bead on both sides, observing the pencil guide line.

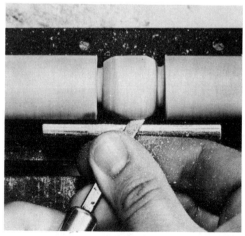

MAKING A BEAD. After rough shape has been achieved, use 60-degree chisel with a light touch to smooth work.

Faceplate turning

Faceplate turnings, as you recall, are mounted on the faceplate and the right end of the workpiece is unsupported. This leaves the face free to be hollowed or otherwise cut.

On a faceplate turning, start cutting on the outside surface rather than on the face. Remember that the first 1/2 inch or so of the turning contains the tips of the woodscrews and should not be deeply shaped. Turn the outer circumference until it is round, then make whatever shapes you want on the outside surface, using normal shaping techniques already described.

Working the face. After rounding the outside surface of the workpiece, work on the face. To get ready, turn the tool rest so that it extends across the face of the workpiece, and at right angles to the lathe bed. Adjust the tool rest height so it is slightly below the centerline.

The first step is to "face off" the piece — that is, smooth the exposed end so that it is straight across. If you are turning a flat planed board attached to the

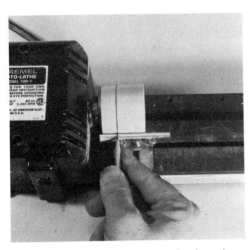

FACE WORK. The first 1/2 inch of work on the faceplate is waste. Mark it and do not work left of the mark.

FACE WORK. Work side before starting on face. Make several passes with chisel to square up the workpiece.

FACE WORK. Turn the tool rest across the face of the work. Begin by facing off (leveling) the work face.

FACE WORK. Work only on the left side (side nearest front) of the workpiece. Use only scraping cuts.

131

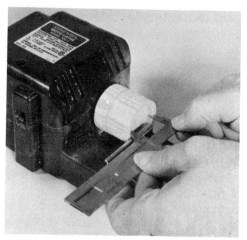

FACE WORK. When hollowing out work, an inside caliper or similar measuring device aids accuracy.

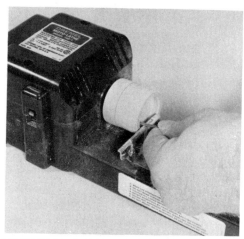

FACE WORK. After reaching desired depth, make the work smooth by light cuts with 60 degree chisel.

faceplate, the end should already be straight across but should be faced off anyway, to correct for mounting errors. If the workpiece was sawed off of a dowel, the facing off is especially necessary, since the saw cut may not have been straight across the dowel.

Use the round end chisel for facing off work, with the blade flat on the tool rest. Take light cuts and move back and forth from the center to the left edge. When it appears that the face is straight, hold a straightedge across it to check.

Remember that in a faceplate turning, you do not work at all to the right of the center, since on that side the workpiece is turning upward. This motion will lift the chisel and you will have no cutting action.

Hollowing a workpiece. To hollow a faceplate turning, you can use any of the four chisels. The chisels selected depend on the final shape of the cavity. To smooth a flat inner surface of a cavity, the 60-degree chisel is often the best tool. A pair of inside calipers can be used to measure the inside diameter of a cavity, such as the inside of a bowl.

To make V grooves, beads, and coves on the face of the turning,

select the appropriate chisel and work on the upper left or forward side of the face only. A template can be used to achieve the desired contours.

Turnings on the woodscrew center are done in much the same way, except that the size of the workpiece is smaller.

Finishing a turning

Once you have shaped any turning, it is somewhat rough, so you want to give it a smooth finish. Go over the turning carefully with the appropriate chisels for a final finishing cut. Touch all surfaces lightly, since you don't want to remove much material during this operation, but only make all parts of the turning as smooth as possible.

For a final finish, use sandpaper in descending degrees of coarseness while the work turns in the lathe. Remove the tool rest before using sandpaper. Hold the sandpaper to the bottom of the workpiece as the work turns or hold each end of a thin strip in one hand and allow the sandpaper to follow the contours over the top of a turning. You can fold narrow strips of the sandpaper for finishing coves and grooves. Emery boards, sold

132

for manicuring fingernails, make fine little sanding boards for getting down into grooves on lathe turnings. Some hardwoods can be polished to a fine finish by holding a pinch of wood chips against the workpiece while it is turning.

Stains, varnish, sealers, wax, and other finishing materials can be applied to wood workpieces while the work turns in the lathe. A soft cloth pad dipped into the finishing material makes a good applicator. Stain usually can be applied full strength, while other material may have to be thinned. Liquids may splatter as they are applied, so

clothing, the lathe and surrounding areas should be protected.

While a cloth makes a fine applicator for finishing materials it can easily be caught and wound up in the turning almost instaneously. For this reason, only a small pad should be used. And it should be kept away from parts like the headstock spur center, which could easily snag the cloth and tear it from your hands.

Metals can be brought to a bright finish by using descending grits of emery cloth, from coarse through fine, while the work turns in the lathe. Plastics can be polished

FINISHING. Work can be made smooth by light touches with the 30- or 60-degree chisel.

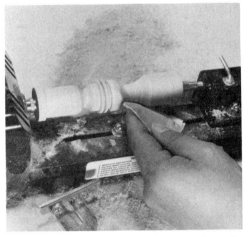

FINISHING. Hold sandpaper to work as it turns to produce high degree of smooth ness. Hold paper to bottom of work.

FINISHING. Strip of emery cloth or paper can be cut to size for finishing grooves and tapers.

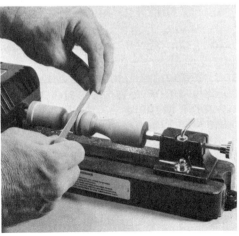

FINISHING. An emery board, used for filing fingernails, is handy for sanding in narrow grooves.

FINISHING. Wax and stains can be applied with cloth pad as lathe turns. Be careful of stain splatter.

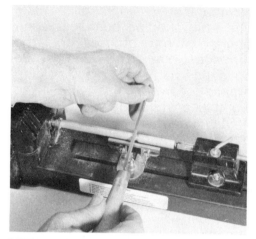

METAL WORK. Soft metals can be worked on the lathe. Use small files rather than chisels for cutting.

while turning in the lathe by using polishing compounds compatible with the material being used.

The use of files

Soft metals such as aluminum, brass and copper and some hardwoods can be shaped between centers on the lathe by using small files. Some grades of aluminum can be turned with the standard chisels. The do-it-yourself aluminum bars and rounds sold in some hardware stores work well in the lathe with the chisels. An ideal turning aluminum for the Moto-Lathe is No. 2001 alloy, bar stock ends of which are sometimes available from screw machine shops listed in the yellow pages. Copper and aluminum will plug up a file quickly so have a file card, a tool available in many hardware stores, handy to clean particles of metal from the file frequently. On some soft alloys, you can minimize clogging of files by first rubbing the file with wax.

Files come in a variety of shapes and sizes, so you can choose the ones to suit your job. When using files remove the tool rest and keep the file in contact with the top of

the turning. Use one hand to hold the file handle. Use the other hand to bear gently on the file, causing it to cut lightly into the turning.

Move the file back and forth over the work to help clear it of metal chips. Holding the file in one place too long will cause the teeth to become jammed full of material.

Never use a file without a file handle or you will risk jamming the tang into your hand. Note that if you have files without handles you can use your Moto-Lathe to make handles for them. Use the handles of the chisels which come with the Moto-Lathe as patterns and make the new handles out of hardwood. Just be sure the necks are wide enough to receive the tangs of your chisels. Drill a hole slightly smaller than the wide part of the tang after the handle has been turned and tap the file, tang first, into it.

A short length of copper or similar thin tubing can be fashioned into a ferrule to prevent the handle from splitting as the tang enters the hole. Turn a short cylinder on the end of the handle, of the same or slightly larger diameter than the inside diameter of the tubing, so the ferrule will fit snugly. Fit the ferrule to the handle before inserting the file tang.

PROJECT. Files should not be used unless they have handles. With the lathe, you can make your own.

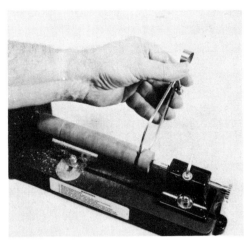

PROJECT. This walnut round is marked with sizing cuts to show top of handle and location of ferrule.

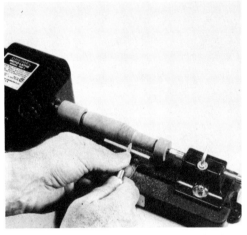

PROJECT. Using the round-nose chisel, the workpiece is shaped by reducing diameter of lower end.

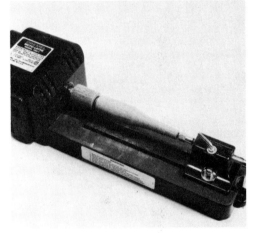

PROJECT. Finale shape of handle is achieved, with right end made to fit inside of ferrule.

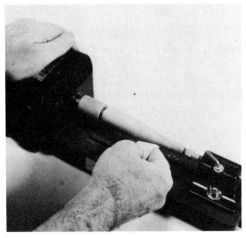

PROJECT. Handle is sanded to finished smoothness. Stain and wax could be applied at this time.

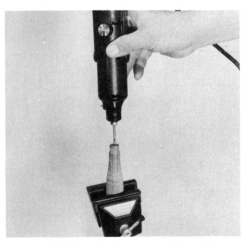

PROJECT. Handle is removed from the lathe and drilled to receive tang of file. Hole is smaller than tang.

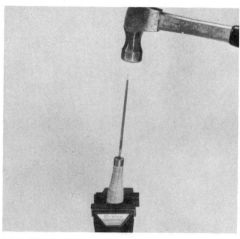

PROJECT. Ferrule made by cutting off small section of copper pipe is hammered down over the handle.

PROJECT. Three-cornered file is tapped into the hole in the handle. Project takes 15 to 20 minutes.

QUICK FIXES

A.

B.

C.

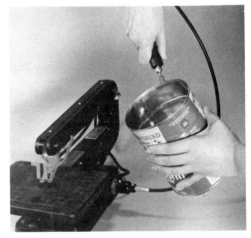

D.

A. If a door in your home has shifted slightly, so that the bolt no longer enters the latch plate properly, one quick way to fix it is to use the Moto-Tool to grind away a little of the lower edge of the latch plate.

B. Ever try to turn a difficult screw and find you have twisted the tip of the screwdriver blade? Restore the blade tip by grinding it on the sanding disc. Just touch the blade intermittently to the disc so it doesn't get hot and ruin the steel. You only want to square off the blade end, not change the shape.

C. Lawn edgers and other garden cutting tools can be sharpened with the Moto-

Tool and a grinding accessory. Make a couple of passes with the tool along the cutting edge of each blade, maintaining the blade edge at the original angle. Note that this is not true sharpening but is a honing to restore squareness to the cutting edges. If you grind too much or change the edge angle, you will ruin the cutting action.

D. Steel coffee and juice cans have a lot of uses, but when opened with a can opener or with a key fastened to the can, they often end up with sharp burrs at points around the lip, which can be dangerous. These burrs can be ground off with a grinding accessory.

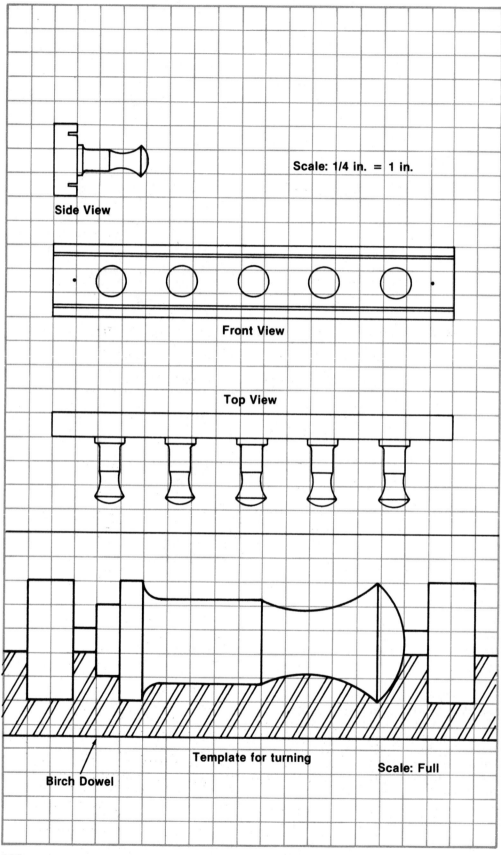

Scale: 1/4 in. = 1 in.

Side View

Front View

Top View

Birch Dowel

Template for turning

Scale: Full

Project 5

Screw this coat rack inside the back door or at the top of the basement stairs. It's like adding a mini-closet to your house.

Materials:
5 Hardwood dowels, 1-1/4 × 5-in.
1 Hardwood board, 1/2 × 3 × 17-in.
White glue
Sandpaper
Finishing materials of your choice.

Tools:
Dremel Table Saw
Moto-Lathe
Outside calipers
Portable drill and 3/4-in. wood bit

This project offers an interesting opportunity to use the Moto-Lathe as you shape the coat pegs. Begin by looking at Plan A, where the upper section (scale 1/4-in. to 1-in.) shows the overall dimensions, while the lower section offers a template (full size) to use in turning the coat pegs. The template shows the scrap allowance at each end of the dowel. Mount each dowel between centers, using the spur center on the headstock spindle. Make a cardboard copy of the template to check the turnings (see Detail A), and use the outside calipers to measure the depth of cuts. After each turning is completed, sand and apply finish while it is still in the lathe. Then remove it from the lathe and saw off waste at each end. Cut the backboard to size on the table saw, then add feature grooves by making two dado cuts on the table saw. See Detail C. Refer to Plan A for location of coat pegs on backboard, then mark and drill them. Use 3/4-in. drill bit in portable drill, and make each hole 1/4-in. deep. Finish the backboard and allow it to dry, then fit coat pegs into holes, using white glue. Wipe away any excess glue.

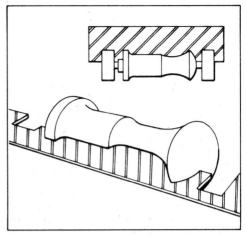

DETAIL A. Make a cardboard copy of the template in Plan A to check shape of each peg in the lathe.

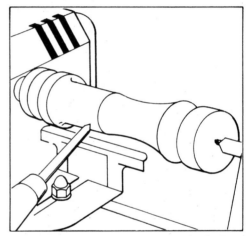

DETAIL B. Finish each peg in the lathe, first with chisels, then sandpaper, and finally, stain or wax.

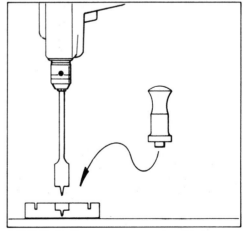

DETAIL C. Coat pegs are glued into 3/4-in. holes drilled in the backboard with a portable drill.

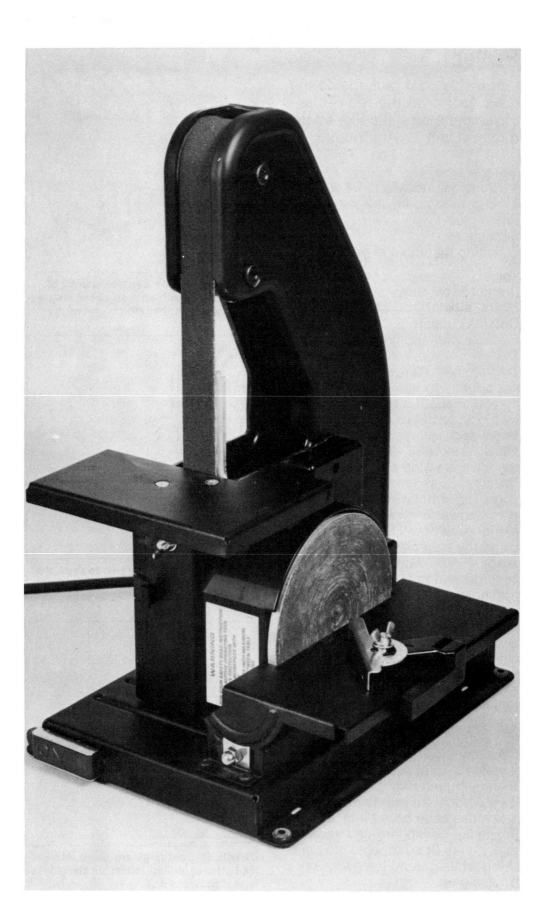

CHaPTeR SIX

The Dremel Disc/Belt Sander

A compact version of the big belt and disc sanders, this tool enables you to shape, sand, polish, clean and sharpen items in wood, metals and plastics, using either the continuous belt or the disc

Woodworkers want both disc and belt sanders because each does a particular kind of work better than the other. The belt sander is great for finishing project components and for finishing projects after assembly. You might, for example, sand an assembled miniature jewelry box with it, or use it for fast sharpening of knives, chisels, and other edge tools, as well as for shaping wood. It does a particularly nice job on the end grain of wood.

The disc sander serves nicely for sanding surfaces to true them up, for fast removal of material, for various shaping jobs and for sand-ing to close tolerances.

The Dremel Disc/Belt Sander is a happy combination, offering both types in one combination tool. It occupies just one square foot of shop space and weighs only 11 pounds. Both the belt and the disc sander can be used on hard and soft woods, metals, and plastics.

A look at the disc/belt sander

The disc/belt sander stands upright on your workbench, with a base that measures 8 × 11 inches. There is a work table for each of the sanders.

The belt sander is ideal for sanding projects, such as this jewelry box, after assembly has been completed.

The disc sander provides control and is good for sanding to close tolerances and truing up surface.

Sander mounted on a 3/4-inch wood base is easy to clamp to workbench and to remove for storage.

The table for the belt sander is fixed at 90 degrees, while that of the disc sander is adjustable from 90 to 45 degrees. The motor operates on standard 110/120 household current, providing a belt speed of 2,700 feet per minute and a disc speed of 4,400 RPM. The belt is 1 inch wide by 30 inches long, and the discs are 5 inches in diameter.

Setting up the sander

Because the sander is light in weight, and you will be applying some pressure to workpieces, it must be securely mounted on your workbench or table. There are two ways to do this.

If you have a permanent workbench, you can drill holes through the bench to match the holes in the base of the sander and then bolt the sander to the bench through these holes. It is best to have the sander mounted at the right end of a workbench so that both tables can be approached with ease.

If you want to be able to move the sander for storage, you can mount it on a 3/4-inch plywood base which in turn is clamped to the workbench or a table with C-clamps. A convenient size for the plywood base is 12 × 15 inches.

Position the tool on the plywood and mark through the four bolt holes in the base with a sharp pencil. Drill at the center of each marked hole with a 9/64-inch drill bit. Next, moisten the rubber feet provided with the sander and twist them into the holes in the base. The smaller the diameter of the rubber feet goes up into the holes, and the larger diameter faces downward.

Attach the disc-belt sander to the plywood base with mounting screws and washers which are furnished. Tighten these screws firmly, but not so firmly that the rubber feet are crushed or distorted. Try to make all screws equally tight, because you don't want to put uneven pressure on any part of the base.

Adjusting the sanding belt

When you first set up the sander and later as you use it and change sanding belts, it is necessary to check or adjust the tracking of the sanding belt from time to time.

Open the cover on the left side of the tool. You will see that there are two fingered pulley wheels, one at the top and one at the bottom front of the sander frame. There are also

The idler pulley wheel over which the belt passes at the back of the sander is spring loaded.

Rear idler pulley is moved to the forward position and belt is relocated as shown for internal work.

The upper flanged pulley is exposed at the top of the sander frame so you can check tracking visually.

The upper Phillips-head adjusting screw is used to adjust tracking when sander is set for internal work.

two idler pulleys, one just below the upper flanged pulley and one toward the lower rear of the sander frame.

The idler pulley at the lower rear is spring loaded, and has two operating positions: Full back and full forward. The idler pulley will balance itself midway between these two operating positions to make it easier to change belts.

The two operating positions permit the belt to do two types of sanding: external, such as removing burrs from a piece of aluminum bar that has just been cut with a hacksaw; and internal, for sanding the edges of an area that is completely enclosed, such as the interior hole left when the letter "D" has been cut on the scroll saw.

If the belt goes over and around both the upper flanged pulley and the upper idler pulley and then under and around the spring-loaded idler pulley in its full forward position and under and around the lower flanged pulley, the sander is properly set up for internal sanding.

One of the best features of the Dremel Disc/Belt Sander is a patented system for pre-setting the internal and external belt tracking adjustments. Once these adjustments are pre-set, their "memory" allows them to return to the last previous setting for either the internal or external modes, with no adjustments required. Many disc/belt sanders similar to Dremel's require tedious re-tracking adjustments every time a change is made from external to internal and back again. The Dremel sander requires only infrequent adjustment to compensate for belt wear, etc.

At the top forward part of the sander frame, the upper flanged pulley is exposed. This serves two purposes: (1) It permits you to sand workpieces that have concave curves and therefore cannot be sanded on the flat side of the belt or on the disc; and (2), it allows you to visually check regularly to determine if the belt is tracking properly.

With your right hand, turn the sanding disc counterclockwise and observe whether the belt in this exposed area remains in the center of the pulley wheel. If it is riding up against or close to either of the flanges, the belt tracking needs adjustment.

On the side of the machine which holds the disc sander you will see a box-like obstruction on the frame, just behind the belt sander work table and to the rear of the disc sander assembly. The front of the box has two openings allowing access to two Phillips-Head adjusting screws.

The upper adjusting screw is for adjusting the tracking when the sander is set up for internal sanding, and the lower is for adjusting tracking when in the external position.

Clockwise adjustment of the upper or "internal" adjusting screw causes the belt to move to the left.

Clockwise adjustment of the lower or "external" adjusting screw causes the belt to move to the right.

Assuming the belt is in the external position, rotate the sanding disc toward you for several revolutions. This will cause the belt to move in a downward motion. Observe whether the belt is too far to the left or to the right. Make whatever adjustment is needed by turning the lower adjusting screw in the proper direction, as explained in the previous paragraph.

Make only a slight adjustment and then repeat the process. Continue to make small adjustments until the belt is running equidistant from the two flanges. Then close the sander cover and switch the motor on. Observe the belt and if it is running slightly more to one side than the other, the final adjustment can be made with the motor running.

The lower Phillips-head adjusting screw adjusts tracking when sander is in the external sanding mode.

This photo shows the location of the belt backing plate. Most belt sanding is done without this plate.

Spring loading on lower rear idler pulley is strong, so moving it takes a firm grasp and heavy pull.

For internal sanding, belt is fed through the workpiece before being placed on the pulleys.

Work was left out of this picture to provide clear view of belt mounting on pulleys for internal sanding.

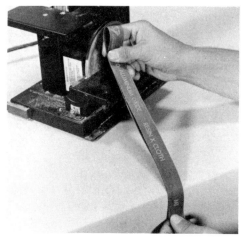

To alleviate stiffness in a new belt, reverse it and draw it back and forth over the edge of the workbench top.

When you've completed the adjustment for the external sanding position, make a similar adjustment for the internal sanding mode. To convert the sander from the external to the internal positions, the belt backing plate must be removed if this has not already been done. (Most belt sanding is done without the use of the plate.) Again, the sander should be unplugged when any adjustments, repairs or maintenance work is being done.

With the left side panel open, grasp the lower rear idler and swing it forward to a center position. This will take the tension off the belt and allow you to rethread it in and around the two flanged pulleys and the two idler pulleys, as shown in the photographs. (If you were making the change from external to internal for the purpose of sanding a closed internal area on a workpiece, at this point you would thread the belt through the hole in the workpiece before continuing with the installation of the belt.

When the belt is properly threaded for the internal mode, swing the spring-loaded idler pulley to its full forward position to put tension on the belt. Check to see that the belt is tracking in the center of the upper idler pulley. If not, make adjustment by slightly turning the upper Phillips screwhead until the belt is running in a central position.

Use the internal position only for internal sanding, since the abrasive side of the sanding belt is in contact with both idler pulleys in this position and causes extra wear.

The belt backing plate can be used whenever you feel it is necessary for external belt sanding. Otherwise it does not have to be in place and you may get better results without it, depending upon the type of sanding you are doing. The belt backing plate cannot be used at all for internal sanding.

When you are installing a new

belt, tracking adjustments can become more difficult. This is partly because the new belt is stiff. To alleviate this problem, turn the belt inside out and draw it lengthwise back and forth over the edge of a workbench top. This will soften it. Do not crease the belt while holding the ends. Work one side of the belt, then turn it over and draw the other side over the edge of the workbench, top.

While the belt is turned inside out, you may see an arrow indicating the proper direction of rotation. If no arrow is seen, the belt can be run in either direction. Belts with arrows should be installed in the sander with this arrow pointing downward as the belt moves over the upper flanged pulley, down past the table and on to the lower pulley.

Safe operation

Like the other power tools discussed in this book, the disc/belt sander must be correctly connected to a properly grounded electrical circuit, as explained in Chapter One. The work area should not be damp or wet, and should be clear of sawdust and other debris.

While working with these tools, do not wear loose fitting clothing or jewelry. Safety goggles and a dust mask are required. There should be no open flame, such as in a furnace or hot water heater, nearby since a mixture of sawdust and air can be explosive.

Do not use any liquids or coolants on the discs or belts.

Sander safety. Always disconnect the sander before servicing or when changing belts or discs. And always make sure the switch is in the OFF position before plugging it in.

Never leave the sander while it is running, even for a moment.

Use only belts or discs recommended and supplied by Dremel.

If you have been sanding wood with the sander and then wish to

grind a piece of ferrous metal such as iron or steel, first remove all sawdust from the inside, the outside and the area surrounding the sander. Ferrous metals throw off sparks when they are ground, and these can cause sawdust to catch fire. Often, the sawdust smoulders for a long time before bursting into flame — and this could be a long time after you've left the area. Nonferrous metals also throw off hot particles, so it is a good practice to remove sawdust before grinding these, too.

Maintain a maximum clearance of 1/16-inch between the face of the

To prevent accident or injury, keep clearance between the disc face and the worktable at 1/16 inch.

sanding disc and the worktable to prevent the work from slipping down between the disc and the edge of the table, where it could bind, causing damage to the equipment and perhaps injury to you.

Do not attempt to hold small workpieces in your fingers to sand them either on the belt or the disc. They can be torn violently out of your hands, striking your body or jamming into the machine. Or your fingers can touch the moving belt or disc, which will quickly remove the skin.

For wood or plastics, use a small cabinetmaker's gluing clamp or a

This simple clamp can be made in minutes to hold small work for sanding on either belt or disc.

One important use of the belt sander is the shaping of irregular or curved surfaces.

similar non-marring clamping device which will hold firmly. A simple non-marring clamp can be made with two short strips of wood into which holes have been drilled about an inch from each end. Insert bolts with wingnuts into these holes. The work is held by clamping it between the two strips of wood.

Belt Sander Operation

The belt sander, in the external setting, has many uses, such as shaping irregular and curved surfaces, carved figures, gun stocks, handgun grips, briar pipe bowls, and similar objects. It can be used for cleaning rust from metal pieces (auto and bicycle parts, for example); removing the sharp edges from castings of model parts, or burrs from a metal piece that has been cut with a hacksaw, and for putting an edge on dull chisels and other cutting tools.

The belt sander can be used with the furnished backing plate placed just behind the belt at table height. Most belt sanding, however, is done without the plate. The plate does give added support to the belt as you press the workpiece into it, and

The disc sander is best for truing up work or making accurate shapes. Here, the edge is sanded square.

can be attached when needed. The backing plate does not create an absolutely flat surface or as square an angle as the disc sander on larger pieces of work. For this reason, when turning up work or making accurate shapes, it is best to use the disc sander. On small workpieces, the belt sander's accuracy is satisfactory.

The internal setting is for sanding the inside edges of a large hole or other closed figure, such as the inside edge of an opening that has been scroll sawed in a workpiece and is inaccessible when the belt is in the external setting. The sander

The inside edge of scroll sawed pieces such as this can be sanded using the internal sanding setup.

should be set up for inside sanding, then used in this setting only until the task is finished, because in this setting, the sanding belt wears the idler pulley faster. The abrasive side of the belt is against the pulley.

When sanding on the belt, do not move the work across the belt, because the belt will flex and move to the side.

Sanding belts. Six different abrasive belts are available for use on the belt sander, ranging from the coarse 50 grit to the very fine 320 grit. These are:

No. 8040, 50 grit. Coarse, for rough sanding hardwood and plastics, and for grinding metals.

No. 8041, 80 grit. Medium, for rough sanding of softwoods and plastics, for grinding of metals, and for deburring.

No. 8042, 120 grit. Fine, for finishing wood and plastics, removing rust, sharpening cutting tools, and finish deburring.

No. 8043, 180 grit. Extra fine, for light polishing and finishing on wood, metal, and some plastics.

No. 8044, 240 grit. Very fine, for fine finishing, polishing on wood, metal, and some plastics.

No. 8045, 320 grit. Fine polishing, for extremely fine final finishing of wood, polishing on wood, metal and

some plastics. Also for honing and sharpening cutting tools.

When finishing work, it is customary to do three or more successive sandings, starting with a coarser grit, then graduating to a medium grit, and finally finishing with the finest grit. This produces the best surface for quality finishes such as varnish.

Polishing. Polishing of metal can be done with a fine grit belt that is completely worn out. In fact, the more worn the belt, the finer the finish will be. For the last bit of polishing, you can use jeweler's rouge (Dremel Polishing Compound

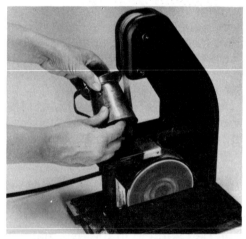

A fine grit belt that is completely worn out takes on a new life when it is used to polish metal objects.

No. 421) or other polishing compound on the worn out 320 grit belts.

The static electricity problem. One annoying problem typical of all belt sanders is the production of static electricity. This happens mostly when the air is very dry — when the furnace is running in midwinter, or when the air conditioning has been running for some days in the summer. The problem can be minimized by humidifying the air in the winter. Static electricity is completely harmless, but the tiny shock it creates can give you a start when you are concentrating on a sanding job. When the humidity is low, you can eliminate this problem by keeping a finger or hand touching some metal part of the sander such as the table. This grounds you and does not allow a static charge to build up.

Using the belt sander

The relative narrowness of the 1-inch sanding belt permits you to power sand in places that would be virtually impossible by any other means. And the length of the belt permits cooler sanding in metals and plastics, as well as on the end grains of wood, all of which tend to overheat where less sanding surface is available. One of its great advantages is the ability to sand internal surfaces that may otherwise have to be sanded completely by hand.

Here are some typical belt sanding operations and how to do them.

Sanding wood — Most wood sanding on the belt is free-hand smoothing or shaping of irregularly shaped objects, such as a figurine or carving, a briar pipe bowl, a replacement handle for a bench plane, shaping a propeller for a model airplane, etc. To do this kind of work, the sanding belt often works best without the use of the belt backing shoe, which can easily be removed. In this way, the flexible belt can take on the same contours as the object being sanded and do a more thorough job.

The best way to learn to use the belt is to practice with scraps of wood. Try creating different shapes and contours as you practice.

You will notice that light pressure, where the sanding grit is allowed to do the work instead of your muscle, will work better.

Do not attempt to move the work laterally back and forth across the belt, because the belt will veer off

course in whichever direction pressure is applied. If you need to sand a convex curve on the belt, for example, stand the work on end so that its edge is parallel to the belt. Then rock the curve up and down vertically, rather than attempting to lay the work flat on the table and move it laterally back and forth.

The same would be true of sanding a flat edge that is wider than the belt. Instead of attempting to sand the edge with the work horizontally on the table and moving back and forth against the belt, stand the work vertically on end and use part of the length of the belt as your

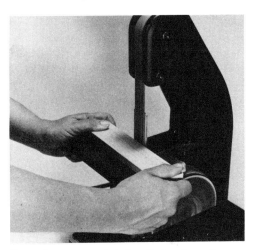

Do not move work laterally back and forth across the belt, but move it straight in with a light pressure.

Sanding a convex curve on a belt can be done by standing the work on its end and rocking it up and down.

Convex curves can also be sanded at the top of the sander, where the belt rolls over the flanged pulley.

When sanding plastics, work in short bursts of just a few seconds at a time to prevent buildup of heat.

sanding surface instead of its *width.*

Convex curves of wood or other materials can be sanded at the very top of the sander, when the belt is visible as it rolls over the upper flanged pulley.

The sanding belt without the belt backing plate works particularly well in smoothing off edges of wood that are intended to be rounded. Do the rough work by tipping the workpiece up to meet the belt while the work rests on the sander table top. Then a quick hand sanding will complete the job.

As you practice with the belt you will begin to get the "feel" of how it works, both with the backing plate and without.

Sanding plastic — Many of the comments made for sanding wood apply equally for plastics. Many plastics, however, have very low melting points. As you work with plastics, sand in short bursts of just a few seconds. If there is considerable sanding to be done on a piece, start at some point, then quickly move on to the next section and the next, allowing the previously sanded areas to cool before you start sanding them again.

Grinding metal — As explained earlier, all sawdust and other com-

bustible materials should be cleaned out of the inside of the sander, off of the outside and from the surrounding area so that sparks or hot bits of metal will not ignite them.

Metal that has just been cut with a hacksaw, cutoff blade or other means often has a sharp edge or burr. A natural use of the sanding belt is to remove the burr or sharp edge. However, if the sharp or jagged edge of the metal is pushed straight into the belt it is likely to tear or cut the belt, thus ruining it. So instead of pushing the metal straight in at a right angle, move in from the side with a light rocking motion until the burr or sharp edge has been removed.

Metal that is being ground tends to build up heat rapidly and to hold it for long periods of time. The heat also spreads, so that you can suddenly feel your fingers growing hot even though you may be holding a workpiece several inches from the point where it is being ground. Frequent dousing of the metal into water will help keep it cool if you have considerable grinding to do.

The metal cutting edges on tools that are allowed to overheat lose their temper — that is, their hardness that allows the edge to take and hold a keen cutting surface —

To maintain bevel on chisels and other tools, use guide as you sharpen them. Grind only beveled side.

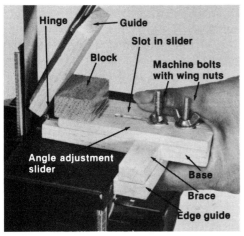

Adjustable guide for sharpening beveled chisels fits on disc sander table. Base of (1/2 × 2-in. stock) is 4-1/2-inches long. Edge guide (1/2 × 1-in. stock) which slides against table edge is 4-1/2-inches long. It is screwed to base from bottom, has brace blocks on either side, as shown. Slider (1/4 × 2-inch stock) is 4-in. long, and has 3/4 × 1 × 2-inch block glued at front end. Slider moves back and forth to change angle of chisel guide as needed. Machine bolts through base ride in slot in slider. Guide itself is of 1/2 × 2-inch stock, 3 inches long, hinged to the base. In use, slider is moved until the guide is at proper angle to hold chisel bevel flat against sanding disc, then wing nuts are tightened. Hold chisel firmly against guide, grind only a few seconds at a time to minimize heat. Plunge in water to help cooling.

and thus are virtually ruined. Thus in sharpening metal cutting edges, great care must be taken to prevent heat buildup. Short bursts of grinding, followed by frequent dousing in water, help considerable in keeping the heat held down. If the cutting edge begins to turn color and shows any shade of blue is visible, especially at the fine cutting edge, the temper of the blade has been lost.

One problem with grinding a cutting edge in short bursts, however, is that the edge must be beveled at exactly the correct angle for that tool. If you have several small hand tools in your shop — wood, lathe or woodcarving chisels, the blade from a hand plane, and a cold chisel, you'll see that, from a side view, that each has a different cutting angle. Each was designed at that bevel for maximum cutting efficiency. Note, too, that the bevel continues across the entire cutting surface in one unbroken line. If you were to attempt to grind edges free hand on such tools with several short bursts, and without the aid of a guide, with each burst you would likely grind away at a different facet, so that your finished job would be a series of uneven facets rather than one smooth unbroken line.

First, for the amateur, do not attempt to grind new cutting edges on tools at all unless they are so badly nicked or dulled that they must either be ground or discarded. If the edge is in relatively good shape, hone the edge regularly to keep the tool sharp. Set aside a place or means where your tools will not be thrown or banged against each other, or with other metal surfaces and thus become nicked. If you are not sure you can properly grind a new edge on an expensive tool, consider taking it to a professional grinding shop to have a new edge ground onto it rather than spoiling it.

If you wish to attempt to grind the cutting edge on the belt sander, do not do so free hand. If you have a set of badly dulled wood chisels for example, all of them will or should have the same cutting bevel. Determine which direction would be best for the blades to attach the belt for best results and ease of handling. If, for example, you attempted to grind the edges so that the belt is moving directly down against the cutting edge, as the chisel is sharpened it may suddenly cut the belt and ruin it. In this case, it would be better to decide on an approach from one of the sides or with the cutting edge pointing downward.

Once you've determined the best direction for approaching the belt, loosely clamp a block of wood onto the table top to serve as a guide. You may have to notch or otherwise alter the wood block to make a firm holding surface for the tool. To obtain the correct grinding bevel for the particular tool you wish to sharpen, hold the tool so the bevel is flat against the blade. You probably will want to use the belt backing plate for this work. When you've set the block of wood at the proper angle for the tool's bevel, tighten the C-clamp to hold the guide firmly in place. Now, as you move the tool's cutting edge against the guide and edge in against the sanding belt for short bursts of grinding, you'll achieve exactly the same angle with each approach. Allow the cutting edges to cool each time before continuing the grinding.

If you have tools or other items that are rusted or pitted, in some cases they can be cleaned up to look almost new. Much rust can be removed from iron and steel with a stiff wire brush wheel used in a bench grinder. This, however, will not remove any pits. To grind away shallow pits, slacken the belt by removing the belt backing plate. Feed the workpiece gently to the belt, holding

it and moving it at the same time so that you won't get a flat surface where a round one is required. Let the work ride gently against the belt so that you have the feeling you are "steering" the loose belt somewhat to keep it running truly. Stop frequently to examine your progress and to allow the metal to cool.

Using disc sander

Keep in mind that while the belt works well for many jobs and is superior for others, many jobs can be done either on the belt or the disc, and sometimes the disc has some advantages.

As much as possible, plan your work so the sanding is done only on the upper, forward quarter of the disc, the part of the disc towards you. If you think of the disc as being the face of a clock, this would be the area where the numbers 9 through 12 appear.

This quarter of the disc moves downward and its rotation tends to keep the workpiece on the table. If you go beyond the center of the disc to the right of center as you face the disc, not only will the work be lifted from the table and perhaps thrown, but also dust and grit will be thrown into your face. It is not impossible to

When using the disc sander, work only on the upper forward quarter of the disc, between 9 and 12 o'clock.

sand across the entire upper face of the disc if the work is held very firmly onto the right side of the table to prevent an uplift. It is much more advisable, however, where a wide or long surface must be sanded, to do half of it on the 9 to 12 o'clock quarter and then flop the workpiece and sand the remaining surface on the same quarter section of the disc.

Most of your work on the disc will be done with the table at 90 degrees. A perfect 90 degree angle can be maintained by periodic checking with a machinist's or carpenter's square. You can adjust the table, however, from 90 through 45 degrees. Use a protractor to measure the angle.

Check the disc sander table periodically to be sure it is at a perfect 90-degree angle. Adjust if necessary.

If you want to sand a workpiece to a duplicate angle of another workpiece, you can use the finished part as a guide. If this is not convenient, you can use a sliding T-bevel, an inexpensive device available in most hardware stores. The T-bevel allows you to pick up the angle from the workpiece being copied, lock the tool to that angle, and then transfer the angle to the disc sander table, which is then locked in place at the same angle.

The miter gauge which slides along the edge of the disc sander table is also used for making precise angles, such as the 45-degree angle used in mitering the corners of picture frames. While there is an angle scale on the miter gauge, it should be used only for rough work. To make precise angles, use a protractor to make the exact setting on the miter gauge. The miter gauge is adjusted by loosening its locking nut to set the correct angle, and then retightening the nut.

Sanding discs. Discs for the sander are available in packages of five, and in three degrees of abrasiveness. These discs are 5 inches in diameter, and are held on the disc with an adhesive. The abrasive on

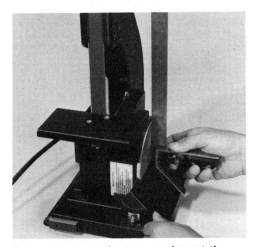

For accurate work at an angle, set the table with measuring device. Here, a combination square is used.

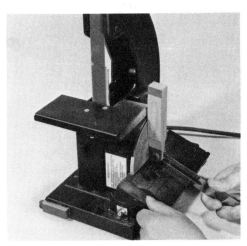

Sliding T-bevel allows you to pick up angle from workpiece being copied and transfer it to the table.

153

Miter gauge on table guides work for angular sanding. For precision, set miter gauge with a protractor.

The Miter gauge is also a help in sanding workpiece ends square. Disc does good job on end grain.

them is aluminum oxide. No. 8050 is 50 grit. No. 8051 is 80 grit. And No. 8052 is 120 grit. The 50 grit is the coarsest paper, and the 120 grit, the finest.

To get the best results from the disc sander, learn which discs to use. A general rule is always to use the coarsest disc which will do the job adequately. Fine grit discs are only good for very fine finishing and polishing, and may actually cause burning on the surface of hardwoods. They may also melt plastics because the fine grit tends to overheat. Also, the fine grit loads up faster when sanding wood that contains pitch (pine, for example) and when sanding plastics.

Movement of the work. When sanding on the disc sander, move the work back and forth on the upper, forward quarter of the disc. This spreads the wear and heat on the sanding disc and assures faster removal of material and longer life for the abrasive.

Replacing discs

The Dremel discs for the disc/belt sander are of the self-adhesive type. Each disc comes with adhesive on the back, covered by a backing paper.

Final sanding of angular cuts is easy with table tilted. Measure table angle carefully for precise work.

To remove disc from backplate, grip edge of paper and peel it away, rotating disc as you do.

To remove the old disc from the backing plate, first unplug the sander. Grip the edge of the paper and begin peeling it away. Rotate the disc and peel again, and continue to do this until the disc comes away from the backplate.

Remove the protective backing paper from the new disc. Carefully slide the disc between the table and the backing plate and position it on the backplate. Then press it into position.

This can be difficult to do. Fortunately, there is an easier way but it takes a little longer. This is by loosening the two cap screws which hold the table clamps, and tilting the table up to slide it out. Do not take the nuts off the screws; just loosen them. If you remove the nuts, the screws will fall out, and you will have to remove the table support for reassembly.

Before applying a new disc, be sure the backing plate is clean and free of lumps of adhesive or pieces of the old disc. To clean the backplate, hold an edge of a hardwood stick against it as it spins. If you choose to use a cleaning solvent, be sure the cord has been unplugged and is left unplugged until the solvent has completely evaporated.

Sanding on the sanding disc

As you first begin to practice sanding wood on the sanding disc you'll note that when your workpiece is near the center of the disc very little material is removed, while when the work is at the very outer edge of the disc, material is removed at a very rapid rate.

This is so because while the entire disc is turning at the same RPM, the outer edge of the disc, being larger in circumference, has to travel farther on each revolution than the center inch or so, which has relatively little distance to cover

An easier but longer way to change sanding discs is to loosen cap screws and remove the table.

To remove table, tilt it upward after loosening cap screws. Do not remove cap screws. Just loosen them.

To clean backplate before applying new disc, hold edge of stick against it lightly as it spins.

155

compared with the outer edge.

The implication of this to the operator is that because the outer edge has to travel more distance with each revolution, more surface feet per minute of sanding material is passing across the workpiece and thus is removing more material faster. This must be taken into consideration when holding a workpiece against the sanding disc. To achieve a 90-degree angle on the end of a wooden workpiece, for example, it is necessary to apply more pressure to the side of the edge which is near the center of the disc. Unlike the belt, the disc is intended to have the workpiece move back and forth across it, either by using the miter gauge or by guiding the work free hand. To start a sanding pass, start by moving the workpiece up against the turning disc just to the left of the center point, and then move the work toward the outer edge of the disc. Use light pressure and repetitive passes rather than trying to remove large amounts of material with one heavy pass.

Jigs and fixtures — Several simple jigs and fixtures can be designed and built to facilitate sanding on the disc.

For handling large workpieces, an auxiliary top of 3/8-inch or thicker plywood which can be clamped to the regular table can be a help.

With such an auxiliary table, perfect circles or parts of circular edges can be sanded on the disc. First rough saw the circle on the scroll saw. Find the center of the circle and drill a hole of about 1/16-inch in diameter. Drive a small finishing nail into the auxiliary top at the approximate point where, when the hole in the circle is placed onto the finishing nail, the edge of the workpiece will come into light contact with the sanding disc. Turn the workpiece in a clockwise direction (as you look downward on it from the top). After you've made one

Auxiliary table of plywood allows such work as sanding perfect circles. See text for details.

By clamping a 2 x 4 to the table, you can sand longer edges. Pass the work along the top of the 2 x 4.

complete revolution of the workpiece, remove it from the finishing nail and examine the edge. If there are places on the edge that have not been sanded, loosen the clamp on the auxiliary table until the finishing nail pivot point is slightly closer to the sanding disc. Repeat this process, until the entire outer edge of the disc is sanded and you'll have a perfect circle. If the hole in the center is offensive, fill it with wood filler and sand until smooth.

If you have a workpiece with a 10-inch long edge you wish to sand you cannot do so with the 2-1/2-inch portion of the disc at table top height and from the center point to the outer edge of the disc. You may, however, clamp a thick piece of wood, a 2 by 4 for example, flat side down to the top of the table, maintaining a 1/16-inch clearance between the wooden guide and the sanding disc. This will leave only slightly more than an inch of the top of the sanding disc exposed. At this point the area of the disc that is exposed is traveling in somewhat of an arced sideways direction, from right to left. Thus much of the lifting action that would occur if you were to sand to the right of the center of the disc, where the disc is moving upward, is eliminated. You then can sand your 10-inch edge by letting it ride along the top surface of the 2 by 4 and meanwhile moving the edge from right to left across the entire exposed part of the upper disc.

With a little planning and thought, you can design other simple jigs and fixtures to help you sand pieces to a uniform thickness or to sand several identical pieces with a pattern attached to the workpiece and a guide block attached to the table. The pattern rides against the guide block while the workpiece encounters the sanding disc.

Sanding plastic — Much of the same information given for sanding wood on the disc and for sanding plastic on the belt applies as well for sanding plastic on the sanding disc. The main concern is to keep the plastic from overheating, by using short bursts of sanding followed by longer cooling periods, or by using extremely light pressure against a very coarse disc.

Grinding metals — Emery cloth works especially well for sanding metals on a disc, but it is not readily available in precut 5-inch discs. You can, however, cut two 5-inch discs from a standard sheet of emery cloth and attach them to the sanding disc.

To cut the discs, scribe two 5-inch discs on the backing with a compass or dividers, or simply by tracing around one of the edges of a regular 5-inch Dremel disc. Cut out the discs using an old pair of scissors or tin snips.

To mount the emery discs use commercial disc cements available at some hardware stores and through large mail order houses which sell a full range of tools. If disc cement cannot be located, a coating of rubber cement on the metal sanding disc as well as on the backing side of the emery cloth usually will work well. The rubber cement permits the disc to be peeled away when it is worn out and the sander's metal disc can be cleaned with rubber cement thinner obtainable from artist supply stores.

The precautions given for grinding metals on the sanding belt to prevent overheating and uneven facets apply even more so with the sanding disc, which has a faster cutting edge. A metal cutting edge or sharp burr which is allowed to cut against the downward spin of the turning sanding disc may quickly cut it or rip it, causing possible damage or injury, as well as ruining the disc.

Grinding of small metal parts on the disc should never be done by holding the part in your hand. A pair of locking pliers makes a good holding device for small bolts, nuts or other pieces which must be ground.

Accurate sanding — Once you've had some experience with sanding on the disc you will find you can do some very accurate sanding to close tolerances without the benefit of guides. To do this, make a very fine line with a sharp knife, razor blade, sharp awl point or similar device. If you are working in wood, you may want to darken the mark with a sharp pencil to make it easier to see.

Approach the sanding disc as you would for sanding with the miter gauge or other guide, but use your eyes to guide the sanding operation. With some practice, you'll find that you can sand exactly to the line you've scribed with only a few thousands of an inch, plus or minus, to spare. Some professional machinists and patternmakers use this system when extreme precision is not required. And you can make near perfect mitered corners and other close fitting work with a little practice, with wood, metal or plastics.

Sharpening metal edges — Follow the same precautions given in the section on belt sanding for grinding metal edges. First, decide whether the work can best be done on the disc or the belt. If you use the disc, make a guide block which can be clamped to the table top and permit you to grind in short bursts, always at the same bevel. Do not allow the tool to overheat.

Other sanding tips

Do not sand wet wood or other composition materials on either the disc or belt. Green wood, that which has just recently been cut from a tree

and which has not yet had a chance to dry, also should not be sanded. If, for any reason, the grit on your sanding disc becomes clogged, a wire or bristle brush can sometimes clean out the material, extending the life of the belts and discs.

You will need to lubricate the rear motor bearing in the disc/belt sander after about every 50 hours of operation. Place one drop of light sewing machine oil in the hole that is slightly to the left of center on the end of the motor casing.

All other bearings in the sander have been lubricated for the life of the tool.

Cleaning

Remove accumulated dust and debris from the inside of the disc-belt sander at frequent intervals.

Remove accumulated dust and debris from the inside of the motor at frequent intervals. To do this, hold a vacuum sweeper hose to the rear motor vents, while tapping the motor housing with a screwdriver handle or light, non-marring hammer to loosen the dirt. DO NOT BLOW AIR INTO THE MOTOR as this will blow dirt into the bearings. Failure to keep the motor clean will result in over-heating of the motor and could result in a fire if the dust is flammable.

To lubricate the rear motor bearing every 50 hours of operation, place a drop of light oil in hole on casing.

QUICKFIXeS

A.

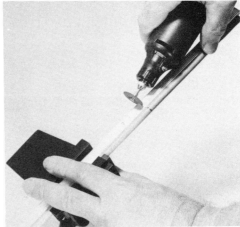

C.

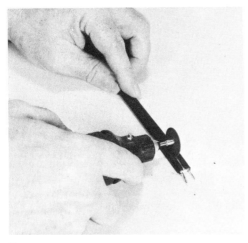

B.

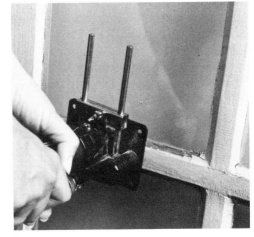

D.

A. When you leave an exhausted battery in a flashlight too long, it drips and can ruin the electrical contacts inside. You may be able to restore the light if, after removing the old battery, you grind the electrical contact points clean. In some cases, the battery acid will have eaten too much metal away to permit restoration.

B. Putting up an TV antenna? The two-wire lead-in cable, either insulated or uninsulated, must be split at the set so wires inside can be connected. You can cut the tough plastic easily with the emery wheel accessory. Be careful to cut between the wires, and only cut deep enough to slice the outer plastic coating. Then pull it away and expose the encased wires.

C. When installing metal weather stripping around a door or window, use the emery wheel (No. 409) to quickly cut through both metal and plastic parts.

D. Replacing old dried-up putty on a window seals leaks and saves energy. Old putty comes out easily with the Moto-Tool and a high speed cutter or if you use the router accessory as shown here. Edge guide on the router can be set for proper depth of cut.

Project 6

The banjo clock has been a favorite since colonial days and now you can make your own, exercising true craftsmanship to individualize it.

Materials:
Clock movement (electric or battery)
1/4 × 2 × 48-in. hardwood or
   hardwood plywood board
2 1/4 × 7 × 9-in. hardwood or
   hardwood plywood board
3 1/2 × 8 × 8-in. hardwood blocks
2 × 2 × 4-in. hardwood block
2 × 2 × 3-in. hardwood block
1/8 × 4 × 10-in. hardwood or
   hardwood plywood board
brass roundhead nails
White glue
Stain and varnish

Tools:
Table saw
Moto-Shop Scroll Saw
Moto-Tool with router attachment
   (optional)
Disc/Belt Sander
Clamps for gluing
Hammer

Examine Plan A and determine dimensions of all clock parts, but before cutting wood, purchase clock movement. It should fit within 2-1/2-in. inside diameter of clock head. If you buy larger movement, increase size of clock head. Make clock head by sawing 3 identical rings with scroll saw. Note the tabs at the bottom of each ring. Saw out centers of rings first. To do so, drill 5/32-in. or larger hole in waste part. Slip saw blade through hole and install in scroll saw, then cut on guidelines. See Detail A. Sand each ring separately on disc or belt sander until all three are of same size and contour. See

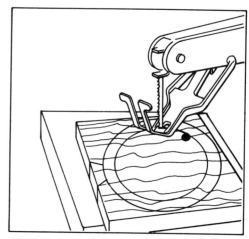

DETAIL A. Cut three identical rings on scroll saw, cutting centers out first, to make clock head.

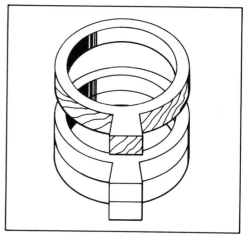

DETAIL B. The three rings are sanded to shape individually first, then glued together and sanded again.

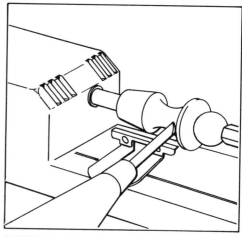

DETAIL C. The finial, in either wood or brass, is turned on the Moto-Lathe and fastened to the top.

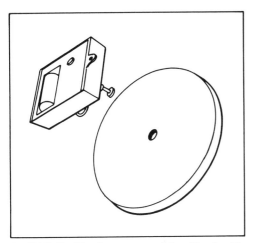

DETAIL D. Clock movement is attached to the back of the face, with clock arbor extended through hole in face.

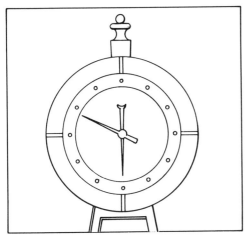

DETAIL E. Brass roundhead nails are driven in around face to indicate hours. Router cuts can decorate face.

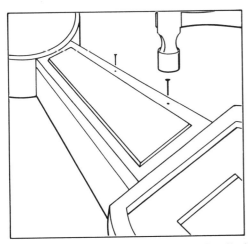

DETAIL F. Front panel is glued and nailed to back. Brass roundhead nails could be used here, too.

Detail B. Glue rings together, clamping until glue sets. Now sand entire head to final shape. Belt sander good for this job. Cut other clock parts next, using either the table saw or scroll saw, as appropriate. Sand each part before assembly. Glue lower box pieces together, using small glue blocks inside of it, and clamp until dry. Then glue upright pieces between clock head and lower box. Again, clamp until dry. Glue 2 × 2 × 4-in. block to bottom of lower box. Cut bottom decoration from 2 × 2 × 3-in. block on scroll saw, then glue it to bottom of clock case. The rear clock case is now finished. Sand smooth, using belt sander. When gluing parts, be sure no glue gets on wood adjacent to glued joints, as this will interfere with staining later. Next make front pieces of clock case. Lower front consists of two pieces cut on scroll saw from 1/4-in. hardwood. The center of the front piece of this assembly is cut out as shown in Plan A, and is glued to the back piece, which does not have the center cut out. This assembly is then glued to the clock case. The middle assembly also consists of two pieces. The larger is 1/4-in. hardwood, while the raised panel (See Detail F) is 1/8-in hardwood. Cut the circular clock face also from 1/8-in. hardwood, and drill a hole at its center for the clock arbor. (See Details D and E). If you choose, you can decorate the face with router cuts. Glue the face to the clock head and use brass roundhead nails to indicate the hours. Turn the finial on the Moto-Lathe (See Detail C) and attach it to top with a small dowel. Plan calls for wood finial but you could turn finial of brass for more authentic look. Before installing movement, stain and varnish clock case.

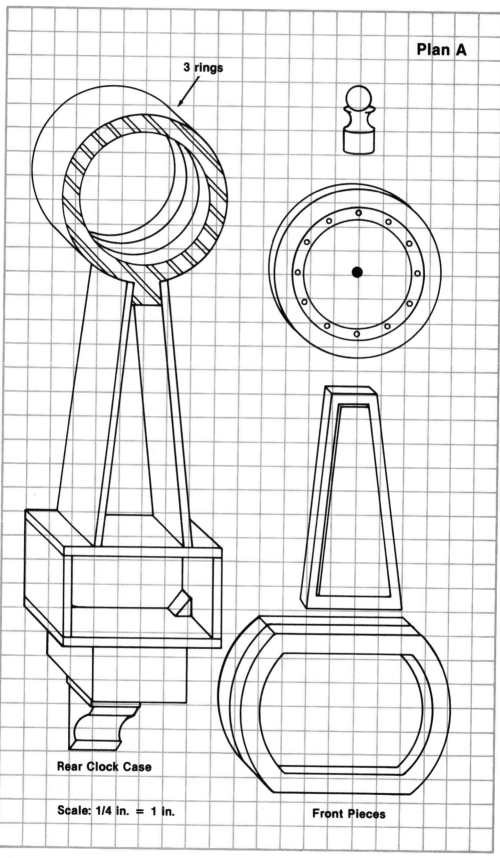

Plan A

3 rings

Rear Clock Case

Scale: 1/4 in. = 1 in.

Front Pieces

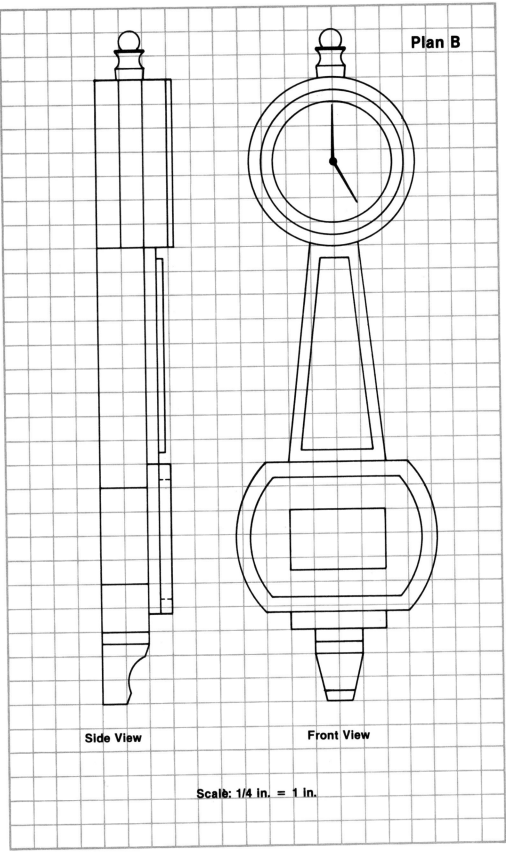

Plan B

Side View

Front View

Scale: 1/4 in. = 1 in.

CHAPTER seven

The Dremel D-Vise and Other Special Tools

For those times when you need a third hand in the workshop, look to the D-Vise. It holds the work in any position and frees your hands to operate tools with greater safety and accuracy. And for special jobs, there are the Chainsaver, for sharpening chain saws; the Engraver, for all kinds of engraving; and the Woodburner, for decorative work on wood.

A look at the D-Vise

There probably is no workshop accessory handier than the D-Vise. It is a vise for your workbench, but it is a lot more than just an ordinary vise. With it you can position and lock work in any position over a 180-degree range and a 360-degree axis, giving you greater control over the work. It is a versatile "extra hand" in your work area, an assistant always ready to hold what you want in any position you want it.

There are some very good reasons for using a vise as you work. First, of course, is the fact that when the workpiece is held firmly in a vise, you can work in greater safety and with much more accuracy. You have both hands free to operate your tools, and the work won't slip away at the wrong moment.

Second is the fact that you can work in more comfortable positions with less fatigue. And third, you can concentrate on your work better, exercising greater control over the tools.

One of the interesting things about the D-Vise is that it has five separate elements. By selecting the elements you need for your work, you can assemble a vise that is "custom made" for your own

The D-Vise gives you a third hand. Here, quick setting epoxy glue is used to repair glass stem.

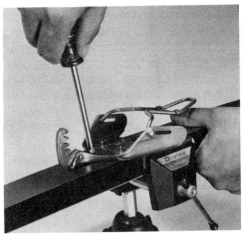

The D-Vise can help even with some large work. Here, adjustments are made on cross-country skis.

needs. The D-Vise with appropriate attachments is used in craft and hobby work, such as trout fly-tying, lapidary work, woodcarving and macrame, as well as in precision business applications like watch repairing, gunsmithing, camera repairing, electronics, optical work and tool and die making. The five elements of the D-Vise are:

The base unit. The base is a sturdy casting, triangular in shape, with a ball swivel built into it. Other elements are installed in the ball swivel, as needed. The base has three mounting holes so that it can be permanently bolted to a workbench if desired.

The vise head. The vise head is the unit which is used to clamp or hold the workpiece. It is fitted into the ball swivel of the base unit by inserting a special 6-sided post into the ball swivel. Thus mounted, the vise head can be rotated a full 360-degrees, and it can be tilted to any angle over a 180-degree range at any point within the 360-degree circle. It can be firmly locked in any of these positions, allowing you to apply pressure to any workpiece.

The Han-D-Clamp.™ The Han-D-Clamp is a metal framework with a clamping screw similar to that on a C-clamp. The framework fits over the flanges of the D-Vise base unit and its lower extension fits under the edge of a table or workbench. By turning the clamping screw, you clamp the vise base securely to the tabletop. Loosen the clamping screw a few turns and the D-Vise is released and ready to be put away until the next use or moved to a new work location.

The Moto-Tool holder. Designed with the same type of post as the vise head, this holder for the Moto-Tool fits into the ball swivel of the vise base. Any Moto-Tool can be clamped into the holder. This means that you can set the Moto-Tool at any convenient angle and

The base unit of the D-Vise, with vise heads (l. and r.), base clamp (top), and Moto-Tool Holder (bottom).

The vise head fits into the ball swivel of the D-Vise base unit, where it can turn 360-degrees.

The vise base clamp fits over the bottom edges of the base unit and clamps to any table edge.

With the Moto-Tool in the D-Vise holder, you use both hands to bring work to the spinning accessory.

bring work to it, holding the work in both hands for greater control. This combination is excellent for many sanding, grinding, and polishing operations.

The Drill press vise. This is an auxiliary vise which can be temporarily bolted to the table of a drill press to hold a workpiece, or which can be permanently bolted to a workbench and used as a small bench vise. It consists of the D-Vise head unit previously described, plus a special mounting plate for attachment to the drill press or bench. Since the base unit containing the ball swivel is not included, this vise does not rotate or tilt. If you are equipping a workbench, it is a solidly made compact vise, ideal for use with the type of work you will be doing with other Dremel compact tools. It is also ideal for holding flat, round and other shaped parts that are to be drilled on the drill press.

Assembling your D-Vise

Select the elements you need to assemble the vise that will handle the kinds of work you will be doing. If you intend to permanently bolt

your D-Vise to the workbench, you don't need the Han-D-Clamp, for example. But if you store your tools between jobs, this vise clamp used with the swivel base is a great idea.

The basic elements of the D-Vise are the base and the vise head. Start with these. If you also foresee times when you will want to clamp your Moto-Tool and carry the work to it, also add the Moto-Tool holder.

If you feel that you won't need the adjustability of the D-Vise, then get the Drill Press Vise and bolt it in place on your workbench or use it on the drill press. If you are mounting the Vise on a workbench, make sure it is fastened close enough to the front edge of the bench top so the handle will turn when the jaws are fully closed.

Depending on the work you intend to do, your collection could include two bases, one for the D-Vise head unit and one for the Moto-Tool holder, and perhaps a Drill Press Vise in addition. Think in terms of the type of work you will do when making these decisions. Think of which combination will bring the greatest added convenience and safety.

Using the D-Vise

The D-Vise is very simple to adjust to any position desired. To rotate the head, hold the vise steady and turn the *clamp ring* on the base counterclockwise until the vise head moves freely. When the vise head is rotated to the desired position, turn the clamp ring clockwise by hand until the vise head is secure.

To tilt the vise head, a similar procedure is used. Hold the vise steady, loosen the clamp ring, and tilt the vise head to the angle you want. Then lock the vise head in position by turning the clamp ring clockwise.

The Drill Press Vise can hold work on the drill press or be bolted in place on the workbench.

To change angle of work, loosen clamp ring, move vise head to new position, then retighten clamp ring.

Adjusting screw on the front of the D-Vise opens and closes vise head. Maximum jaw opening is 2-1/2 inches.

Obviously, there will be many times when you want to rotate and tilt the vise head at the same time. Follow the same procedure, loosening the clamp ring, tilting the vise head and rotating the assembly to the positions you want. Then lock the D-Vise head in place by tightening the clamp ring.

To open or close the D-Vise jaws, turn the adjusting screw handle on the front of the vise head. The maximum jaw opening is 2-1/2-inches.

The D-Vise jaws come with soft jaw pads on each jaw face. These permit you to clamp delicate pieces and to protect fine finishes. These pads slide off the jaws.

The removable steel jaws of the vise contain vertical and horizontal V-grooves to enable you to clamp round or irregularly shaped objects. Place the object between the jaws in either the horizontal or vertical grooves, depending on how you want the work positioned. When you tighten the jaws, the workpiece will be securely held in place.

The D-Vise can be tilted to hold long bar and rod stock in a vertical position. The vise should be mounted on the edge of the workbench or a table. Then tilt the vise head so that the jaws are in a vertical position. Tighten the jaws on the long stock, which can extend all the way to the floor if necessary.

The great versatility of the D-Vise, such as the above capability, will become apparent as you work with it.

Mounting the D-Vise. You can bolt the D-Vise to your bench, or clamp it in place with the Han-D-Clamp™ In either event, place the D-Vise so that one of the three straight edges of the base is aligned with the edge of the table or workbench.

If bolting the D-Vise down, position it on the table and insert a pencil through each of the base bolt holes and mark the hole locations.

Drill 1/4-inch holes at these marked spots, and fasten the D-Vise to the bench with No. 10 carriage bolts, along with proper washers and nuts.

You also can mount the D-Vise on a 10 × 10-inch board of 1/2-inch plywood, following the same procedure as described in the last paragraph. This board can then be clamped to any table using two C-Clamps.

If using the Han-D-Clamp,™ install the three rubber feet which come with the D-Vise in the base bolt holes. The narrow ends of the feet are twisted into the bolt holes from the bottom. These will protect the tabletop to which the D-Vise is clamped. Put a small square of wood or a thick felt pad on the head of the clamping screw, to protect the bottom surface of the table.

A look at the engraver

The Dremel Electric Engraver was designed to allow you to do engraving on glass, metal, ceramics, plastics, wood, and other materials. Operating at a speed of 7,200 strokes per minute, the engraver permits you to write, print, or draw. You can engrave whole landscapes with it, if you choose, or simply use

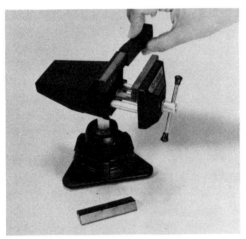

Soft jaw pads fit over the steel jaws of the clamp, allowing you to clamp delicate work safely.

Rubber feet on the D-Vise base protect work surfaces when vise is clamped to table or bench.

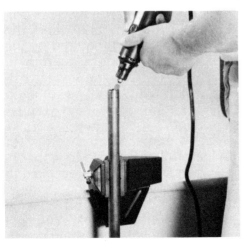

The D-Vise can be tilted to hold long bar and rod stock in a vertical position when necessary.

it to engrave your name on television sets, radio, and other valuables in your home to discourage thieves.

Because of its speed and the carbide tip furnished with the engraver, along with the fact that you can control the depth of engraving to suit the material on which you are working, the engraver makes fast, solidly-scribed lines. You won't have to go back and forth over the same area to make the lines appear solid and continuous. The pencil-like grip allows you to control the engraver for fine, delicate engraving.

Using the engraver

Most models of the engraver use regular 110/120-volt household current. Models designed for use with other voltages such as 220V, 50-Hz are clearly marked on the nameplate.

Hold the engraver pretty much as you would a pencil, in your thumb and forefinger at a slight angle. Rest your arm comfortably on a table top or other work surface and hold the engraver lightly, controlling it with your fingers — again, as you would a pencil.

Touch the engraving point to the work. Do not press down. Use a light touch and guide the point over the work somewhat slower than you normally write.

There are two controls on the engraver. The ON-OFF switch is on the back panel. The stroke length control is the dial on the side of the housing.

The stroke length control. This control actually determines the length of the point stroke in order to control the depth of the engraving. It should not be used as an ON-OFF switch.

Determining the correct dial setting is a matter of some experimentation with each job. Determining

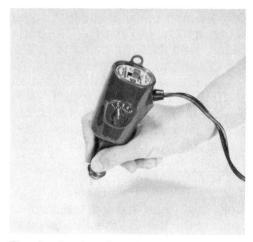

The depth control on the engraver controls the length of the point stroke and depth of engraving.

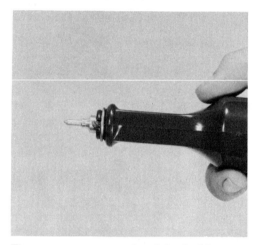

The engraver comes furnished with a carbide point. A diamond point is available for special work.

factors are the hardness and brittleness of the material, and the depth of engraving required by the work you are doing. The rule of thumb is to select the lowest setting which will produce a deep enough engraving to meet your requirements.

Obtain some sample scraps of the material you intend to work on, and spend a few minutes making sample experimental engravings. Change the settings and observe the effect on the work. You will quickly learn which setting is best. (Note that the lowest number indicates the shortest stroke.)

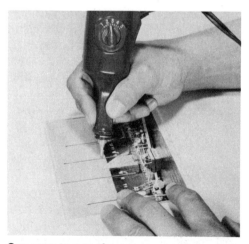

One way to use the engraver: slip a photo under glass and then use it as a guide in engraving design.

A carbide point is furnished with the engraver. It works well for most materials. A diamond point, Part No. 9929, works especially well with glass and is available from Dremel as an accessory.

To remove a worn point and install a new one, simply loosen the set screw located on the point holder and pull the point out. Insert the new point and retighten the set screw.

To lay out work before engraving, it is often helpful to draw the intended design or guidelines on the workpiece. A felt-tip pen, a grease pencil, or crayons may be used for this. Remove the marks after the engraving has been completed. Straight guidelines for printing can be improvised with transparent tape. For engraving clear glass, a picture or design can be attached to one side and then traced or copied with the engraver from the opposite side.

Project Theft-Guard

Project Theft-Guard is a national effort to protect against theft by permanently marking items that are frequently stolen from homes. It has been adopted by many police departments and has been proven

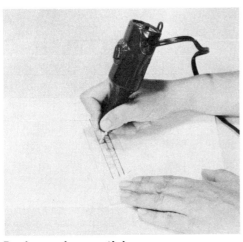

Begin use by practicing on scrap materials. Change depth settings to observe effect on the work.

to be a successful crime deterrent. The Dremel Electric Engraver is frequently used for this purpose.

The idea is to engrave your name, driver's license number or social security number on all valuables — electronic gear, cameras, binoculars, bicycles, clocks, and any other valuable property which might be stolen. At the same time, you alert thieves with Project Theft-Guard stickers. Two of these stickers, one each for your front and back doors, are packed with each engraver. Additional stickers, both for the home and for the valuables, can be ordered from Dremel.

A potential thief, seeing the Project Theft-Guard stickers on your home, or valuables, should realize that he will have trouble selling whatever he steals, and will turn away to more profitable targets.

A "fence," a criminal who buys stolen goods for resale, will offer a thief little or nothing for an item that is clearly engraved with an identifying mark.

If a marked item is stolen and later recovered by the police, you will have little difficulty identifying it as your own.

The Chainsaver

The 1246 Chainsaver kit contains a portable electric chain saw sharpener that operates from normal 115V household current. It should be used only in properly grounded receptacles and with properly grounded extension cords, as explained in Chapter One. Proper grounding is especially important if the chain saw is being sharpened out-of-doors, where the earth may be damp, or in any wet or damp location, for that matter. The 1241 Chainsaver kit contains a 12 volt tool designed to be attached to an automotive battery so it can be used in locations where there is no available household electrical

Engrave identification number on valuable equipment, then affix a Project Theft-Guard sticker.

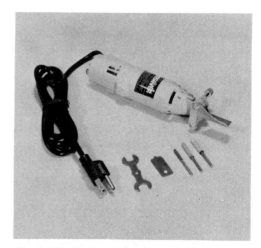

The 1246 Chainsaver is an electric chain saw sharpener kit, also available in battery-operated model.

current.

Both Chainsaver models have a gauge which shows the user if the sharpening guide is properly positioned. The sharpening guide is built in and indicates the correct angle to hold the tool to get a sharp cutting edge on each tooth.

Using the Chainsavers

To use a Chainsaver, first examine the chain to determine its chain number. Usually this is marked on a certain number of the chain drive links. The chart supplied with the tool identifies the correct grinding stone to use. Three grinding stones come with the tool, along with necessary spacers. "See owners manual for correct positioning of spacers."

With the pink (7/32-inch diameter) stone, use two spacers.

With the orange (3/16-inch diameter) stone use one spacer.

With the blue (5/32-inch diameter) stone, use no spacers.

When you have identified the stone to use and the number of spacers to use with it, the sharpening tool can then be assembled. It consists of a clamp which goes over the nose of the chainsaver; the spacer or spacers required; and the

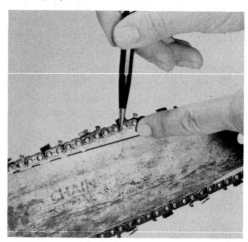

Examine chain to find its number, usually found on a certain number of the chain drive links.

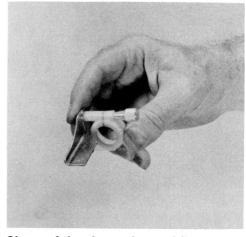

Clamp of the sharpening tool fits over the nose of the motor and holds spacers and sharpening guide.

sharpening guide, assembled in that order. They are held together by a short screw on one side and a long screw and clamp knob on the other.

The grinding stone is inserted into the collet (for collet information, see Chapter One), with approximately 1/4-inch of the shank exposed between the chuck cap and the stone.

A gauge is furnished with the tool to be used to determine if the sharpening guide has been properly positioned. You are ready to begin sharpening when the guide has been properly adjusted.

If your chain saw is electric, it must be unplugged when the chain is being sharpened. If your chain saw is gasoline powered, the switch must be off and the spark plug lead wire disconnected.

Set the saw on a flat surface, positioned so you are looking at the chain bar, with the motor on your right. The chain tension should be adjusted as directed in your owner's manual which usually will suggest that the chain be loose enough so that it can be turned by hand on the guide bar, but not loose enough so that it sags noticeably.

Before starting to work, refer to the diagram in the Chainsaver manual to identify which shape of cutter teeth are like those on your chain saw. There are four possible shapes. For two of them, sharpening is done with the grinding stone held horizontally. For the other two, the grinding stone is tilted 10-degrees. You can identify the shape of the cutters from the drawings.

The teeth on the near side are sharpened first. The guide should be laid flat on each tooth, with the *index line* aligned with the chain by eye, as shown in the accompanying photograph. With the Chainsaver motor running; take two or three light strokes across the chain.

Unless the cutters have been damaged, this should be enough grinding.

The teeth on the far side are sharpened next, with the saw kept in the same position. For these teeth, the *angular* edge of the guide should be aligned with the chain, as shown on the accompanying photograph.

When all of the teeth on the top of the bar have been sharpened, advance the chain, using a glove or rag to protect your hand, by pulling the chain toward the end of the bar. Repeat this until all teeth have been sharpened.

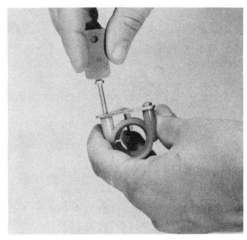

The assembly is held together by a short screw on one side and a long screw on the other side.

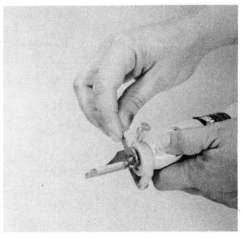

Grinding stone is inserted into collet with 1/4-inch of shank exposed between the cap and the stone.

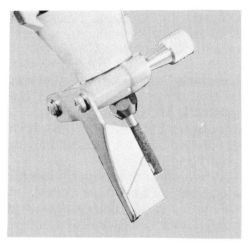

Refer to chain guide in owners manual for correct size of grinding stone to use.

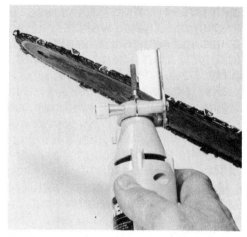

Teeth on the far side are sharpened after those on the near side, with the saw kept in the same position.

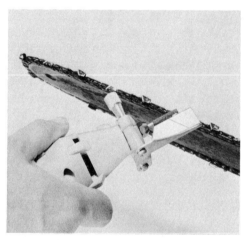

Align the index line on the guide with the saw chain by eye. Teeth on near side are sharpened first.

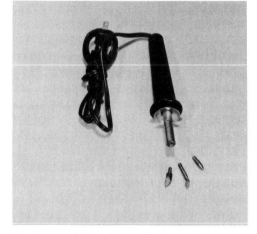

The Dremel Woodburning Tool comes with three woodburning points which cover majority of burning needs.

As you work, try to sharpen all teeth equally. Use the same number of strokes and the same amount of pressure on each tooth.

The Woodburning Tool

The woodworker who is looking for an additional way to decorate his work should consider the Dremel Woodburning Tool, which developes point temperatures up to 950-degrees F. to burn or char wood faster and darker.

The woodburning tool comes

You can find plaques with designs already on them to start work with the woodburning tool.

with three woodburning points: An all-purpose point which permits contrast, line variation and depth, and fine detail work; a grading point that is ideal for gradation and makes even, golden burned shading and special effects possible; and a script point for lettering, script writing, and the drawing of circles and swirls.

The tool has a balanced pencil grip that reduces fatigue and helps in control of the point. The short shaft, only 2-inches long, brings the work closer, and also is an aid in better point control.

With adult supervision, even a child can make attractive pictures, plaques and signs with the woodburning tool. An easy way to lay out a picture is to find something you'd like to copy from a book or magazine. Trace the picture's outline using artist's tracing paper and a pencil. Then, using typewriter carbon paper, transfer the tracing to the workpiece directly from the tracing paper. Then follow the carbon lines on the workpiece with the woodburning tool and add any extra details that appeal to you. Headline lettering traced from newspapers and magazines can similarly be used to make signs of many kinds with the woodburning tool.

Artisans as well as children can use the woodburning tool to enhance their work. Woodcarvers may find a detail added here or there with the tool can greatly improve the appearance of their project. Furniture makers who add carved details to wooden parts can burn in details as well as carve them. And master furniture builders can burn in their signatures and the year of construction of a piece, just as some of the old timers did on furniture that now is a valuable antique, worth all the more because the builder's name and the date add to the authenticity.

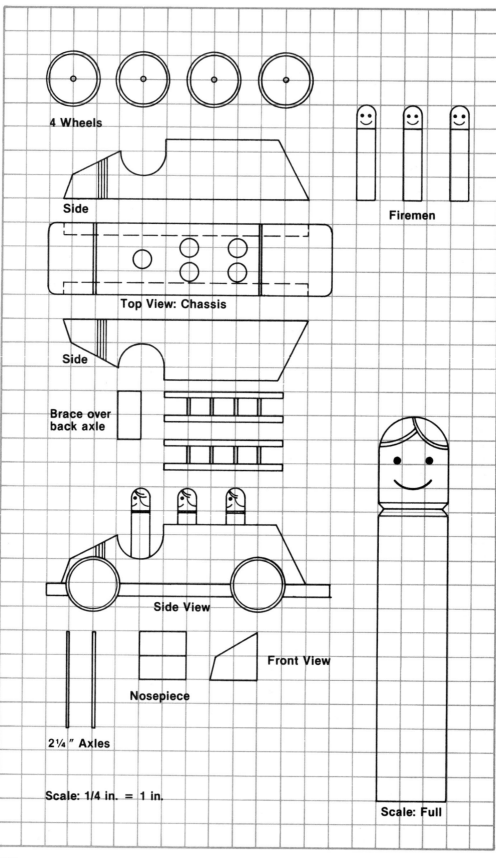

4 Wheels

Side

Firemen

Top View: Chassis

Side

Brace over
back axle

Side View

Front View

Nosepiece

2¼″ Axles

Scale: 1/4 in. = 1 in.

Scale: Full

Project 7

TOY FIRE TRUCK
This imaginative and colorful toy fire truck will bring a lot of pleasure when you give it to a child as a Christmas or birthday gift.

Materials:
Softwood board, 1/4 × 3 × 36
Dowels (1/8, 1/4 and 3/4-in.)
White glue
Several colors of latex enamel

Tools:
Table Saw
Moto-Shop, Woodburning Tool
Moto-Tool, with No. 409 emery
  wheel and 1/8-in. drill bit
Moto-Lathe
Electric drill
3/4-in. wood drill bit
Hammer

There are a lot of parts to this toy, so study Plan A first, to identify them and make note of their dimensions. Saw all pieces to the sizes shown on the scroll saw or the table saw, as required. Sand each piece on the disc sander. Cut two slots, 1/4-in. wide and 1/4-in. deep on chassis to serve as axle housings. Do this by making a series of cuts on the table saw.

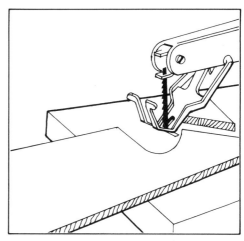

DETAIL B. In cutting out various parts, you can use both the scroll saw and the table saw.

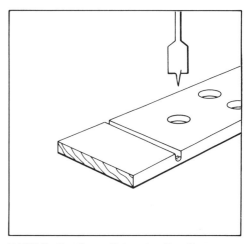

DETAIL C. "Seats" for the five firemen are bored with a 3/4-in. flat wood boring bit.

Detail for woodburning

DETAIL A. This sturdy toy fire truck and its five firemen can become some child's favorite toy.

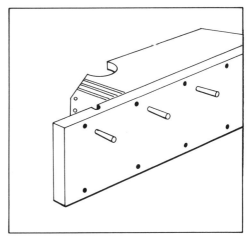

DETAIL D. For strength, body is assembled with 1/8-in. dowels glued and driven in.

177

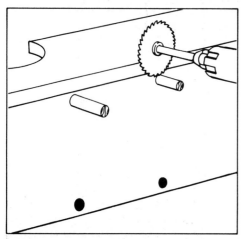

DETAIL E. After glue dries, ends of dowels are cut off with saw or emery wheel accessories in the Moto-Tool.

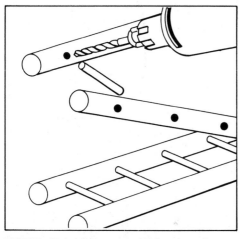

DETAIL F. Ladders are 1/4-in. dowels drilled to receive 1/8-in. dowel rungs. Drill press would make job easy.

Use the electric drill and 3/4-in. wood boring bit to drill five holes, each 1/4-in. deep, in top of chassis board for firemen. See Detail C. For location of holes, see Plan A. Turn the 5 firemen on the Moto-Lathe, using 3/4-in. dowels. You can use the woodburning tool to draw their faces and also to decorate the fire truck, if you choose. Assemble truck body on the chassis board, using 1/8-in. dowels glued and hammered into place. See Details D and E. Saw off ends of dowels after glue has dried, using Moto-Tool and emery wheel No. 409 or steel saw accessory. Sand dowel ends after cutting. Next, insert axles (1/4-in. dowels) into housing slots. Drill center holes in wheels, then glue wheels to axles. Ladders are made next, using 1/8 and 1/4-in. dowels. See Detail F. You can now glue the firemen in place, or allow them to remain loose and removable. Use bright enamels to finish the project — red for the fire truck, yellow for the ladders, black for the truck trim, etc.

QUICKFIXES

Using grinder to clean rust spot.

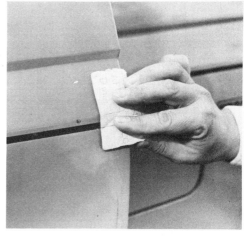

Rubbing out undercoating.

Feathering edge of adjacent paint.

Apply final finish coat.

When doing necessary touch-up painting on your car, begin by grinding the exposed area clean to bare metal, using an abrasive wheel. Carefully feather the edge of good paint adjacent to the rust spot. Then apply a coat of automotive undercoat. When it has dried, sand lightly, and again feather edges. Finally apply the matching final coat and rub out with 0000 sandpaper after it has dried completely.

Applying undercoat.

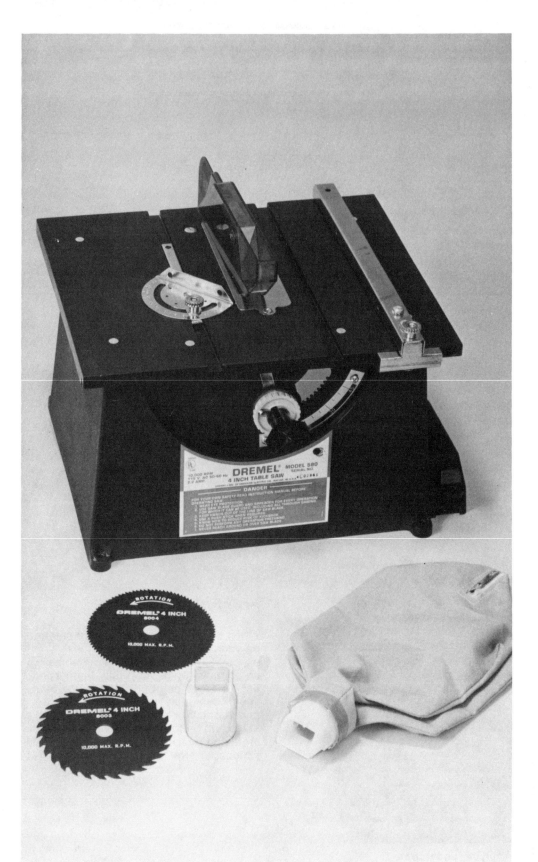

CHAPTER EIGHT

The Dremel Table Saw

Here is a 4-inch tilt arbor table saw that can do bevel cuts, miter cuts, tongue-and-grooving and other wood joints, as well as all the other work you expect of a table saw, making cuts up to 1 inch in depth.

In almost any woodworking project, sawing is the task most frequently performed. Most woodworking saws cut in a straight line, usually to make a board either shorter or narrower to fit the dimensional requirements of the project. The table saw is the bench power tool most frequently used for straight-line sawing, and the Dremel Table Saw is a good choice to serve as the workhorse of your compact power tool workshop.

There are six basic straight-line saw cuts: the crosscut, the rip, the miter, the bevel crosscut, the bevel rip, and the bevel miter. All other straight-line cuts are variations or combinations of these. The Dremel can perform each of the basic cuts with ease. How these cuts are done will be explained later.

The table saw is also excellent for making a wide variety of wood joints, such as the rabbet, the tongue-and-groove, the miter and others which can give your project added strength as well as a professional touch.

The chief difference between the Dremel saw and its larger brothers is one of capacity. The 4-inch circular saw blade is smaller, the motor less powerful, the table dimensions not so big, etc. But the Dremel saw has some advantages, too. It excels at smooth, accurate sawing for hobby work and maintenance chores around the house. Its compact size requires less space in the workshop, and it can be moved and stored easily.

It can cut through stock a full 1-inch thick in one pass, and its small, thin blades allow it to cut thin materials better than some bigger, more powerful models.

Table saw guides and controls

Cuts on a table saw should never be made free-hand, without benefit of a guide (either the miter gauge, the rip fence, or a specially-made jig made to serve the purpose). Free-hand cuts cannot be done accurately or safely on the table saw.

The miter gauge is a protractor-like head which pivots on a metal bar. This metal bar rides in either of the two grooves on each side of the saw blade, that span the table top. A locking knob holds the protractor head in place at the angle selected for making a cut.

Cuts made with the miter gauge are most often at 90 degrees across the short dimension of the work-

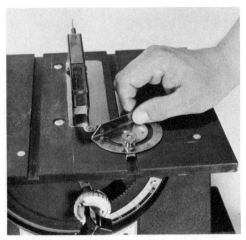

Miter gauge rides in either groove in the saw table top, and the head can be locked at the selected angle.

Rip fence spans the saw table and can be locked in place on either side of saw blade to guide rip cuts.

Height adjustment knob is at the front of the control assembly located on the front of the saw.

piece and across the grain of the wood. However, since the head of the miter gauge is adjustable, work guided by it can be made at a range of angles.

The rip fence is the metal guide bar which can be locked in place on either side of the saw blade. It is always parallel to the sides of the saw blade and reaches from the front to the back of the saw table. Cuts made with the rip fence usually are made along the long dimension of the workpiece and with the grain of the wood.

The Dremel Table Saw is a *tilt arbor* saw. This means that the blade itself can be tilted while the table remains flat. Cuts made in this manner are bevel cuts.

In addition to tilting, the blade also can be raised and lowered. Both of these adjustments are made from an assembly on the front of the saw base. The black knob on this assembly is the *height adjusting knob.* By turning the knob clockwise, you raise the blade. Turning it counterclockwise lowers the blade.

The tilt lock, is located immediately behind the height adjusting knob and the *tilt knob* is behind it. To tilt the blade, loosen the lock and turn the tilt knob clockwise. An indicator on the scale on the front of the table shows the degree of tilt — from 0 to 45 degrees. When the desired angle is reached, the tilt lock is tightened and the cut can be made.

Before tilting the blade, the blade height must be set 1/4-inch or more below its maximum height. Otherwise, the nut which holds the saw blade in place can damage the table insert plate.

When any workpiece is sawed through, the blade should be set just high enough to completely penetrate the work — about 1/16-inch higher than the thickness of the wood. Thus, to saw through 1/2-inch plywood, set the blade height at 9/16-inch.

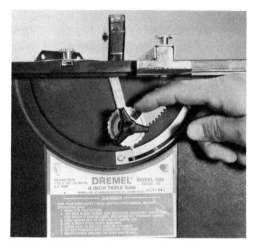

Behind height adjustment knob is the tilt lock lever, which locks blade after tilt adjustment has been made.

Protective assembly on the saw includes plastic blade guard, spreader, and anti-kickback spurs.

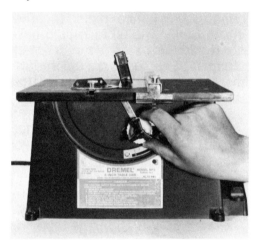

Tilt knob is turned to set tilt of the blade from 0 to 45 degrees. Indicator scale shows angle of tilt.

When workpiece is sawed through, blade is set 1/16-inch higher than thickness of workpiece.

The two guide devices, the miter gauge and the rip fence, along with the tilt and height controls, permit you to make all six of the basic straight saw cuts.

Also on the table top with the miter gauge and rip fence is a protective assembly consisting of three elements: the blade guard, the spreader and the anti-kickback spurs.

The blade guard is a transparent plastic shield which covers the saw blade. You can observe the cut being made through it without having sawdust or loose knots thrown in your face, and the guard protects your fingers from injury.

The spreader is a thin, vertical strip which enters the saw cut, or kerf, after the workpiece passes through the blade. The spreader holds the saw cut open and prevents its binding or pinching the blade. It is needed because some woods tend to close up, especially on rip cuts, after the cut has been made, due to internal stresses released by cutting. Binding can cause the wood to be kicked back toward the operator. By keeping the cut open, the spreader helps prevent this.

The anti-kickback spurs serve a similar purpose. They permit the

183

work to pass freely through the blade but if, for some reason, the work binds on the table and a kick-back starts, the spurs dig in and help prevent it from being thrown or "kicked back" toward the front of the saw where the operator stands. Spurs do not hold on smooth surfaced work like hardboard or plastic.

The blade guard and spurs lift up out of the way when a board to be sawed is pushed under them. The entire protective assembly tilts when the blade is tilted for a bevel cut.

Almost all cuts on the table saw can and should be made with these protective devices in place. Some specialty cuts, such as grooving, require the assembly to be removed. But for your own protection, it should be installed again as soon as the work being done permits.

Also, even though the table saw is equipped to prevent kickbacks, they sometimes still do occur. For this reason, the operator and workshop visitors should never stand directly behind or in front of the blade whan a cut is being made.

The ON-OFF switch of the Dremel Table Saw is at the lower right side of the saw as you face the table. Be familiar with its position, so you can turn it off by feel while

ON-OFF switch, located at lower front of saw table, has hole for padlocking of saw in OFF setting.

keeping an eye on the workpiece and the spinning saw blade. A hole in front of the switch permits it to be padlocked in the OFF position to prevent unauthorized use.

Setting up the table saw

The table saw should be placed in the work room with several feet on each side, in front, and in back of it to allow room to maneuver larger workpieces. If the saw is permanently set up in one location, it is best to build or buy a heavy duty bench to hold it. An adequate bench can be built with inexpensive 2 × 4 construction lumber nailed together into a table. The table should have no tendency to tip over or creep along as workpieces are fed through the saw. The legs should be level so the saw does not teeter or wobble during work.

For most operators, the table top should be about 34-inches from the floor, the approximate height of most kitchen counter tops. Taller or shorter persons can adjust this height for comfort, but for safety and ease of operation, the table top should not be more than waist high.

If the saw is not bolted permanently to a work table or bench, you should mount it on a 3/4-inch plywood board measuring 12 × 14-inches or larger. To use the saw, clamp the plywood base to a table top with two or more C-clamps. Do not use just one clamp, since this might allow the saw to turn accidentally as you apply pressure to a workpiece. When you finish using the saw, it can be quickly unclamped and stored in a safe location.

As explained in the table saw manual, the saw should be mounted either on a workbench or plywood base using the rubber bushings and hold down screws provided. The bushings help control noise and vibration.

Table saw safety

The table saw manual provides full safety information, but the following are especially important rules for safe saw operation that merit review:

1. Always wear safety goggles to protect the eyes from sawdust.
2. The saw should always be unplugged when not in use, and when changing blades or performing any service work.
3. Never wear loose clothing or jewelry around the saw, and keep long hair firmly in place.
4. Use only Dremel saw blades or accessories. Do not use unauthorized dado or moulding heads, cutoff wheels, sanding discs, or any similar attachments.
5. Do not cut metal or other extremely hard substances with your saw.
6. Keep your hands at least 3-inches from the saw blade at all times.
7. To avoid injury from kickbacks, never stand directly behind or in front of the spinning blade.
8. When making rip cuts, never release the material between the blade and the fence until the work has completely cleared the blade.

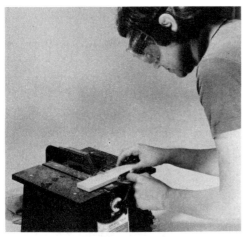

Always use safety goggles to protect eyes from sawdust, knots and splinters when working on saw.

9. Always use a pushstick when cutting narrow or short material.
10. Do not make conventional cuts on round, dowel-like objects, warped boards, or materials that do not have a straightedge to ride along the rip fence.

Choice of saw blades

Two blades, which cover a wide range of common cutting operations, are available:

The combination blade. This is part No. 8003. It has 30 teeth and is a general purpose blade which can be used for rips, crosscuts, bevels and miters.

The fine blade. Listed as Part No. 8004, this blade has 100 teeth and is designed for smooth sawing of materials that splinter or chip easily — plywood, paneling, fiberboard, some hardboards, plastics and other manmade materials. It makes smooth crosscuts and miters in softwoods and some hardwoods, and is useful for making close-fitting wood joints. It should not be used in ripping because its chip clearance is too small, so it cuts slowly and may bind or overheat.

Neither of these blades should be used on any type of metal nor on filled plastics because the filler is often an abrasive, such as sand or fiberglass. Also, do not use the saw on plastic laminates, the hard plastic sheets used for counter and table tops.

To change blades, follow the instructions in the manual carefully.

Making the basic saw cuts

Crosscut. A straight or right angle crosscut is made with the miter gauge set at 0 degrees and the blade tilt also at 0 degrees. The workpiece is held against the miter gauge and pushed toward the blade,

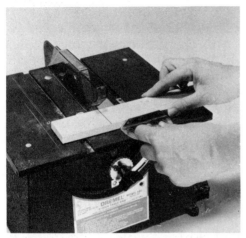

CROSSCUT is made with miter guage set at 0 degrees and blade tilt angle set at zero degrees.

BEVEL MITER CUT, with both blade and miter gauge at an angle. Cut made with guard down. Guard up to show cut.

BEVEL CROSSCUT, with miter gauge at 0 degrees and blade tilted. Guard lifted so cut can be photographed.

RIP CUT is made using rip fence as a guide. Most rip cuts are made along long dimension of workpiece.

MITER CUT is made by setting angle on miter gauge and holding work against it as gauge is moved toward saw.

BEVEL RIP CUT, with blade angled. Guard, down during cut, lifted so photo can show blade in workpiece.

with the miter gauge sliding in one of the two table grooves serving as a guide.

Bevel crosscut. If the miter gauge remains set at 0 degrees and the blade is tilted to any setting other than 0 degrees, the resulting cut is a bevel crosscut. In this cut, the work also is held against the miter gauge and pushed toward the saw blade with the miter acting as a guide.

Miter cut. If the blade tilt remains at 0 degrees, but the miter gauge is set at any reading other than 0 degrees, a miter cut will result. Again, the miter gauge is used to guide the work toward the saw blade.

Bevel miter. If both the miter gauge and the blade are angled, then the cut you achieve is a bevel miter.

Rip cut. The rip cut is made usually with the grain of the wood and along the long dimension of the workpiece. To make it, the blade tilt is set at 0 degrees, and one side of the workpiece is held against the rip fence, which serves as a guide. In the typical rip cut, the rip fence is set the distance from the blade needed to produce the desired finished width. The workpiece, held against the rip fence, is pushed toward and through the saw blade, where it is "ripped" or cut into two pieces.

Bevel rip cut. If the blade were tilted at any angle other than 0 degrees whan a rip cut is made, the resulting cut is a bevel rip.

Extension tables

The Dremel Table Saw is intended to be used chiefly with relatively thin, short pieces of material. Its 10 × 12-inch table works well with lumber up to 1-inch. When larger and heavier pieces are either ripped

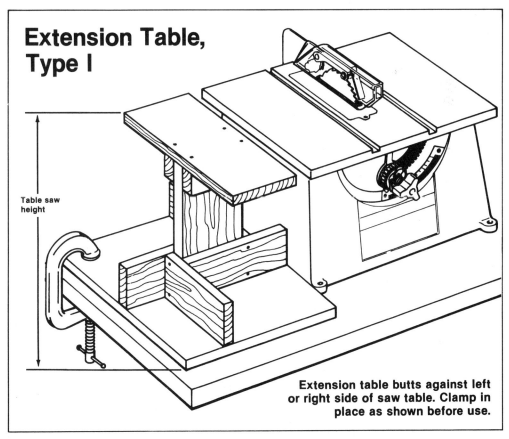

Extension Table, Type I

Table saw height

Extension table butts against left or right side of saw table. Clamp in place as shown before use.

Extension Table, Type II

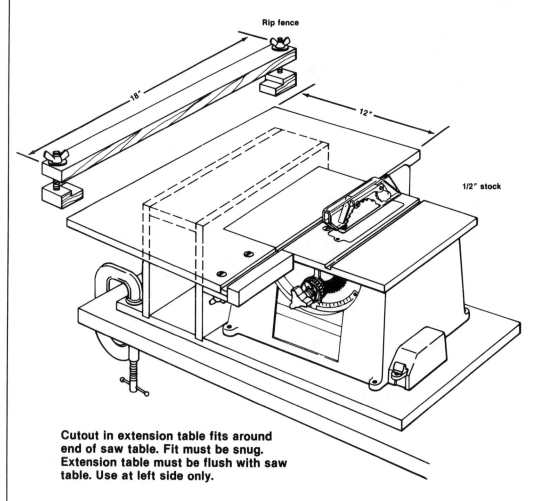

Rip fence

18"

12"

1/2" stock

Cutout in extension table fits around
end of saw table. Fit must be snug.
Extension table must be flush with saw
table. Use at left side only.

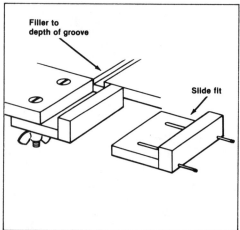

Filler to
depth of groove

Slide fit

Edge of table serves as extension of miter
gauge groove. This adjustable piece
completes the groove.

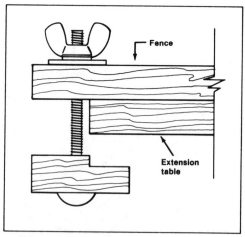

Fence

Extension
table

Larger rip fence is needed with extension
top. This shows how fence is clamped on
extension table edge.

or crosscut, supporting the work becomes cumbersome and difficult. One solution is to extend the size of the table by adding a plywood extension. You can make these extensions yourself and sketches of two types are included in this chapter. Both will work with either a permanently mounted saw or one mounted on a baseboard and clamped to a table for use.

The Type I extension is simply a plywood addition to the table built on a pedestal the height of the table. It is butted against the saw table at either side to provide needed additional table space. It should be clamped in place to prevent movement during work.

The Type II extension is made to "wrap around" one side of the table, and provides additional table space to one side and to the front and back as well. Note than an adjustable extension of the miter gauge track is shown in sketch, along with details for the larger rip fence which is needed on the wider table.

Both tables can be made of 1/2 or 3/4-inch plywood. Dimensions can be whatever you need, but for Type I, the extension should add from 4 to 8-inches to the table width. Type II should be about 12 × 18-inches in finished form. It is important that each extension be perfectly level with the saw's table top. They must be made so that either the miter gauge or rip fence can be used for every cut.

Other accessories to build

You can increase the efficiency and capabilities of your table saw with other accessories in addition to the extension tables. These include pusher sticks, stop blocks, miter boards and miter extensions.

Pusher. A pusher is a stick or other device used to push the work-piece into the saw blade. Its purpose is to keep your fingers away from the blade. When sawing short or narrow pieces, use two pushers at the same time, one in each hand.

The basic, most used pusher is a flat stick, about 12-inches long, with a V-notch cut in one end. The notch permits you to hold the work edge during the pushing operation. An old yardstick can be cut into excellent push sticks.

Stop block. A stop block is a block clamped to the saw table during crosscutting when you are cutting a workpiece to a dimension. In this operation, the rip fence should not be used as a gauge against which one end of the workpiece slides. The reason is that the work can bind easily and be thrown from the blade, and injure you or damage the saw blade.

Instead of the rip fence, use a stop block as a gauge. Accompanying illustrations show how this is done. The workpiece is guided by the miter gauge during the cut. The stop block, a simple block of wood, is clamped to the table so that the distance between the cut line on the workpiece and the edge of the stop block is the dimension you require in the finished workpiece.

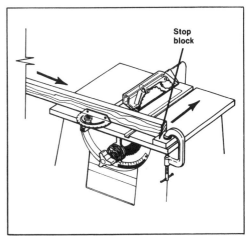

Stop block

Do not use rip fence as gauge when crosscutting. Instead, use stop block clamped to table as shown.

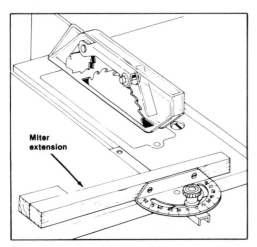

Miter
extension

This extension of the miter gauge allows easier feeding of larger work to the saw for crosscutting.

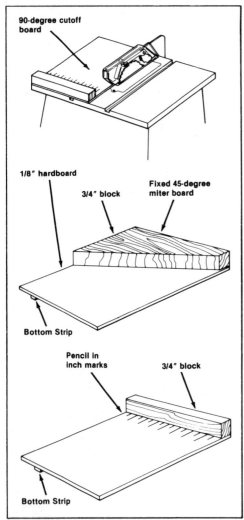

90-degree cutoff board

1/8″ hardboard

3/4″ block

Fixed 45-degree miter board

Bottom Strip

Pencil in inch marks

3/4″ block

Bottom Strip

Miter board and 90-degree cutoff board each have bottom strip which fits into groove on saw table top.

As the workpiece is moved toward the saw blade, it loses contact with the stop block. However, the length of the cut has already been set, and as long as you hold the workpiece firmly against the miter gauge and do not allow it to shift position, the cut will be correct.

Miter extensions. The miter gauge on the table saw is made with two screw holes in it. For better control of larger work during cuts, you can make an extension of the miter gauge and attach it with screws. The illustration shows how the extension is made.

Miter boards. When faced with the necessity of making a number of miter cuts at the same angle (as when making a group of picture frames), or when cutting a number of dimensioned pieces at 90-degrees, you can assure greater accuracy and produce the work much faster by working with miter boards.

Two miter boards are illustrated, one for making 45-degree cuts and the other for 90-degree cuts. If you need cuts at angles other than 45-degrees, you can make boards incorporating the angles you want.

The 45-degree miter board consists of a 1/8-inch hardboard base. A strip of wood which fits into the table top groove is glued to the underside of the board, carefully positioned so that when it is in the groove, the edge of the hardboard is next to the saw blade but not quite touching it. On top of the hardboard, a block of 3/4-inch wood cut at a 45-degree angle is glued, as shown in the drawing. It is a good idea to glue sandpaper to the face of the angular side of this block, against which the wood is held during cutting. The sandpaper prevents the work from slipping or "creeping" as it is cut.

In use, the miter board is placed in the groove on the table, and the work is held against the angular edge while the entire miter board is moved toward the back of the table. Successive pieces cut using this board will have exactly the same angle of cut.

The 90-degree board is constructed in the same manner, using 1/8-inch hardboard and a 3/4-inch wood block, as shown in the illustration. The difference is that the block of wood on this board is set to make straight 90-degree cuts. If you mark the board with rule marks, using a ruler as a guide and a pen to make permanent marks, you can quickly measure pieces to be cut right on the board, without hunting for a ruler to do the job.

In use, the work is placed against the guide, with the length to be cut off extending beyond the inner edge of the board. The work is held against the block on the board and the board is moved toward the saw blade. The guide on the bottom of the board slides in the groove on the table top. This board enables you to make perfect 90-degree cuts every time, and also to quickly measure short workpieces for cutting.

Good table saw practices

The following is a quick list of good practices to follow when using the table saw. They will result in better and safer work.

1. When adjusting the height of the blade, the final height adjustment should be made with a raising rather than a lowering motion.

2. For a crosscut, the rip fence should be removed or at least placed well out of the way of the work.

3. Always measure and mark the workpiece before cutting. Make the mark on the top and front edge — the edge that meets the saw blade first — to make it easy to move the workpiece so the line meets the edge of the saw blade exactly.

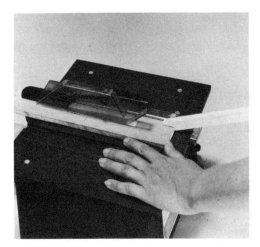

Pusher stick should be used to push narrow or small work through saw. Keep fingers 3 inches from blade.

For very narrow or small workpieces, use two pushers. Here, long, narrow rip cut is being made.

Stock block clamped to corner of table as piece of picture framing is crosscut, guided by miter gauge.

Small miter extension attached to miter gauge facilitates bevel cut. Guard raised for photo purposes only.

Always mark workpiece before cutting, then make cut on waste side of guide line for accuracy.

When crosscutting wide workpiece, reverse the miter gauge in the table groove so work pushes gauge.

To set up rip cut, set rip fence at approximate setting, then measure exact distance from saw to fence.

4. The kerf should always occur on the waste part of the workpiece. If the cut mark you make is exact, the kerf should be on the waste side of it, and the pencil line should be just visible on the end of the finished piece. If the cut is made on the other side of the line, the finished piece will be too short by the width of the kerf.

5. Always make a complete cut, moving the work through the blade in a smooth, steady motion until the work has been cut in two. Do not stop or hesitate part of the way through the cut.

6. When a crosscut is finished, slide the work still being held in the miter gauge slightly to one side, away from the saw blade, without releasing it. Then slide the miter gauge and work back to the front of the table. This provides complete control at all times.

7. To crosscut a wide workpiece, reverse the miter gauge in the table groove, so that the work is pushing the miter gauge instead of the reverse. The gauge will still hold the work square during the cutting.

8. When making rip cuts to dimension, slide the rip fence to the approximate width of the cut to be made, then use a ruler to measure the exact distance between the side

of the rip fence and the tip of one of the saw blade teeth set in the direction of the rip fence.

9. If the work being ripped permits less than 3-inches between the rip fence and the saw blade, use a push stick to advance the work toward the blade.

Other saw cuts

You can do many types of cuts in addition to the six basic ones outlined earlier. Some of these are:

Chamfer cut. A chamfer cut is one where part of the edge of a workpiece has been cut off at an angle. You might use it to make a fancy edge for a table top or to edge a plaque. To make a chamfer rip cut, the saw is set up for a bevel rip, but the fence is set at a distance from the blade so that only the top portion of the edge of the workpiece is cut away. A chamfer need not be a rip cut. A workpiece can be chamfered across its ends as well as its sides. The ends would normally be chamfered using the miter gauge, set either at 0-degrees or at whatever angle the stock was previously cut to.

Rabbet. A rabbet is a groove cut along the edge or end of a workpiece. The sides of the rabbet are normally at right angles to each other, and frequently the rabbet is made as part of a wood joint in which two rabbeted edges are fitted into each other.

To make a rabbet along the long side of a workpiece, the rip method is used, and two rip cuts are made. After the size of the rabbet has been determined, the rip fence is set up so that it cuts the dimension of one side of the rabbet. The blade is raised or lowered so that it cuts only part way through the workpiece, at a predetermined height.

The workpiece is then passed through the saw blade for a "blind" rip cut, one where the work is not

CHAMFER CUT trims part of edge of workpiece at angle. Blade at angle, fence set back slightly for this cut.

RABBET is started by ripping this blind cut to the correct depth. Guard removed so cut can be seen.

RABBET second cut made with work on end. Guard is removed to make cut. Waste is on side away from rip fence.

RABBET now completed. Rabbet joint is made by fitting edges of two rabbeted workpieces together.

V-GROOVE requires two cuts at an angle. Here second cut is made. Guard must be removed for this cut.

V-GROOVE is shown completed. After first cut is made, blade must be lowered slightly for second cut.

cut through. The workpiece is then turned over on its side and the blade and the fence are readjusted so that the second cut will just remove a waste scrap piece and leave a perfect 90-degree groove along the edge of the board.

When making a rabbet, plan the work so this waste scrap piece is not trapped between the blade and the rip fence when it separates from the workpiece at the end of the second cut. Otherwise it can be caught by the saw blade teeth and propelled back toward the operator at a rapid speed. All such rabbet rips should be made so the scrap piece is cut loose on the side away from the rip fence, and falls harmlessly on the table top when cut free from the workpiece.

You can also form a rabbet by making a succession of cuts, each the width of the saw blade kerf. The first cut is made and then the rip fence is moved so that the next cut will saw away another strip the width of the kerf. The procedure is continued until the rabbet groove is the desired width.

A rabbet on the end of a workpiece is usually easiest to cut using the succession of cuts method but holding the workpiece against the miter gauge instead of the rip fence. In this operation, the blade is set at a height to achieve a rabbet of the desired depth.

Groove or slot. The groove and the slot are two other types of blind cuts where the height of the saw blade is set so it does not cut all the way through the workpiece. These are actually the same cut, with the term "slot" used to describe a narrow furrow, and "groove" to describe a wider one. Both are channels cut along either the short or long dimension of a workpiece at some place other than the edge or end of the workpiece.

V-grooves. V-grooves can be cut on the table saw using either the miter gauge or the rip fence. To begin with, the blade is tilted to the desired angle of the side of the groove, and set at a height that will achieve the desired depth of groove. The first cut is made, then the blade is lowered just slightly, so that the second cut will saw only part way into the kerf of the first cut. With the blade tilted at the same angle, the work is reversed and realigned so the second cut saws the opposite side of the V-groove.

Keep in mind with rip cuts that a piece of waste or scrap will be cut away just as the cut is completed. This can be hurled back toward you.

As you increase your skills with the Dremel Table Saw, you will find yourself wanting to know how to make the more advanced cuts such as tapers, wedges, coves, etc., and how to make wood joints such as dovetails, lap joints, splines, box joints, mortise-and-tenons, tongue-and-grooves, and others. You will find advanced texts on woodworking available at most libraries and bookstores which will help you learn these and other complex cuts which can be made on a table saw.

Controlling dust

Your work area can be a lot cleaner if you collect the sawdust as you work. This can be done neatly and conveniently by installing a Dremel Dust Bag on the saw. An adapter is included with this accessory so that the dust bag can be readily attached to a chute near the bottom of the motor.

Installation is easy. Simply tilt the adapter over the top of the chute and hook the ribs located in the adapter end over the ribs on the sawdust chute. Then carefully press the adapter down over the chute opening until the opening is completely covered.

From that point on, dust sucked

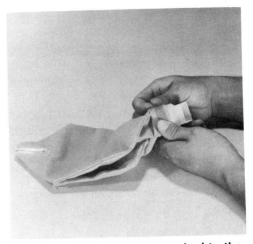

The Dremel Dust Bag is attached to the back of the table saw, collects saw dust to keep work area clean.

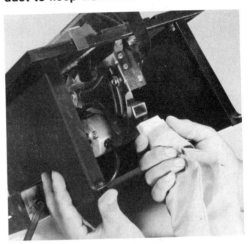

The dust bag quickly snaps over a chute located at the back of the saw table, gathers dust when motor is on.

Household or workshop vacuum cleaner can be attached to table saw by means of this special adapter.

from the table is collected in the bag.

Using your own vacuum cleaner. You can even employ your own vacuum cleaner to help draw saw dust from the table saw. To do this, purchase the Dremel vacuum hose adapter, Catalog No. 8013. This makes it possible for your vacuum to replace the dust bag. It is attached to the sawdust chute on the saw in the same manner as the dust bag.

Cleaning

Remove accumulated dust and debris from the inside of the table saw at frequent intervals.

Remove accumulated dust and debris from the inside of the motor at frequent intervals. To do this, hold a vacuum sweeper hose to the rear motor vents, while tapping the motor housing with a screwdriver handle or light, non-marring hammer to loosen the dirt. DO NOT BLOW AIR INTO THE MOTOR as this will blow dirt into the bearings. Failure to keep the motor clean will result in overheating of the motor and could result in a fire if the dust is flammable.

QUICK FIXES

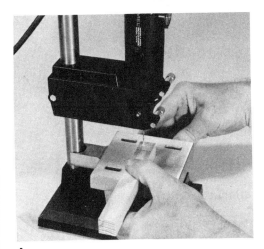

A.

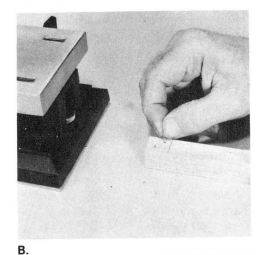

B.

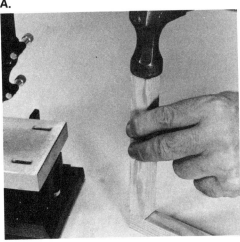

C.

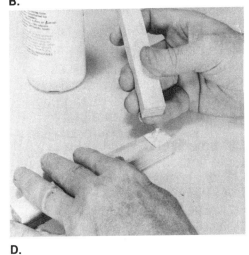

D.

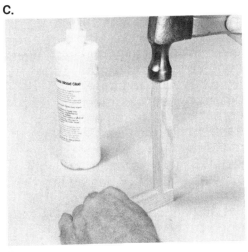

E.

Toothpick dowels are great for making joints in small work. The trick is to match the dowel holes. Here is a good way to do it: First drill holes in one side of the work. Then insert wire nails with points upward in those holes. Then tap other piece of work down on the nails to mark spots for drilling opposing holes. After drilling, insert dowels made from hardwood toothpicks, and join the wood with glue.

Project 8

The Parsons Table has been popular for 250 years. Now you can make a version especially for chess, checkers, and backgammon.

Materials:
3 × 4-ft. square, 1/2-in. birch plywood
8 metal corner braces
1/4 × 1/2-in. flat molding
Finishing nails
Wood putty
Latex enamel

Tools:
Table Saw
Disc/Belt Sander
Hammer
Nailset
Woodburning tool

Have birch plywood sheet cut at lumber yard into two 18 × 48-in. pieces. On table saw, cut each of these into two 18 × 18 and one 12 × 18-in. panel. Cut all table parts from these panels. Refer to Plan A for dimensions of side pieces of table and cut these on table saw. Get dimensions for all leg pieces from Plan A and cut 4 sets on table saw. See Detail A. Construct table sides, using lap joints at the

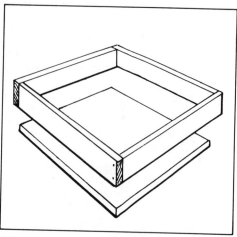

DETAIL B. Assembled sides of table are fitted over top as shown here and attached with corner glue blocks.

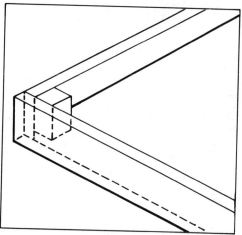

DETAIL C. Glue blocks are 1-in. squares glued so as to adhere to both sides and the table top.

corners. Table top is 16 × 16-in. square of plywood. After sides are assembled, place frame on workbench over the table top, as in Detail B. With the top fitted between the sides, glue 1-in. square corner blocks to top and sides at each corner. See Detail C. Next, make the 4 legs as shown in Detail D. The pieces of the leg are assembled with 90-degree lap joints, glued and nailed together. Set all nailheads and fill holes with wood putty. After putty dries, sand smooth. Now fit each leg to the table (see Detail E), gluing it to the corner block, sides and top. Use

DETAIL A. Have plywood cut at lumber yard into 18 × 48-in. pieces. Cut project parts from these on table saw.

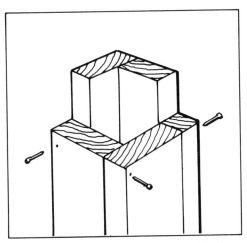

DETAIL D. Leg pieces are assembled using full lap joints as shown here, then glued and finish nailed.

two metal corner braces screwed to the leg and the underside of the table top additional bracing for each leg. To make the gameboard, cut a 13 × 13-in. square of 1/2-in. plywood. Center it on the table and fit a frame of 1/4 × 1/2-in. molding around it. After mitering the corners of this frame, nail it to the table-top with wire nails. It will serve as a fence for the double-sided game-board. Make a chessboard (see Plan B) on one side of the gameboard and a backgammon board on the other. Use the woodburning tool to make dark areas on the game-boards. After burning, varnish the board. Sand the entire table, then finish with colorful glossy enamel.

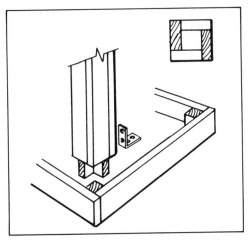

DETAIL E. Assembled legs are glued to top, sides, and glue blocks, and also secured by two corner braces.

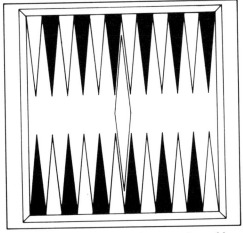

DETAIL F. The reversable game board has this backgammon board burned on one side, chess board on the other.

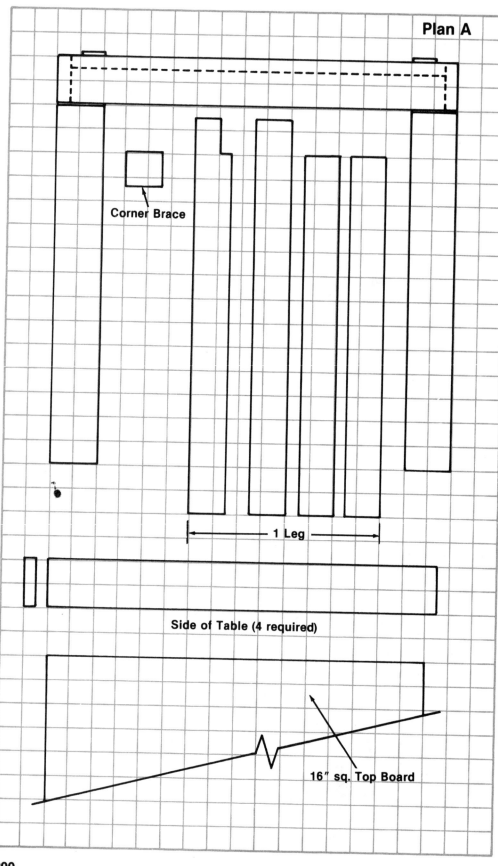

Plan A

Corner Brace

1 Leg

Side of Table (4 required)

16″ sq. Top Board

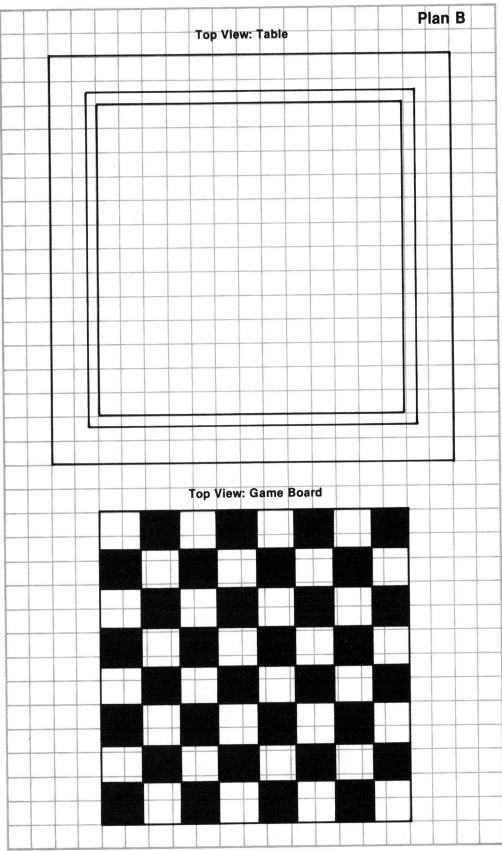

Plan B

Top View: Table

Top View: Game Board

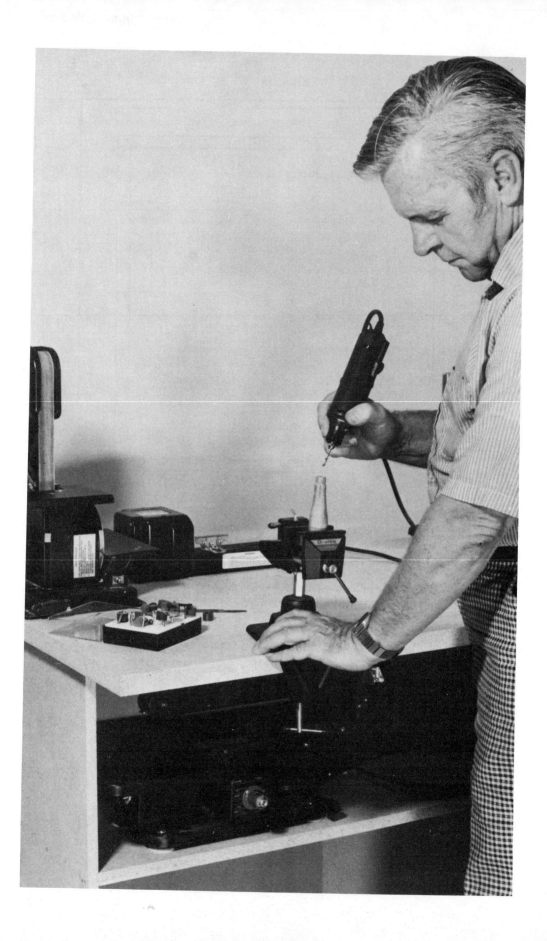

CHAPTER NINE

Building a Mini Power Workshop

Here are suggested workbench plans, and fold-up storage ideas for people with limited space. With a little effort and these plans, you can build a convenient workspace in which to use and store your compact power tools.

Each of the compact tools described in the earlier chapters of this book will perform certain tasks, but when you expand from doing occasional repair jobs around the house to building projects on a regular basis, you will find that a collection of power tools becomes a great asset. One project, for example, might require routing, sawing, sanding, wood turning and drilling, as you make a variety of different parts and assemble them into a single finished product. Then you will need a well-organized, well-equipped workshop.

The home woodworking shop has been a long-standing American dream. It is a place with enough room and equipment so that the craftsman or woman can exercise that urge to create and translate ideas into real things. It is a place dedicated to work, always there and ready, away from the daily stream of life in the rest of the house. It is the inevitable dream of everyone in creative work, whether it be sewing, painting or woodworking.

But it is often a dream which doesn't come true because of space limitations. The woodworker, to build a workshop, must have room for all those tools. Compact power tools can help to solve part of the problem simply because they don't need as much space. The projects, of course, in a compact workshop are scaled down to the size of the tools, but to a majority of woodworkers this is not a serious hinderance. For one thing, much of their work is small in scale to begin with. For another, the ability to have a workshop, even though compact, outweighs the disadvantages of having no shop at all.

Planning your workshop

In thinking about a workshop, you need to consider a couple of things:

1. The kind of work you intend to do.

2. The space, or lack of it, available.

The kind of activity will dictate the power tools you need. If you are a woodcarver, for example, you will need the Moto-Tool with a set of high speed cutters. But you could also use a table or scroll saw to cut the work before carving, a sander to shape and smooth the uncarved portions, or a router for precarving some areas. If you intend to make useful wood or plastic items — perhaps toys, picture frames, candle holders, salt and pepper sets, and the like — you might need a lathe for turnings, along with a router, a table saw and a sander. One purpose of this book is to preview the various compact tools available and their uses to help you plan.

Space needs can present several problems:

If you have plenty of space — perhaps a room or a large area in the basement — the problem is one of designing an efficient layout. You probably have room for all the tools you want, but they should be placed so they are convenient to operate.

If you have limited space, you may have to decide which tools are most important, and make permanent space only for those. Planning the efficient use of the space, of course, is critical, since you want to get the most out of every square foot you have. You should be particularly interested in tools such as the Moto-Shop, which do double duty. These can cut your space requirements without reducing your work capabilities.

The third possibility is that you have no spare space available for use as a full-time workshop. Your answer will have to be a roll-away shop of some kind — which can disappear between projects and in which all of your tools can be conveniently stored. Fortunately, foldup and rollaway workbenches can be practical when you use compact power tools.

Other considerations when thinking about workshop space include:

1. *Adequate electrical service.* If you plan an extensive shop — a whole room with a large array of tools — you should have two or more electrical circuits, one for lighting and one or more for the operation of tools. For the typical compact workshop, the second circuit probably won't be necessary, but you will need enough conveniently located wall outlets to run all

tools. The electrical outlets, of course, should be properly grounded.

2. *Adequate ventilation.* Power tools generate dust. A dusty atmosphere is not safe for breathing and can be explosive. You may also be using finishing materials such as paints, stains and lacquers which give off fumes. All of these dictate a workshop area with excellent ventilation. The best for most workshops is an exhaust fan mounted in the window, or attached to a ventilating duct (as a kitchen or bathroom fan is).

3. *Storage space.* Tools and scraps of material lying about on workbenches and on the floor are a major cause of workshop accidents. Look for ways to keep tools stored when not in use. Provide a bin or drawer space for collecting scrap materials.

4. *A means of locking tools.* This is another safety precaution, especially if there are children in the house. All tools, and especially power tools, should be locked up when not in use. This means locking the tool switches in the OFF position or moving the tools to a cabinet which can be locked.

First planning steps

The first step in planning a workshop is to make a scale drawing of your available space on graph paper. You can do a workable set of plans on paper ruled in 1/4-inch squares, letting each square represent one foot of the room. Draw in all walls, doors and windows, and indicate the location of any electrical outlets.

If you are able to convert a whole room to a workshop, let this plan show the room empty. If you expect to use only a part of a room, or use it only part time after rolling your workshop out of a closet, the plan should show what furniture will stay in the room while the workshop is set up. Draw squares to show the space occupied by this furniture, and then you can see the space remaining for a work area.

Next, think about the bench or table space you will require. You will need a flat, open table surface for working, and some surface space for each power tool.

Some work is done while you sit and some while you stand. If you plan to do wood carving, for example, you will probably sit down as you work. This means the work surface should be at a good height for sit-down work.

Cutting on a lathe or a scroll saw, on the other hand, is usually stand-up work, and the tools need to be situated on surfaces at a height that is comfortable as you stand in front of the equipment.

Determining work surface height.

One good thing about making your own workshop is that you can construct it to the height you like best and that suits your physical build. There are established standards for surface heights, and it can help in your planning to know some of them:

Dining room table: About 30 inches.

Kitchen counters: About 36 inches.

Typing table: About 26 inches. This places the typewriter keys at about 30 inches.

Typical card table: About 26 inches.

Typical workbench: About 36 inches.

Bathroom sink or vanity: About 31 inches.

Sewing machine table: About 27 inches, which places the sewing height at about 31 inches.

These measurements can help you to decide the heights to plan in a work area, but you don't have to follow them. Some typists, for example,

find it easier to work when the machine's keyboard is 25 or 26 inches high rather than 30. You may have discovered that in work where you tend to lean close, such as wood-carving, a surface height of between 25 and 27 inches works best. For stand up work, you'll find 33 to 36 inches, depending on your own height, is most comfortable. If you are quite tall, the higher work surface would be better. If you are short, you might plan a lower work surface. The important thing is to be relaxed and comfortable as you work. You shouldn't have to stretch or bend unnecessarily.

Amount of surface you need

The basic working surface is a clear area free of tools where you do assembly, gluing, etc. As a matter of convenience, you should have hand tools, glue, nails, screws, etc., near this area, preferably on a wall rack behind it or in convenient drawer. A Pegboard wall rack keeps pliers, rule, screwdrivers and other tools in plain sight. (One way to keep these tools where they belong is to paint a silhouette of the tool on the board. This tells you, or anyone using your shop, just where to put the tool when it is being replaced. You also can tell at a glance when some tool is missing. This beats pawing through a tool box or drawer to find what you want.)

Small parts storage is always a problem, but there are good cabinets available with whole banks of small plastic drawers. They aren't expensive and are a big help in keeping the work area clean and free of clutter.

Planning for power tools. Each power tool requires a certain amount of space, not only for mounting but also for handling workpieces. A

Dremel table saw, for example, takes a mounting space of 12 × 14 inches, but you have to allow room on either side and in back of it so long workpieces can be cut. Adequate surrounding space for long work is also needed for a shaper table, if you build one to hold your Dremel router. The Moto-Shop has a throat 15 inches deep, so you can cut in the center of a workpiece nearly 30 inches wide. You can turn the scroll saw blade in the Moto-Shop and make very long cuts from either the left or the right. Therefore, you must allow room around the Moto-Shop when you mount it for these large workpieces. Since the Moto-Shop is portable, of course, you can move it for special long cuts.

When planning a workshop for full-scale power tools, the usual advice is to locate tools in the center of the shop floor space so as to have sufficient room for material handling. Because you don't work ordinarily with such large workpieces in a compact workshop, this won't be quite so necessary, and will make floor planning easier.

When planning to place one of the compact tools on a bench surface, look first at its base dimensions. Then consider the space on either side needed for maneuvering larger work pieces. With these in mind, place the tool on the surface, located close enough to the front of the work surface so you don't have to reach to work.

If you have the luxury of plenty of space, then all power tools such as the Table Saw, Moto-Shop, and Disc/Belt Sander, should be bolted permanently in their own places on the work surface. Each tool comes with holes for such bolting.

If, however, you have limited space, then you may plan on making a power tool work area. This area would be designed so that you can clamp the power tool you need in place, do the work, then remove the tool and store it. The most convenient arrangement is to have a storage area under the work surface for each tool. If the tools are pre-mounted on plywood and ready to clamp in place with C-clamps, switching from one tool to another is quick and easy.

Buying a workbench. You can build your own workbench or benches, and we have presented sketches for three benches in this chapter. You also may buy ready-made workbenches at some hardware and home center stores as well as from mail order houses.

Workbenches you can buy range from plain types, made of particle board and 2 × 4s, to fancy ones made of hardwoods with built in clamping devices. The inexpensive ones are usually shipped knocked down and you assemble them. You can alter the dimensions on these easily. The expensive ones usually are already assembled and so beautifully constructed that you won't want to alter them.

You may find some good workshop ideas in furniture that wasn't intended for workshop use. An example would be a sewing center. These are listed in most major mail order catalogs, and are designed to be compact pieces of furniture which can be opened up to provide work surfaces when needed. There is good storage space for the sewing machine and other sewing paraphernalia. Dozens of different designs are available and many are sturdy enough to handle compact power tools.

Look critically before you buy. Be sure that the work surface sits solidly after being pulled out or unfolded. Folding legs or leaves should lock in place, so there is no danger of a collapse as you work. Check the storage space to see that it is big enough to store the tools you want to put away. Most of these units fold down into space-saving, attractive cabinets that you won't mind having in a living area. So as not to mar work surfaces, power tools should be clamped in place rather than permanently mounted with bolts.

Workshops you can build

The accompanying sketches show three workshops you can build yourself. These are simple designs intended for easy construction. They were not designed to be built with compact tools, though there are many parts which can be made with your Dremel tools.

Materials used are pine or fir for legs and crossbraces, and plywood or particle board for doors and side and top panels. Particle board is the least expensive, but has some drawbacks. It is dense and therefore very heavy. The surface is coarse and rough, and will soak up paint like a sponge. It should not be used in an area that is moist or humid unless it is well sealed, since it tends to absorb water. Unpainted long shelves made of it, for example, will sag in a short time in a humid basement. Plywood costs a bit more, but generally is more satisfactory.

In all of these designs, use woodscrews as fasteners rather than nails. Screws hold better. Use flathead screws and countersink the holes so that the screw heads are at or below the surface when driven.

Use these sketches as springboards or starting points, and modify the designs to suit your own purposes. You can, for example, change the dimensions to fit your own work areas. The Fold Away Work Bench, as sketched, is 24 inches wide and 18 inches deep, but it could be modified easily to 30 × 18 inches if that size would fit your space better.

Fold Away Workbench

This is a workbench which folds into a unit that occupies only 18 × 24 inches of floorspace when not in use, and opens up to 24 × 36 when you need it. It has good tool storage space in its base, and can be equipped with casters so you can roll it into a closet.

The sketches show a hinged door on one side which gives access to the storage compartment. The compartment can be equipped with shelves of adjustable height, and you can add a storage box which slides into the bottom to hold scrap materials.

You can provide even better access and storage by hinging both side panels. If you decide to make the unit 30 or 36 inches wide, you certainly should hinge both panels. Another modification could be the compartmentalization of this storage area. For example, make one compartment of the right size to store a disc/belt sander and another to store the table saw. By careful measurement, and access from both sides, you could easily create permanent storage compartment for half a dozen compact power tools. If, as suggested earlier, you mount each tool on a plywood base, then bringing each tool up to the work area as you need it would be easy.

The cabinet itself is 30 inches high, and when mounted on casters would give you a work surface about 33 inches high. This is minimum height for stand-up work.

Before building the cabinet, decide what height the work surface should be. If you plan to do sit-down work, then make the cabinet from 24 to 27 inches high, and add 2 or 3 inches for casters (depending on the size you buy). If you plan to stand at the bench, the 30 inch

Fold Away Workbench

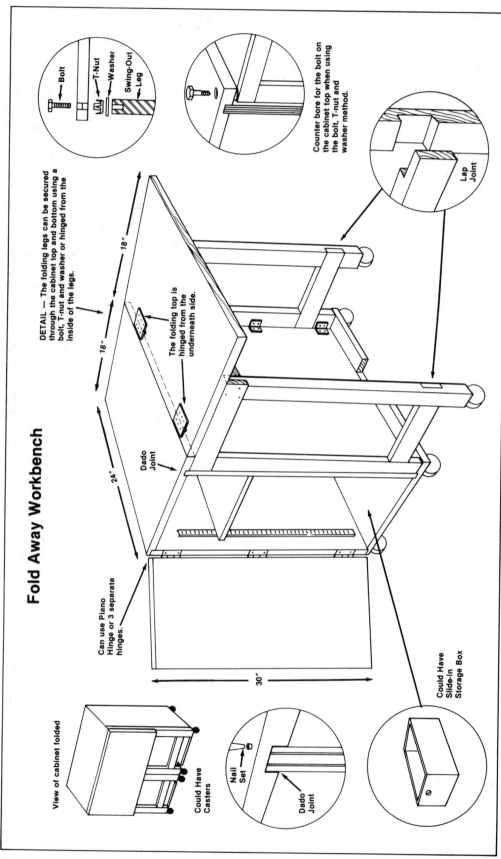

Bolt

T-Nut

Washer

Swing-Out
Leg

Counter bore for the bolt on the cabinet top when using the bolt, T-nut and washer method.

Lap Joint

DETAIL — The folding legs can be secured through the cabinet top and bottom using a bolt, T-nut and washer or hinged from the inside of the legs.

18″

18″

24″

The folding top is hinged from the underneath side.

Dado Joint

Can use Piano Hinge or 3 separate hinges.

30″

View of cabinet folded

Could Have Casters

Nail Set

Dado Joint

Could Have Slide-In Storage Box

cabinet with its 33 inch work height might be right, or you could add up to 3 inches to it if you need to.

You can also vary the size of the extension table. It is planned to be 18 inches wide. You can, however, make it wider, extending it all the way down to the bottom of the swing- away legs.

The basic cabinet is a plywood box (1/2, 5/8 or 3/4-inch). Note the details of the side on which the extension is mounted. Here, a dado is cut into the top and bottom panels. The side panel fits into these dados and is secured by using woodscrews through the table top into it. Countersink the screw heads. Finishing nails could be used in place of the screws if you like. Apply glue to all joints as you assemble and before driving screws or nails.

If you look at the sketch, you will see that this dado is cut so that the lip beyond it is the same width as the wood legs. Thus, if the legs were 2 × 4s, this lip would measure 3-1/2 inches (the actual measurement of a 2″ × 4″ is 1-1/2 by 3-1/2 inches). Allow enough additional room for the corner of the leg to swing.

You could also make the legs out of 1 × 3 lumber (dressed size is 3/4 × 2-1/2 inches). Then the lip would be 2-1/2 inches. The choice of leg size is yours. If you want an extremely sturdy bench, the 2 × 4 leg is better. However, for most people, the 1 × 3 legs are more than strong enough, and make a better looking bench.

The doors and the extension top are attached to the cabinet with piano hinges. The swing-out legs, as shown in the detail drawings, are hinged by means of a T-bolt down through the top. The top of the T-bolt should be countersunk. Note that a T-nut is driven into the underside of the extension top, and that a washer is inserted between it and the top of the door. The T-bolt should extend down into the door

about 1/2 inch. The same T-bolt assembly also is used at the bottom of each swing-out leg.

As the detail sketches show, lap joint construction is used in the assembly of the swing-out legs. Apply white glue to these joints as you assemble them, and clamp them until the glue is dry.

Wall mount workbench

This is an interesting workbench for people with floor space problems. The bench folds up neatly into the face of the wall-mounted cabinet when not in use. The cabinet doesn't have as much storage space as the Fold Away Bench, but it provides a nice 3 × 4-foot work surface.

The sketches show a wall cabinet 48 inches high, 15 inches deep, and 36 inches wide. These dimensions can be varied to suit your needs, but keep in mind that if you make the cabinet bigger, you increase its weight. Plan on using extra lag bolts and additional base mounts to take care of this extra weight when you mount the cabinet on the wall.

Again, 1/2 to 3/4-inch plywood is the best material for the cabinet and extension table. The wall cabinet is a backless box consisting of two side panels and a top and bottom. The extension table folds up to become the door of the cabinet, and the swing-away support leg folds against the door.

The swing-away support leg is secured to the extension table with a piano hinge, and the extension table is secured to the wall cabinet in the same manner. Note that corner brace locks are used on each side of the unit to lock the support leg when the extension table is down and ready for work.

You can put two or three shelves into the cabinet, using adjustable shelf bracket strips. You can store

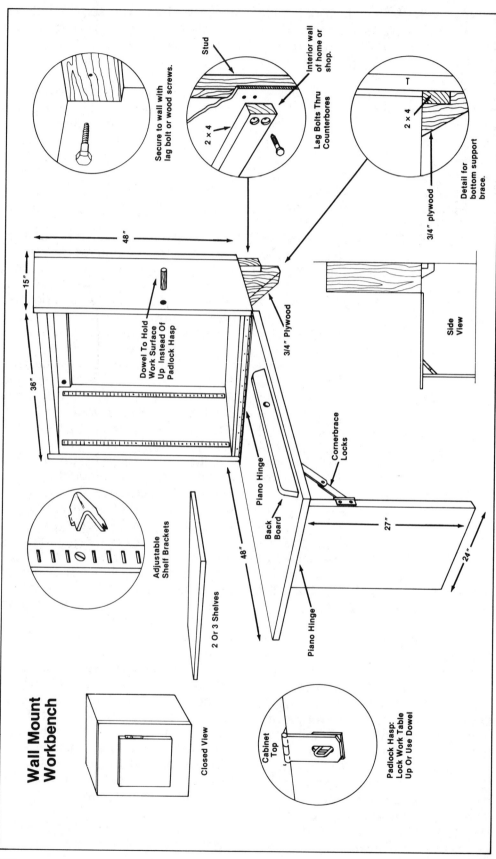

Wall Mount Workbench

Closed View

Cabinet Top

Padlock Hasp: Lock Work Table Up Or Use Dowel

2 Or 3 Shelves

Adjustable Shelf Brackets

Piano Hinge

Back Board

Cornerbrace Locks

Piano Hinge

48"

27"

24"

3/4" Plywood

Dowel To Hold Work Surface Up Instead Of Padlock Hasp

48"

15"

36"

Side View

Secure to wall with lag bolt or wood screws.

Stud

2 x 4

Interior wall of home or shop.

Lag Bolts Thru Counterbores

3/4" plywood

2 x 4

Detail for bottom support brace.

compact power tools on the bottom shelf, and add a shelf above this space for a small parts cabinet. (Your Moto-Tool cutters and other accessories can be neatly stored in the plastic drawers of this type of cabinet.)

If you plan to sit down to work at this bench, mount it on the wall so that the extension top is at the work height you want. The length of the support leg is determined by this measurement. If you want to sit as you work, cut the support leg 25 to 28 inches long. If you intend to stand up, mount the cabinet with the work surface 33 to 36 inches from the floor — and cut the support leg accordingly.

Note that two ways are suggested to hold the extension table and support leg in the upright or folded position. One version calls for a padlock hasp, screwed to the top of the cabinet. When the extension table is closed (in the upright position), the hasp hinges down over it and over the padlock eye which is screwed to the underside of the extension table. The other version calls for a dowel to be inserted through a hole in the side of the wall cabinet. The dowel (3/4 inch diameter) would extend into a matching hole drilled in the "back splash" board attached to the extension table surface.

Mounting the wall cabinet. The wall cabinet must be attached to wall studs by means of large lag bolts through the 2 x 4 that is located at the back inside top of the cabinet.

After determining where you want the cabinet located, and remembering the height of the work surface from the floor, tap the surface of the wall with a small hammer to locate the wall studs. You can tell where they are because of the dull sound when you tap the wall over a stud. If the wall is of drywall construction, the studs can be located with a stud finder, an inexpensive tool available in most hardware stores. Predrill holes through the 2 x 4 support member in the cabinet for the lag bolts, carefully locating these holes so that the lag bolts will turn into the wall studs.

Support the finished cabinet on saw horses or by moving another cabinet under it. Place the supported cabinet in position, with the lag bolts over the studs, and turn the lag bolts into the wall. Wall studs are ordinarily located every 16 inches in a wall and you should use a pair of lag bolts for each stud the cabinet crosses, as shown in the sketch.

To further support the cabinet, insert 3/4-inch plywood support brackets under the cabinet, as shown in the sketches. These provide additional support when the extension table is opened up.

The standard workbench

The third design shown here might be described as a standard workbench, though it has a few interesting features which actually make it more than that. One interesting feature is the suggested use of hardwood flooring for the top surface. Another is the storage space enclosed by sliding doors.

The dimensions of the bench are optional. It is suggested that you make it anywhere from 18 to 30 inches wide, with 24 inches as the most practical width. And you might make it from 48 to 60 inches or more in length. Determine the dimensions by the space you have available.

This workbench is intended chiefly for stand up work, and therefore should have a top surface at least 33 inches from the floor, and 36 inches if that height is most comfortable. The legs and cross members are 2 x 4 lumber. The back and side panels

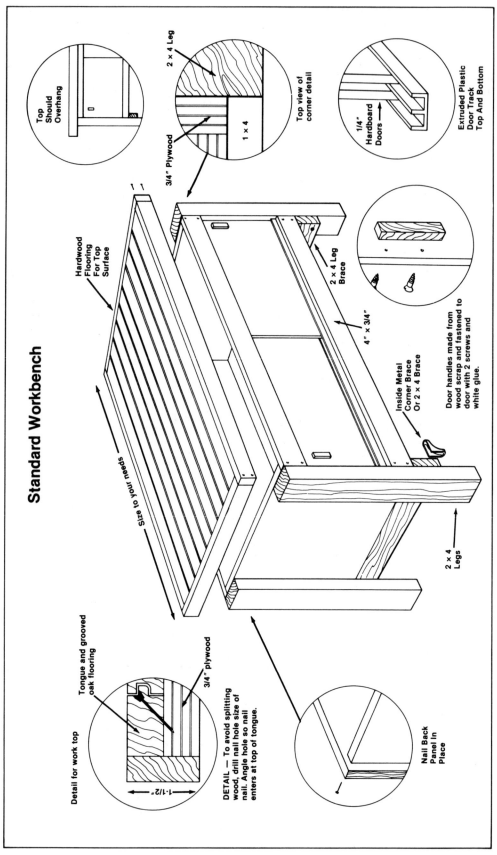

Standard Workbench

Top Should Overhang

2 × 4 Leg

3/4" Plywood

1 × 4

Top view of corner detail

1/4" Hardboard Doors

Extruded Plastic Door Track Top And Bottom

Hardwood Flooring For Top Surface

Size to your needs

2 × 4 Leg Brace

4" × 3/4"

Inside Metal Corner Brace Or 2 × 4 Brace

Door handles made from wood scrap and fastened to door with 2 screws and white glue.

2 × 4 Legs

Detail for work top

Tongue and grooved oak flooring

3/4" plywood

1-1/2"

DETAIL — To avoid splitting wood, drill nail hole size of nail. Angle hole so nail enters at top of tongue.

Nail Back Panel In Place

could be either 1/4-inch plywood or 1/8-inch hardboard. These are not weight bearing panels, and serve only to enclose the storage area. For strength, the bottom shelf should be 1/2-inch or thicker plywood.

The legs and lower cross braces are 2 × 4 lumber. The wood braces across the front are 1 × 4 lumber or can be cut from 3/4-inch plywood. The sliding doors are of 1/4-inch hardboard, which slide in plastic door tracks. (You can buy such track at your hardware store or home center.)

To assemble the bench, first screw the lower 2 × 4 cross braces to the legs, making two end assemblies. Then attach the end panels to each of the assemblies. Now join these two assemblies with a bottom shelf. This shelf cannot be seen in the sketches, but serves as the bottom of the storage compartment. Next, install the back panel, and then the two front cross braces.

The top is assembled separately and put on last. The framing for the top is 1 × 2 lumber, and the dimensions of the top should be large enough so that there is about a 2-inch overhang on all four sides of the table. The top is a sandwich consisting of a sheet of plywood inside a frame of 1 × 2 lumber, which is topped with hardwood flooring. You could finish the top with hardboard, plywood, or particle board instead of hardwood flooring if you choose.

Anchor the top to the bench by driving a woodscrew through the top and into the legs at each corner.

Put gliders on the bottoms of the legs as an aid in moving the bench without damaging the floor under it.

Finishing a workbench

Most workbenches are left unfinished. However, yours can be given a better appearance by applying a finish. One way would be to stain the wood dark and then apply several coats of penetrating resin. Penetrating resin is a manmade coating, similar in appearance to varnish after it dries. When applied it soaks into the top 1/16-inch or so of any softwood. When it sets, the resins harden and cause the surface of the wood to turn hard. The hard surface resists dents and scratches and lasts longer under hard use than the soft surface would. One brand is Watco Danish Oil Finish, which comes in walnut and natural colors.

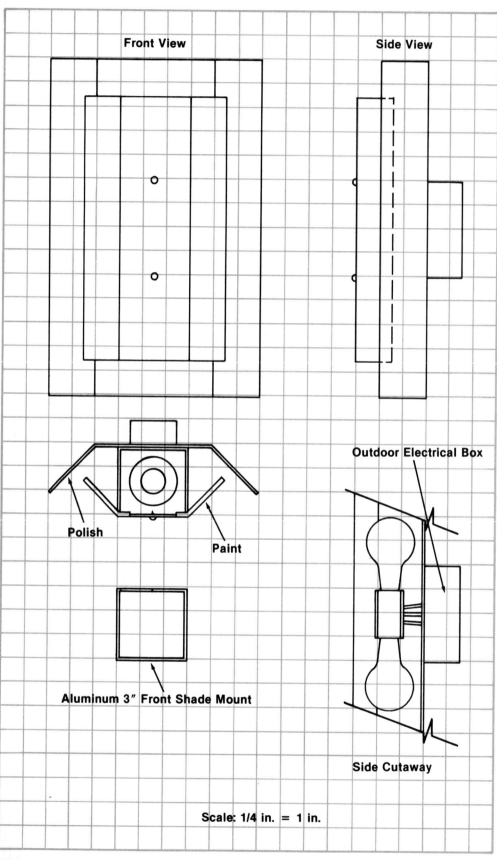

Front View

Side View

Polish

Paint

Aluminum 3″ Front Shade Mount

Outdoor Electrical Box

Side Cutaway

Scale: 1/4 in. = 1 in.

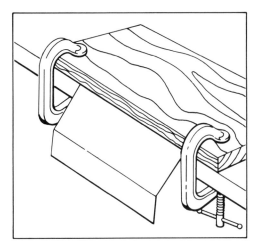

DETAIL A. Here is how to set up a quick sheet metal press on workbench edge for bending aluminum.

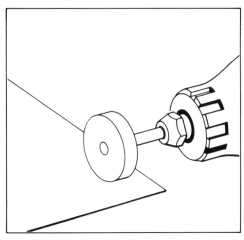

DETAIL B. Bring all reflective surfaces to a high polish using the cloth polishing wheel and compound.

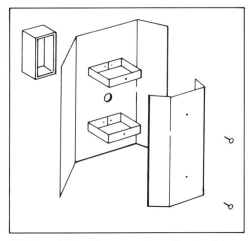

DETAIL C. Brackets are riveted to backing sheet. Front reflector is attached by sheet metal screws.

Project 9

PORCH LIGHT

Not every home can boast of a unique, handcrafted porch light, but yours can if you embark on this project.

Materials:
Sheet Aluminum stock
Sheet metal screws
Aluminum rivets

Tools:
Moto-Tool
1/8-in. drill bit
No. 423 cloth polishing wheel
No. 402 mandrel
No. 932 wheel point
Polishing Compound No. 421
Sheet metal snips, Hand riveting tool, Screwdriver, C-clamps

Refer to Plan A for size and layout of sheet aluminum parts of the porch light. Transfer these to aluminum stock and then cut stock with metal snips. After cutting, smooth all edges with Moto-Tool and No. 932 wheel point. Clamp those aluminum parts to be bent to the edge of your workbench, using a straightedge held by C-clamps. Then bend as shown in Detail A to the necessary angles. Polish reflective surfaces to a high sheen with the Moto-Tool, No. 423 Polishing Wheel, and polishing compound. See Detail B. After polishing, coat area with clear lacquer to prevent oxidization. Refer again to Plan A, and mark all hole locations. Drill these with Moto-Tool and 1/8-in. drill bit. Attach brackets to backing sheet with rivets and riveting tool. Next attach front reflector with sheet metal screws. See Detail C. You can paint non-reflective surfaces if you like. This fixture requires weatherproof outside lamp sockets and wiring, and could be a fire hazard if wired improperly. Have the wiring for your fixture done by a competent electrician.

CHAPTER TEN

Service and Maintenance

Routine care and maintenance can extend the life of your tools and keep them working at peak efficiency. Here are tips on how to give your compact power tools the care they deserve and how to make minor repairs.

Dremel compact power tools have been designed to require minimum maintenance so that with only a little time and effort on your part they can be kept in peak operating condition. The Owners Manual with each tool provides specific instructions on the care of the tool. Read the manual when you purchase the tool, then store it in a convenient location near your work area. Refer to it frequently until you have become thoroughly familiar with the operation of the tool.

Make a habit of pulling out the manual occasionally and reading it again to refresh your memory, even after you have become so proficient with the tool that manual reference isn't necessary. You will find information and hints that you have forgotten, particularly in the area of tool maintenance.

Electrical maintenance

Power cords on all electrical tools and appliances are subject to strains and hazards, and should be checked frequently. The most frequent problems are accidental nicking or cutting by a sharp blade, bench edge, or other sharp item; accidental contact with an operating power tool; exposure to high heat; strain resulting from pulling the cord to disconnect the plug rather than pulling the plug itself; strain from carrying the tool by the cord; and bending of prongs or blades.

Much of the damage outlined above is the result of improper or careless handling of the power cord, and can be avoided by good workshop habits. You can think of these good habits as "preventive maintenance," since by avoiding damage, they eliminate the need for some maintenance.

Make it a habit to know where the power cord is whenever you work. Be sure that it doesn't pass close to any source of high heat (a soldering iron, for example) and that it doesn't have to cross any sharp edges. (The underside of the edge of a metal table can be sharp and can cut when anything is pulled across it.) Lay the power cord in gentle natural curves, without kinks or knots, from the outlet to the tool.

When operating hand power tools such as the Moto-Tool, always arrange the work so that the power cord comes from behind or well to one side of the work area, and does not cross the work area or come near to the spinning accessory. If the tool should hit a knot of wood and jump suddenly, it might accidentally nick the power cord if it is too close.

When operating several power tools, you may have a number of power cords running to the same wall outlet. Care must be taken not to develop the "spaghetti bowl" effect, where you have too many power cords running together, sometimes intertwined, that begin to look like a collection of black spaghetti. This situation creates a number of hazards.

First, there are too many wires and it is difficult to keep them clear of hazards. Second, plugging and unplugging of any equipment becomes complicated because it is difficult to know which cord leads to the tool to be unplugged. This tempts you to pull on the cord rather than the plug, and can cause a separation of connections at the plug. Third, a multitude of plugs in one outlet can result in an overload of the circuit if a number of tools are used at the same time.

As a safety measure, you are advised to unplug any tool when changing accessories, belts, blades and the like, or when performing maintenance chores. Just turning the tool switch to OFF is not enough because there is always the chance of a short in the switch or of accidentally brushing against the switch and turning the tool ON while you are working on it.

Since you will plug and unplug a tool a number of times during a work session, you should make the plugging convenient. If working in a temporary work area — the kitchen, for example — arrange to work within easy reach of a wall outlet. If you are setting up a workshop, plan to run the electrical circuit to the workbench area and install outlets at workbench height on the wall behind the bench.

When using compact power tools, only plug in the tool you are using at the moment. If you have several tools in your collection, leave the others unplugged until needed. This eliminates all of the spaghetti bowl problems and makes for much safer operation all round.

Make an examination of all power cords on a regular basis, preferably before each work session. For a quick check:

1. Look at the plug. Check to see that the grounding prong and blades are straight, and are firmly mounted. Look at the power cord entry point to see that there is no break or sign of separation.

2. Run your fingers the length of the power cord, feeling for nicks, cuts, breaks or other damage. If you feel any, look at the damaged site carefully. If the damage has penetrated the protective outer surface of the cord, it is dangerous.

3. Look at the place where the power cord enters the tool, again looking for signs of strain or separation.

If during the examination you find any damage, do not use the power cord until it has been repaired. Return the tool to a Dremel Service Center for installation of a new power cord.

Extension cords. All maintenance suggestions apply to any extension cords as well as to tool power cords.

Always remember that there is a power drop as electricity runs through an extension cord. This means that less power will be delivered to the tool being run on a long extension cord than is available at the wall outlet.

When electric motors are run at voltages lower than normal, they tend to run hot and could burn out. To avoid this problem, purchase long extension cords made of larger wire. Larger wire offers less resistance to the electricity, and thus produce a lower voltage drop over the run of the cord.

For Dremel compact tools, the *minimum* wire size for extension cords should be:

Under 50 feet No. 16 wire
50-100 feet No. 14 wire

The smaller the wire number, the larger its diameter and its electrical carrying capability. Thus, a No. 12 wire is larger than a No. 14. A label or tag on the extension cord should inform you of the size or capacity of the wire used in its construction.

Storage of tools

A compact power tool can be stored easily, which is a great convenience. But you should take care to store under the proper conditions to prevent later operating problems.

Do not store tools in an area of dampness or high humidity. In many areas of the country, the air is dry in the winter, but quite moist and humid in the summer. If your work area is in a basement, it is likely to be very dry during the winter, but humid and musty in the summer. Storage in the basement in the winter would present no problems. But if you allow the tool to stay there for the summer, the moisture might seriously affect its later operation.

Always remove all accessories from the Moto-Tool when storing. If an accessory remains in place, oxidization or rust may make the collet difficult to operate after a period of time. Moisture also may penetrate and affect electrical connections within the tool, possibly causing a short circuit.

Accessories, collets, saw blades, attachments, exposed shafts, etc., can be sprayed with rust inhibitive material, available from hardware stores, for storage. The parts should be wiped clean before being used again.

While locking stored tools is not a matter of maintenance, it is a very sensible precaution. Keep tools that are not in use locked so that curious children cannot try to play with them and either damage the tool or injure themselves.

Tools should be covered when stored, to protect them from dust. Use the carrying case for storage, if one came with your tool, or save the original box for storage purposes. If you don't box the tool, cover it with a plastic bag or sheet during storage to protect it from dust. Dust entering the motor may cause it to run hot.

Cleaning motors

All compact workshop tools run in an atmosphere of dust and at times, some dust may collect in the motor. The usual signal for this is that the motor smells hot.

To clean sawdust from a motor, use a hose equipped vacuum cleaner. With the cleaner running, bring the hose close to the motor air vents. Tap the motor firmly with a screwdriver handle or small non-marring hammer to dislodge dust, which will then be sucked into the vacuum.

If a vacuum is not available, the motor housings of the Dremel Moto-Tool, Scroll Saw/Sander and Disc/Belt Sander may be struck with a screwdriver handle or other non-marring device while the motor is running. The built-in motor fans will help remove some of the dust.

Do not attempt to clean a motor by blowing the dust out with an air hose. This method may blow dirt into the bearings and cause them to overheat and fail.

When operating the Moto-Tool, be careful not to cover the vent holes in the housing as you work.

219

You do not want to shut off the air flow to the motor, nor impede its ability to blow dust out.

As a preventive measure, help keep the motor clean by keeping sawdust and chips at a minimum in the work area. Brush the area frequently and don't allow excessive debris to accumulate.

Changing belts

Some compact tools operate with drive belts between the motor and the operating parts. These tools include the table saw, and the disc-belt sander.

Drive belts tend to stretch over long periods of time, and will wear with use. Because the stretching and wearing usually occur very gradually, it can be difficult to spot belt problems until they reduce the efficiency of the tool very considerably. The most noticeable symptoms are excessive vibration when the belt is worn, and loss of power when the belt is loose.

To keep the tool at good operating efficiency, check the belt frequently. Look for signs of wear, cracks or nicks, and flat spots. If you have become familiar with the appearance of the belt when it was

DISC/BELT SANDER. To change drive belts on disc/belt sander, remove cover by taking out screws inside housing.

DISC/BELT SANDER. Second screw to be removed is in back wall, in front of drive belt and below sander table.

DISC/BELT SANDER. With screws out, cover can be removed from disc sander side of the tool.

DISC/BELT SANDER. Drive belt is located behind sanding disc. New belt goes on over disc, then rolled on motor pulley.

new, irregularities are easier to spot. If stretching begins to cause slippage during operation, resulting in a slight loss of power, you will know the problem and can replace the belt before the loss seriously affects tool operation.

When ordering a new belt, refer to the parts list in the tool manual and specify the correct part number. Use only the Dremel belt listed and never substitute a belt that "looks like it fits." Any small variation in belt cross section or diameter or in belt size or belt material can result in either poor operation or eventual damage to the tool.

Follow the instructions in the tool manual carefully when replacing a belt. In each case, the instructions provide step-by-step guidance for rolling the belt on or off the pulleys.

Dropped tools

If a tool has been dropped or fallen from a table, do not attempt to operate it until you have carefully inspected it. Many times, the tool will operate when turned on after a fall, but damage caused by the fall may make operation unsafe.

After a Moto-Tool has fallen, look for small cracks in the housing, and look also for any sign that the shaft has been bent. The cracked housing may mean that parts inside are no longer in proper alignment. Even the slightest damage to the shaft will cause it to run out of balance, especially at high speeds, and create a dangerous situation.

To be safe, if you suspect any damage at all, return the tool to an authorized Dremel Service Center for inspection and replacement of damaged parts.

Tools such as the Moto-Shop, the table saw, and the disc-belt sander may be bent slightly out of alignment as the result of a fall. Inspect carefully, looking at corners

(of the table saw, for example) to see that they are still perfectly true, and at the fit of bolt holes for alignment. If you see even a slight indication of misalignment, send the tool in for an evaluation and repair by one of Dremel's Authorized Service Centers. The operation of any tool with misaligned parts could be extremely hazardous.

To help prevent damage from falls, bolt or clamp table model tools securely in place during use. Be very careful when moving tools to storage areas. Take your time, never carry more than one tool at a time, and use both hands when carrying heavier tools. The Moto-Shop should not be moved about using the top arm as a handle. The suction cup feet can stick tight enough to cause the top arm to be bent out of alignment when it is picked up in this way.

Replacing motor brushes

Inside the motor of the Moto-Tool, two spring-loaded carbon brushes make electrical contact with the motor's commutator. In all motors of this type, it is normal for these brushes to wear in time and require replacement.

You can tell that brush replacement time is approaching when the tool starts to run sporadically, makes strange noises, loses power and runs at reduced speed. In Moto-Tool models 260, 270, 280, 370, 380 Series 5 and later, the brushes have been designed so that they stop making contact with the motor's commutator when the brushes are worn. This prevents the motor from continuing to run until new brushes have been installed.

Earlier models do not have self-limiting brushes and should be removed and checked about every 10 hours of operation. When brushes

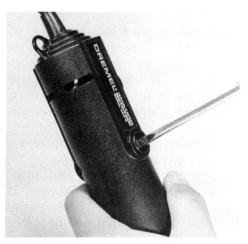

MOTO-TOOL. Brushes in the Moto-Tool are housed in case, and are removed by unscrewing brush cap.

MOTO-TOOL. After old brush is removed, new brushes are inserted in brush housing and cap replaced.

are removed for inspection they should be carefully marked so they can be replaced in the same hole and in exactly the same position as when they were removed. Otherwise, it will be necessary to allow them to re-seat themselves again before the tool will provide full power.

Models 245 and 250 have exceptionally good brush life and will normally last for the life of the tool. If either of these models begin to sputter and run poorly, they should be returned to an authorized Dremel Service Center for examination and possible brush replacement as quickly as possible. Otherwise the commutator may become damaged.

If your Moto-Tool is one of the previously mentioned Models 260, 270, 280, 370, 380 Series 5 or later, you can replace the brushes yourself. Order the Moto-Tool Repair Kit (Part No. 990880), which contains the necessary brushes, replacement brush caps and four collets (1/8, 3/32, 1/16 and 1/32 inch). Some early Dremel models also can be repaired with those brushes. Check your Owner's Manual or a Dremel Service Center.

The brushes are located under two screw caps, one on each side of the tool housing. To inspect the brushes, carefully mark the posi-

tion of the brush underneath the cap. Unscrew the cap carefully because it contains a spring which can fly out and become lost when the cap is unscrewed. Remove only one brush at a time. The brush does not look like a "brush" in the normal sense of the word, in that it has no bristles. This brush is simply a square shaped piece of solid carbon which is dark gray or nearly black in color. Its end will be slightly concave in shape where it fits around the circular commutator.

If the brush is less than 1/8-inch long or the end that contacts the commutator is rough or pitted, it should be replaced. If the brush is longer than 1/8-inch and the contact end is smooth, the problem is not in the brushes. Send the motor to a Dremel Service Center for examination.

Usually, the brushes do not wear out simultaneously but when one brush is worn, both should be replaced.

Instructions for proper positioning of the brushes are in the operating manual. Follow them closely. If the brushes are improperly installed, the tool will not run after the brush caps have been replaced.

Once the brushes have been installed, plug the tool in and allow it to run freely for 15 to 30 minutes to let the brushes "seat" properly. Do not use the tool during this run-in period. Instead, place it in a Moto -Tool holder or on a safe, clean surface and simply let it run.

Dremel service

Dremel has established two Service Centers in the U.S. and tools requiring service may be sent to either location. If you have misplaced your manual, you can write to these centers for replacement parts lists.

Addresses of the Centers are:
Dremel Service Center
4915 Twenty-first St.
Racine, WI 53406
                    and
Dremel Service Center
1345 Calle De Maria
Palm Springs, CA 92262

For the address of Service Centers outside of the U.S. consult the store at which the tool was purchased or write:
Dremel Division of
    Emerson Electric, Co.
Export Dept.
4915 Twenty-first St.
Racine, WI 53406

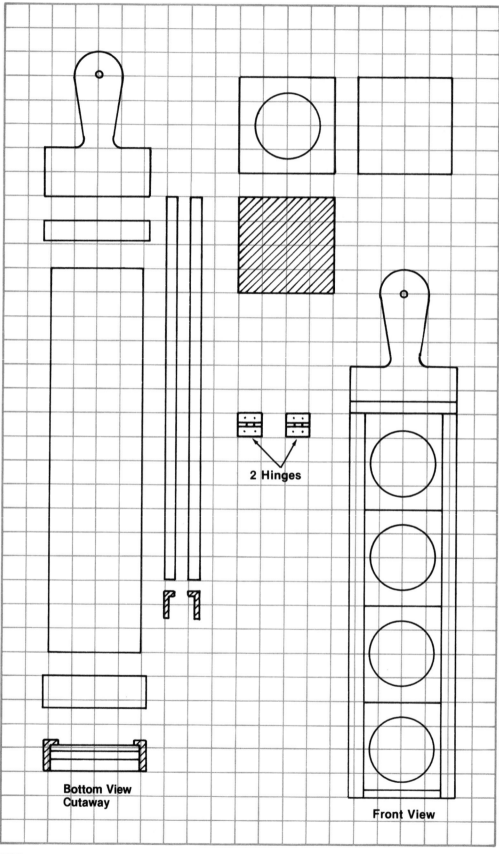

2 Hinges

Bottom View
Cutaway

Front View

Project 10

Where can you store coasters when they aren't in use? This project offers one answer: Hang them on the wall.

Materials:
4 1/4 × 12-in. decorative wood
4 1/4 × 12-in. common wood
1 1/2 × 4 × 14-in. common wood
  board
1 1/2 × 2-1/2 × 6 decorative wood
  block
2 1-in. × 16 corner bead molding
1 pr. 1-in. hinges
Sheet cork material
Small wire nails
White glue

Tools:
Moto-Shop Scroll Saw/Sander
Table saw
Electric Drill and 1/4-in. bit
C-clamps
Hammer
Hobby knife
Screwdriver
Straightedge

Four cork-faced coasters slide into this convenient rack. Begin project by cutting four 4-in. squares of 1/4-in. walnut (or other decorative wood) and four 4-in. squares of birch (or other common stock).

Using scroll saw for an inside cut, cut 3-in. diameter centers out of walnut squares. Using Moto-Tool and drum sander accessory, sand all edges smooth. With hobby knife and straightedge, cut 4-in. squares of sheet cork material. Paint common squares with white glue, then place cork squares on them. Paint underside of walnut squares with white glue and place them on cork. Clamp this sandwich with C-clamps until glue dries. Then sand each coaster, and finish as you like. To make the hanging rack, cut parts to size and shape indicated on Plan A, using table

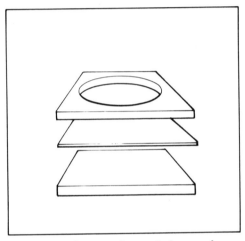

DETAIL B. Coaster is made by sandwiching cutout top piece, cork, and solid bottom piece.

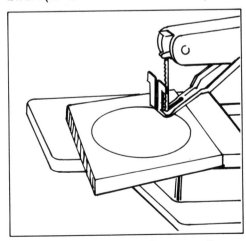

DETAIL A. Make an inside cut on the scroll saw to remove centers of four walnut squares.

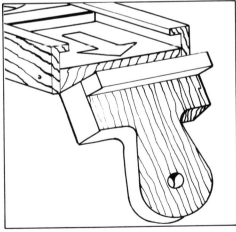

DETAIL C. Handle is hinged to top of rack, and when opened, allows coasters to be taken from rack.

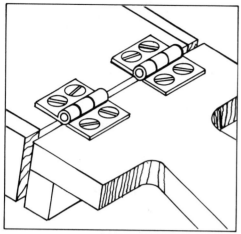

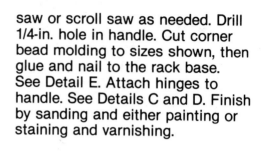

saw or scroll saw as needed. Drill 1/4-in. hole in handle. Cut corner bead molding to sizes shown, then glue and nail to the rack base. See Detail E. Attach hinges to handle. See Details C and D. Finish by sanding and either painting or staining and varnishing.

DETAIL D. Hinges are screwed to handle and back from the back side, as shown here.

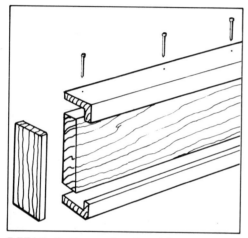

DETAIL E. Corner bead molding makes track in which coasters slide. It is nailed and glued to base piece.

QUICK FIXES

A.

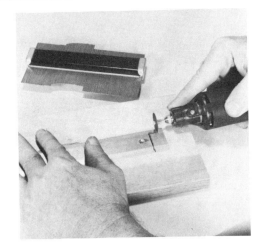

C.

B.

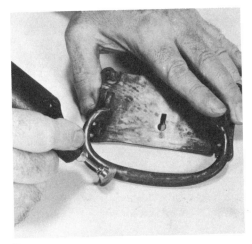

D.

A. Put a new edge on rotary lawn mower blades by grinding with one of the abrasive wheel accessories. Grind along the original angle, not on the reverse side of the blade. If there are nicks in the blade, grind these down and contour them into the blade.

B. The aluminum oxide wheel point No. 952 is the perfect tool for cleaning the burrs on the interior edges of a small pipe after cutting with a hacksaw. One quick insertion of the point in the end of the pipe cleans it. Then the burrs on the outside edges can be deburred almost as quickly.

C. When installing floor tile, install a threshold bar in each doorway to bridge gap between tile and rug in next room. A quick way to cut bar to fit between door stops is to use wire profile transfer tool to copy shape, then trace shape on the bar end. Finally, cut shape with emery wheel accessory. To use, press wires against shape and they assume the pattern.

D. Solid brass antique furniture hardware can be restored by cleaning with a wire brush accessory. Then polish the brass with a cloth wheel and polishing compound. To retain the luster, coat the hardware with clear lacquer.

227

CHAPTER ELEVEN

Materials, Supplies and How to Use Them

Before you start a project, discover the working properties of the materials you will handle. Then you can select the right accessories to do the work most efficiently.

Once you have decided to make something, you immediately face the decision of what materials to use in the project. On the surface, the decision appears to be simple. You say to yourself, "I'll make it out of wood (or plastic, or aluminum, or whatever)". However, the basic knowledge you already have of materials has been put to work in making this decision. In computer fashion, your brain has stored information based on your experience and now puts this to work.

If you decided to work in plastic, you did so because you know something about some of the properties of plastic and about its usage and appearance. In milleseconds, your brain scans this data and suggests that, based on your experience, plastic would be a good material for this project.

The objective of this chapter is to add more data to what you already know about some common materials. In most cases, books can be written about any material, and if you choose to specialize in a material, go to bookstores and the library to learn more. The information here is general and useful but not exhaustive.

Wood

What kind of wood should you select to make a toy? To turn a decorative candlestick? To carve a duck decoy? To carve a horse head in relief on a plaque?

The answer isn't simple. To select the best wood for any project, you must consider the requirements of the project itself and the characteristics of the various woods that are available. Your job is to match the wood to the project's requirements.

Every species of wood is different from all others. Each type of wood has characteristics, some of which make it very desirable and some of which can cause problems.

Some of the fundamental characteristics of wood are (1) hardness; (2) color; (3) grain; (4) weight; (5) smell.

Hardness. By scientific definition, the wood of all trees with broad leaves, rather than narrow needles, is called hardwood. The wood of coniferous or needle-leafed trees is called softwood.

In woodworking practice, this definition doesn't hold up very well. The fact is that woods range over a wide scale from very soft to very hard. Most of the very soft woods are coniferous, and all of the very hard woods have broad leaves.

In the list of common woods that follows a little later in this chapter, we will specify woods as hard, medium, or soft, according to the way each works and feels.

One important note on softwoods of the coniferous variety. Most of these woods contain resin, while none of the broad leafed hardwoods do. The resin runs in tiny canals, too small to be seen without a microscope, through the wood. It gives the wood a "turpentine" smell and makes it a little sticky at times when it is worked. Carvers call this kind of wood *pitchy.*

The chief reasons for considering the softness or hardness of wood for a project are:

Softwood is easier to cut and to work. It is more readily available. It is less expensive. But it is also easier to dent or mar, and cannot take heavy stress.

Hardwood wears better and does not show dents or mars easily. It may work more evenly, depending on the species. It has a broader range of colors and finishes to a finer appearance. And it is stronger in most uses.

The question is, which of these various properties of hardwoods or softwoods are most important in your project.

Color. Wood colors range from black through reds and maroons to white, and include lovely pinks, purples, ambers and browns. If you are making a project for appearance, one reason for selecting a wood would be the natural color it lends to the finished work. If, however, the finished work is to be painted, then the natural color is of no significance.

Grain. The way the grain runs in woods affects its workability and appearance. Woods with pronounced irregular grain can be difficult to carve or to split. For the woodcarver,

then, woods with fine, even grain are important. These grains won't suddenly lead their knives or power cutters off in an unwanted direction. It is best to avoid wild grained wood if you are doing fine carving work.

Grain often lends character to the wood's appearance, as it does in oak or in burled walnut, and may be the wood's outstanding characteristic. Your choice of wood can be affected by both the need for good workability and the desire for exceptional beauty.

Some woods, such as oak and ash, have open or porous grains which must be filled to achieve a perfectly smooth surface. Others, such as hard maple, have a very tight grain and require no fillers. One consideration when selecting a wood is whether or not you want a natural wood look. Currently, for example, much oak furniture is made without fillers. The rough grainy look is popular. In past years, oak was always filled before finishing. So, in your project, what look do you want?

Weight. Wood varies surprisingly in weight. As a general rule, the harder the wood, the heavier it is, since harder wood is denser. On a per cubic foot basis, aromatic red cedar is just about the lightest of the commonly used woods, weighing only 23 pounds per cubic foot. Hickory, at 42 pounds per cubic foot, is one of the heaviest of the domestic species. Douglas fir rates at 26 and white pine at 25, while white oak is at 40. The weight could make a difference to you in larger projects.

Smell. Nearly everyone enjoys the smell of wood, but in certain species, the smell can be a highly prized characteristic. Cedar is the best example. It is used for lining closets and making storage chests, because the smell is pleasant and keeps moths away. Rosewood is another fragrant species, with a delicate perfume reminiscent of roses to add to its colorful beauty.

Wood characteristics

The following is a list of the most common woods and the individual characteristics of each.

Ash. Medium hardwood that runs from white to brown in color. Bends easily when steamed and maintains flexibility, so archers use it for bows. Sands to a good finish.

Basswood. Soft, with a mild, straight grain, basswood is cream-colored with a very fine texture. Easy to work, it is excellent for carving and turning on a lathe. Fairly strong, takes paint well. Seldom used in a natural finish because of bland appearance.

Birch. Mild, close grained and very hard, birch is also cream-colored. Very durable. Carvers like it. Similar in texture to hard maple and often used in furniture making, it usually is finished to look like maple or mahogany.

Butternut. Light, softwood that runs from amber to cream in color. Has a grain structure much like walnut. Easy to work and carve. Sands well. Not easy to find.

Cedar. Fine textured, aromatic, light softwood running from red in the heart to cream-colored at the sapwood. Both colors often present in workpieces. Used to line closets, make storage chests, toys, furniture. Works easily and takes a fine finish. Usually finished naturally, without stain. Red cedar comes from the western states and from Tennessee. White or eastern cedar is less aromatic but has excellent working properties. It machines and carves well.

Cherry. A medium hardwood, cherry has a lovely warm red-brown color and takes a beautiful finish. Dense grain, fine texture, often exhibiting wavy or curly pattern. Highly prized as a furniture wood and for decorative accessories. It is

often used by pattern makers because it carves so well.

Cypress. Rich, red-brown softwood that is highly weather resistant. Very apt to splinter when worked by hand, but can be worked if care is taken.

Elm. Medium hardwood used in furniture making. Has a heavy grain, tends toward tan to brown color. Can be difficult to work, either by machine or by hand. Not recommended for carving.

Fir. Light, soft, creamy orange wood. Generally even textured but can have a wild grain. Much used in plywood and for framing. Can be worked easily, but with care because of grain vagaries. If carving fir, select wood carefully to avoid grain problems.

Gum. A dense, fine-textured medium-hardwood noted for good carving qualities. Dark, reddish brown in color, sometimes available with interesting grain figures. Has a smooth texture, and is easily worked. Minimum tendency to split. It is strong and durable, but should not be exposed to weather as it may warp or twist.

Hickory. The heavy hardwood used to make baseball bats and tool handles, hickory is white to light yellow in color, with very straight grain and uniform texture. It bends well under steam. Not often used for carving.

Mahogany. Light to dark reddish brown in color, mahogany is a medium hardwood with an even fine grain. It works easily with and against the grain. Can be carved. Chief uses are in furniture, mantles, doors, where carvings are common. It takes a beautiful finish.

Maple. Hard maple is heavy, strong and very hard, with a fine wavy grain texture. Excellent for carving by the skilled carver, but not for the beginner. Turns well. Used for furniture and bowling pins. Hard on cutting tools, which must be sharpened often as you work maple.

Oak. Three types — English brown, white and red — all rate as very hard, heavy, strong and durable. Can be carved by an expert. Grain is pronounced and has a tendency to open at board ends (checking). Requires a wood filler for smooth finish. Recently has regained popularity as a furniture wood.

Pine. White and yellow pines are most available, but dozens of varieties exist. White pine, rated as the best all around domestic softwood, is very light, soft, and easy to work. Yellow pine is light but medium hard with a pronounced grain. Because the annular rings are much harder than the wood between them, they can turn the carver's knife unexpectedly. Beginning carvers often start in white pine, but even in white pine, selection of the piece to be carved is important. Yellow pine is not good for fine work but is satisfactory for construction uses.

Poplar. A white softwood that is easy to work but not very durable. A little harder than the pines, with a relatively mild grain. Finished naturally, it has a bland look, so often it is stained for more character.

Redwood. Light, fairly strong and dry (as opposed to pithy or "pitchy" pines), redwood is weather resistant, excellent for use in projects to be used outdoors. Has a mild, straight grain, works easily, excellent for carving. Its natural red color is usually enhanced by clear finishing. Large blocks can be purchased for big carvings.

Spruce. White spruce is similar to white pine and has the same uses.

Walnut. Probably the finest American furniture wood, walnut is rated as medium hard. Comes in a variety of grains, depending on source of wood and way it was cut. Natural light chocolate brown in color, darkens when finished. Excel-lent material for the practiced carver, and good for decorative projects. Turns well in a lathe.

The fancy woods. There are hundreds of beautiful woods from the forests of other parts of the world, all scarce and expensive, and some rare. These include such species as ebony, rosewood, vermillion, purpleheart, cocobolo and zebrawood. Many of these exhibit lovely colors and patterns that enhance anything made from them. Rosewood, for example, has a beautiful light rose coloring, heavily striated with black, and zebrawood is light yellow brown with strong dark brown stripes. Most of these are hardwoods, not easily worked by hand, but good for machine carving and turning. They are useful in the hands of the expert carver. If you are interested in these woods, read the books on rare woods, listed later, and become familiar with their characteristics before buying.

Buying wood. The average lumber yard deals in construction lumber, millwork, plywood and other materials in common use. To buy the majority of woods mentioned in this chapter, you must go to sources which specialize in supplying materials to the craftsman. These suppliers generally do business by mail, print catalogs frequently, and advertise in many of the do-it-yourself publications. Check the ads in these magazines and send for catalogs.

Many of these suppliers make a nominal charge for their catalogs. In addition to wood, they offer veneers, special tools and other materials not easily found.

Two excellent books on rare woods are:

What Wood is That? by Herbert L. Edlin, 1969, The Viking Press, New York.

Know Your Woods by Albert Constantine, Jr., 1975, Charles Scribner's Sons, New York.

Lumber Chart

When you buy lumber, you customarily ask for the nominal size, which is the rough size before the wood is planed to final dimensions. What you actually receive has been planed and is smaller in size. When drawing plans for a project, you must know the actual size of wood, not the nominal size. Check this chart:

Nominal size	Actual size
1 × 2	3/4 × 1-1/2″
1 × 3	3/4 × 2-1/2″
1 × 4	3/4 × 3-1/2″
1 × 5	3/4 × 4-1/2″
1 × 6	3/4 × 5-1/2″
1 × 8	3/4 × 7-1/4″
1 × 10	3/4 × 9-1/4″
1 × 12	3/4 × 11-1/4″
2 × 2	1-1/2 × 1-1/2″
2 × 3	1-1/2 × 2-1/2″
2 × 4	1-1/2 × 3-1/2″
2 × 6	1-1/2 × 5-1/2″
2 × 8	1-1/2 × 7-1/4″
2 × 10	1-1/2 × 9-1/4″
2 × 12	1-1/2 × 11-1/4″
4 × 4	3-1/2 × 3-1/2″
4 × 6	3-1/2 × 5-1/2″
4 × 8	3-1/2 × 7-1/4″
4 × 10	3-1/2 × 9-1/4″
4 × 12	3-1/2 × 11-1/2″

Note that these sizes have been changed in recent years, and these are the newer dimensions. In days past, a 2 × 4 was actually 1-5/8 × 3-3/4″. Now it is 1-1/2 by 3-1/2.

These dimensions apply only to softwood. When buying hardwood, the actual dimension generally is 1/8-inch less than the nominal dimension, but there is no standard as there is in softwood. Thus, a hardwood 2 × 2 would actually measure 1-7/8 × 1-7/8″.

Wood is hygroscopic. That is, it absorbs moisture from the air around it. All lumber and wood measurements reflect the size of the wood in a low humidity. When wood has been stored in high humidity, it may swell slightly. This can affect the size of the wood you receive.

Furniture grade hardwood ideally should be stored in the room in which the furniture will be used for about two weeks before being finished. This permits it to stabilize at that room's average humidity and thus minimizes later problems of expansion, shrinking or warping. Once finished, the wood's tendency to shrink and expand is lessened. While you may not be making furniture, this could be important if making smaller items with close tolerances.

Plywood

Plywood is a sandwich made of thin sheets of wood bonded together. The thin sheets are shaved from logs by large knives. In assembling the sandwich, each sheet is laid down with its grain at right angles to the sheet under it. This type of construction prevents later warping of the sheet.

The great advantage of plywood is that it provides large wood panels for covering big openings and making surfaces such as table tops. While it is possible to make large solid wood panels by edge-gluing boards, solid wood tends to warp, and plywood does not.

Plywood comes in interior and exterior grades. Exterior grades are made with waterproof adhesive, minimizing the effect of weather on the panels. Interior grades, made with other adhesives, will come apart if subjected to excessive moisture.

Plywood made of fir or other softwoods comes in thicknesses ranging from 3/16 to 3/4-inch. Standard panel sizes are 4 × 4, 4 × 7 and 4 × 8 feet. Other sizes, up to 12 feet long, can be ordered.

Fir plywood is graded by a two-letter system, A being the top grade and D being the bottom. Each face of the panel is graded. Thus, a panel rated A-A is cabinet quality without blemishes on either face. A panel rated A-D has a top quality face on one side and a poor quality face on the other, and is used where only the front face will show and the appearance of the back face is unimportant. Lower grades, such as C-C Exterior, are intended for such jobs as concrete forms. Grade C-C or C-D Interior would be used for interior sheathing, floor underlayment and the like.

Hardwood plywood generally is made with a common hardwood as a core and the decorative hardwood, such as walnut, on the face. Most lumber yards stock the common varieties of softwood plywood and can order hardwood plywoods for you.

Working with plywood. Sawing plywood presents one problem: The saw blade, whether a power saw or a hand saw, will often cause a splintered cut on at least one side unless certain precautions are taken.

The important thing to remember is that the good or finished side should get the smooth cut. The rule to follow is: The point of each saw tooth must enter the wood on the good or finished surface. On a table saw, feed the plywood into the saw with the teeth rotating towards the work and with the good or finished side facing upward. With a portable circular power saw, place the good or finished side facing downward. When using a saber saw, look at the direction in which the teeth point and have them enter the good or finished side.

A saw blade with fine teeth and no set to the teeth can be used on plywood for a good cut on both sides.

Another solution, good when you are cutting smaller pieces, is to clamp two pieces of plywood together. For a table saw, place the workpiece on top and the extra piece on the bottom. For a portable circular saw, place the workpiece on the bottom. The ragged cut will then appear on the extra plywood sheet, and both cuts on the workpiece will be smooth.

You also can minimize splintering by applying a strip of masking tape along the line where the panel is to be cut. Saw through both the tape and the plywood, then remove the tape.

Finishing plywood edges. Two methods are used to give the edges of plywood sheets a good finish. One is to nail or glue a molding of the correct size, mitered at all corners, to the sheet. The other is to cement special wood edging tape to the raw edge. This tape is actual wood veneer 1/32-inch thick with a pressure or heat sensitive adhesive backing. The molding method is most often used with softwood plywoods; the tape method with hardwood plywoods. Tapes are available in birch, fir, oak, walnut, and mahogany.

To apply the heat-sensitive wood veneer tape, strip off the backing paper and position the tape on the plywood edge. Then apply an ordinary household iron set at 250 or 300-degrees to the tape to activate the adhesive. Once the tape is bonded in place, sand off any excess that extends above or below the plywood surface, and sand the corners smooth.

Particleboard

Sometimes called chipboard, particleboard is a manmade wood product. Wood chips are mixed with resin and then pressed into boards of different thicknesses. The result is a very heavy, stable board which, when sealed, resists warping. It is less expensive than plywood.

It is used to make inexpensive knockdown furniture, and sold for shelving. Covered with plastic sheets printed to look like walnut and other fine woods, it is being used in the manufacture of inexpensive furniture. It also is now used as the core for some plywoods with faces of fine wood.

It comes in 4 × 8 sheets and in various plank lengths and widths. The most available thicknesses are 1/2 and 3/4 inches, though it is made in thicknesses up to 1-1/2 inches.

Some particleboard reacts badly to water, disintegrating after being soaked. One solution is to seal the board so that water can't get into it. And another is to keep the board away from places where it can contact water.

Used as shelving, it must be supported at 3 to 4-foot intervals or it will sag in time. Be cautious when using fasteners within an inch of the edge of particleboard, and when driving nails into the edge. In both cases, there is danger of cracking or splitting. Always predrill holes before driving screws to lessen the chance of splitting.

Particleboards vary from manufacturer to manufacturer as to density and to surface smoothness. Surface smoothness runs from very rough to mildly rough. To transform the rough surface into a smooth one requires the use of a wood filler to fill the crevices, several coats of shellac or other quick-drying primer to seal the surface, and then several coats of paint. If you attempt to paint the surface without sealing it, you will use large quantities of paint before achieving a smooth finish because the material soaks up paint like a sponge.

Any manmade wood product, especially those made with resin, is very hard on cutting tools. Cutting edges dull very quickly in contact with it. If you plan to cut much particleboard or hardboard, be ready to have your saw blades and cutters sharpened frequently. Some lumber yards refuse to cut these materials for customers because of this prob-

lem, yet for a small fee will cut plywood and lumber to order.

Do not attempt to turn pieces made of particleboard on a lathe.

The weight of particleboard should be a consideration. If you make a workbench, for example, with a particleboard top, sides and back panel, the total weight could run more than 75 pounds. If the bench is to stay in one place and is intended to be sturdy, this is no problem. But if you must move the bench frequently, this much weight could be prohibitive.

Particleboard is used for broad coverage of openings and for large surfaces — table tops, shelves, partitions, doors, etc. It is not used for small project work such as knick-knack shelves, nor is it carved or worked in any fashion.

Hardboard

Hardboard was the first of the manmade wood products and has found an important place in the wood world. It is made by reducing wood chips to their component fibers in a blast of steam. These fibers remain encased in lignin, the natural bonding agent of wood, and are matted under high heat and pressure to form tough, smooth, grainless panels. These panels are equally strong in all directions and have no knots or other imperfections.

Hardboard can be curved to fit a wood frame. It doesn't readily splinter or crack. And it can be nailed or screwed.

A number of types have been developed over the years:

Standard. This product is a light brown color with a smooth, fairly hard surface on one side and a rough screen impression on the other. It should not be used where moisture is expected and should not be subjected to serious abrasion. It is available in thickness of 1/8, 3/16, 1/4, and 5/16 inches. Most readily available are 1/8 and 1/4 inch. Most lumber yards carry 4 × 4, 4 × 7, and 4 × 8-foot panels. It can be had with both sides smooth for special applications.

Specialty hardboards. Hardboards for special purposes have been developed. These include board for use as flooring underlayment; hardboard tile panels, grooved to look like 4 × 4-inch wall tiles; embossed hardboard, with a design embossed on one side; filigree hardboard, a die-cut panel in various filigree designs; and perforated hardboard, widely used to make wall storage racks.

Working with hardboard. Use the highest saw speed possible and carbide tipped saw blades when cutting hardboard. If cutting it regularly, have saw blades sharpened frequently. The denser the board, the quicker it dulls the blade.

Use twist drills, not auger bits, when drilling hardboard, and always drill from the finished side toward the screened side. In fastening, you can use any kind of nail, screw or rivet, but always insert the fastener at right angles to the surface. Don't toe nail or drive nails at an angle. Install all fasteners at least 3/8-inch from any edge to guard against tearing or splitting.

All joints, where two edges of hardboard come together, must be supported by framing because of the material's flexibility. When butting two hardboard panels together, allow 1/8 inch or so between edges for expansion due to moisture absorption. Tightly butted joints may buckle during expansion.

One advantage of hardboard is that panels can be bent or curved to simple, one-directional curves of moderate radii. For greater curves, the board can be soaked in cold water for 40 minutes before bending. Standard 1/8-inch hardboard can be bent to a 12-inch radius when dry, with the smooth side fac-

ing out, and to a 10-inch radius with the smooth side facing in. After soaking, it can be bent to a 7-inch radius with the smooth side out, and a 5-inch radius with the smooth side in.

Do not attempt to laminate pieces of hardboard for turning on a lathe.

Marble

Marble is a limestone with a texture tight enough to be polished. Pure marble is white, and impurities produce colors, including green, red, black, gray, blue and mottled. It is used for counter tops, large and small table tops, lamp and figurine bases, as wall and floor tile and in a wide variety of decorative situations.

Recently, 9 × 9-inch marble tiles 1/4-inch thick, imported from Italy, have become available in the do-it-yourself market. This gives the craftsman a new source of the material and an opportunity to include it in a wider selection of project designs.

You may have to do some detective work to find supplies of marble. Begin by checking the Yellow Pages under "Marble." Also check firms specializing in statuary, church repairs, marble cleaning and antique furniture repair. You can often get leads to marble sources from some of these.

Marble weighs about 170 pounds per cubic foot, can withstand heat up to 1,200 degrees F., and has a crushing strength of 5 tons per square inch. It can be cut with a carbide tipped saw and worked with a Moto-Tool and tungsten carbide cutters. Silicon carbide abrasive accessories from Dremel also will cut and shape it.

Always wear safety goggles when cutting, polishing or shaping marble and use a breathing mask to prevent inhalation of the dust.

When cutting blocks of marble, don't attempt to do the job in one pass. Instead, make a number of successive shallow cuts no deeper than 3/8-inch. When shaping or hollowing, follow the same procedure, making a series of small passes to remove material. Allow the saw or cutter blade to work at its best speed, and do not force the cuts. This will minimize chipping.

Do not try to make curved saw cuts in marble. Instead, mark the desired curve on the marble and make a series of straight cuts tangent to the curve. Then make the curve smooth by grinding off the peaks with a coarse abrasive.

Polishing marble. Marble is polished with abrasives, using successively finer grits. Begin with an 80 grit (an abrasive block rather than sandpaper is used by the experts) and sand by hand in a steady back and forth motion. Then switch to 120, 200, and 320 grits. The first two grits should be hand sanded. After that, you can switch to power sanding.

Sponge the surface frequently to prevent clogging of the abrasive and also to see how the polishing is going. The wet marble surface provides a preview of the final appearance. Change from one grit to another when the abrasive marks appear to be evenly distributed. Don't cut the coarse sanding stages short or you will have to prolong the final stages.

If you are restoring a marble piece, and the marble is only slightly pitted, begin sanding with the 220 grit. If there are no pits but the marble is dull looking, sand only with the 320 grit.

Experts save all marble dust and mix it with resin to make a patching compound for filling holes and repairing chipped edges.

Broken marble can be repaired using polyester resin adhesives, most of which come in two parts (the resin and a hardener) which must be mixed according to directions. Marble dealers have one designed especially for this kind of repair. It dries translucent and makes a repair which is nearly invisible. This same adhesive is used to bond marble to wood. After the resin sets, polish the marble to help the repaired area blend in with the rest of the surface.

Glass

Glass in shapes other than panes is not readily available to the craftsman. Thus, most projects involve cutting sheet glass and colored glass, and cutting glass products such as bottles.

Ordinary window glass comes in two thicknesses, single (.085 to .100 inches) and double (.115 to .133 inches). Heavy sheet glass comes in thicknesses of 3/16, 7/32, and 1/4 inch. Plate glass can be bought in thicknesses ranging from 1/8 to 1-1/4 inches. Glass dealers are listed in the Yellow Pages.

Working with glass. As any glass ages, it becomes harder and more brittle. This makes older glass more difficult to cut. You will need to use more pressure on the wheel of the glass cutter, and there is a greater chance for cracking and chipping.

Always wear safety goggles when cutting glass, since there is the chance that slivers or chips may fly from the cutter. And also wear canvas gloves to protect the hands.

Cutting flat glass. Cutting glass is easy when you have the knack and seems difficult when you don't. Panes of glass are not cut in the normal sense, but are scored and then snapped along the scored line. The knack involves holding the glass cutter properly and applying the right pressure when making the scored line, and it can be acquired with a few practice cuts.

First, the glass must lie on a perfectly flat surface. A straightedge should be used to guide the glass cutter, and should be placed just far enough from the intended line of cut so that the wheel is on the line. And finally, the glass should be clean.

When measuring the glass and marking the scored line, you can make small nicks with the glass cutter near the edge of the glass or mark the edge with a grease pencil. Make these nicks or marks on either side of the scored line.

Hold the straightedge with one hand. With the other, grip the cutter between the first and second fingers and steady it with your thumb. Hold it so the axle of the cutter wheel is parallel to the glass surface, with the cutter handle inclined a little toward you. Make the scored line by drawing the cutter down the glass toward you. Press down firmly, but not hard enough to produce a ragged furrow. What you want is a clean scored line with no skips in it. With practice, you can score glass in one pass. If the first score has skip marks, it is better to turn the glass over and score the other side rather than attempt to redo the first score.

A line with skips, or the need for heavy pressure on the cutter, usually indicates a dull glass cutter. Throw the old one away and buy a new one.

Dip the cutter wheel in oil or kerosene before cutting. You can help prevent crazing (fine cracks) by rubbing the same lubricant along the line of the intended cut.

An easy way to snap the glass along the scored line is to place it over a pencil on a table, with the scored side up and the pencil aligned with the score. Apply a light, snapping pressure to one side while holding the other side down on the table. The glass should break cleanly along the score.

Another way is to move the glass to the edge of the table, with the scored line facing up and aligned with the table edge. This places the part of the glass to be cut off beyond the table edge. Hold the glass on the table and apply a light, quick snapping motion to the part beyond the table edge. The glass should separate cleanly.

Professionals tap the glass under the score, using the metal bulb on the cutter handle, to start the separation. This takes some care since it can cause chipping or permit the glass to break away from the score.

If cutting too near the edge of a pane, breaking along the score is difficult. As an alternate, grasp the narrow strip with pliers near one end of the line to apply pressure for the break. If the break isn't clean, use the pliers or the notches in the cutter head to remove the glass in small bites or "nibbles."

After cutting, use the Moto-Tool and a silicon grinding point to grind the new edge smooth.

A dull cutter is best for cutting textured or figured glass. This minimizes chipping and flecking. Do not attempt to cut tempered glass. On glass that is 1/2 inch or more thick, score both sides before snapping. If cutting colored glass, be careful. This material has a tendency to be slightly bowed and not quite flat. Make cuts on the concave side and don't apply pressure to both ends or sides at the same time.

To cut small diameter glass tubing, score the glass at the point of the cut with a glass cutter or, better yet, a three-cornered file. Then grasp the tube in both hands, with the thumbs immediately behind the score and snap the tubing with a quick light movement.

Cutting bottles. To cut a bottle, you must score around the circumference of the bottle at the point of separation, then apply heat above or below the score. The glass on the heated side of the score will expand and hopefully cause a crack at the score. You may have to help it along by tapping on the scored line.

You can make a guide for cutting the scored line around a bottle by wrapping a perforated steel strap around the bottle and tightening it with a nut and bolt through two of the holes. (This is the same pipe-clamp method used to secure radiator hoses in a car, and you may be able to purchase such clamps of the right size.)

Drilling glass. Holes can be drilled in glass with tungsten carbide drills. Lubricate the tip of the drill with water to keep it cool, don't apply much pressure, and make intermittent contact with the glass to avoid a buildup of heat.

A recommended drilling practice, especially for thicker glass, is the dam method. In this method, make a small dam around the area to be drilled, using putty or clay. Pour water into the dam to both cool and lubricate the carbide-tipped drill. Bring the drill down to the glass, applying light pressure, and touch it to the glass intermittently. When the point of the drill barely breaks through the glass, reverse the work and drill from the other side. You can remove the dam once the glass has been perforated, but brush water on the tip and into the hole as drilling continues. Reverse the glass several times until the hole has been drilled clean and to the desired diameter.

Another method of drilling glass utilizes a piece of soft copper, brass or aluminum tubing and an abrasive slurry. In this method, a slurry of oil or water and an abrasive material is put into the dam and the tubing is rotated in the slurry, causing it to grind the hole.

Cutting glass circles. To cut circles of glass or to cut circular holes in glass panes, you need a glass circle cutter — a movable arm which holds a glass cutter and which has a center post that sticks to the center of glass by means of a suction cup. Most hardware stores carry these or can get them for you. The swing of the arm is adjustable to the size of the circle desired.

Once the glass circle has been scored, the only trick is in removing it from the pane. The easiest way is to make a scored line from the edge of the circle to the edge of the pane. Hold the glass on either side of this score and exert a slight snapping pressure. This should separate the glass and allow the circle to drop out. Be careful, because the circle may drop suddenly. Hold the pane no more than an inch or so above the table and use a soft cloth or foam rubber sheet to pad the table so the glass won't break as it falls.

To cut a circle out of a pane, scribe the desired score, and then make another from 1 to 2 inches inside of it. Make several scored lines across the inner circle, then tap these lines until these inner pieces separate and drop out. Make half a dozen radial scored lines between the inner and outer circles, and after the center glass has dropped out, apply pressure to the segments between circles until they separate. Cutting a hole in glass in this manner is not easy because it is possible to get bad breaks. Sometimes the application of heat to the inner or outer portion helps.

Be careful of all cut glass edges. Most of the time, the separation is clean, but occasionally a tiny jagged edge, almost invisible, is left. This is why you should wear gloves as you work with glass, and also why it is a good idea to run the Moto-Tool with a silicon grinding point a few times over every cut edge.

Whenever you grind glass edges, remember that heat builds up quickly at the point of grinding. This can cause the glass to crack. To avoid the heat buildup, keep the grinding point moving back and forth.

Glass etching. The art of engraving glass could require a separate book. In general, glass can be engraved with the Moto-Tool and various tungsten carbide cutters and silicon grinding points. For beginners, one easy technique is to fasten a photograph, drawing or design on one side of a transparent pane of glass, a drinking glass, clear ash tray or other item and then copy the design on the other side of the glass, using the Moto-Tool and proper accessories.

Plastic

The plastic material most often used by craftsmen is clear acrylic, available in sheets; round and square tubing; round, triangular and square rods; and spiral twist rods. It can be bought in clear and an assortment of colors, in a wide selection of sizes. Marketed under brand names such as Plexiglas and Lucite, it softens at temperatures between 290 and 340-degrees F., and should not be exposed to temperatures of more than 180-degrees F. in use or storage.

Acquiring plastic for craft work can present some problems. Some well-equipped hobby shops carry a limited assortment of rods and sheets. To get many of the colors and sizes available, it is necessary to find a plastics supply company. These supply plastic materials to industry, but usually can provide small amounts to the craftsman. Look in the Yellow Pages under *Plastics* to locate one near you.

Hardware stores and home centers carry sheet acrylic for use in windows. Note, however, that there are two different types of acrylic sheets. One is made specifically for glazing and *cannot* be capillary cemented. The other is a general purpose material used in craft work and *can* be capillary cemented. Capillary cementing will be explained later. Plexiglas G, for ex-

ample, is the general purpose material. Plexiglas K is the glazing grade. If you intend to cement the material, be sure you have the right grade.

You can, of course, make your own plastic stock by casting it. This is the best way when you need odd shapes or have no supplier nearby. To do this, purchase a liquid casting plastic kit containing the plastic resin and a hardener to be mixed with it. Hobby shops have them and craft suppliers advertising in do-it-yourself magazines sell them by mail. Follow the directions for mixing that come with the kit. Then pour the mixture into a mold and allow it to set. Follow the directions in regard to materials which can be used to make molds, since different mixtures may have different requirements. Usually, paper drinking cups and similar items are satisfactory.

Working with plastic. Some plastic, as has been noted, becomes soft or melts when heated. Therefore, when using saws, high speed cutters or drill bits to work plastic, reduce the speed of the Moto-Tool to reduce heat build-up if needed.

The easiest way to cut sheet plastic is on the table saw. It also can be cut with a saber saw, or a reciprocating scroll saw like the Moto-Shop. Do not remove the protective paper before cutting. If the paper has already been removed, apply masking tape to both sides (top and bottom) of the line of the intended cut. This reduces friction and gumming behind the blade.

If you use a portable saber saw, the plastic must be solidly supported or it may crack.

Dremel scroll saw blades have 15 and 25 teeth to the inch. The 25 teeth-to-the-inch blade works well for cutting thin plastics. In the Dremel Table Saw, use the No. 8004 blade, recommended for finish cuts on plywood and veneers. It has 100 teeth and cuts plastic smoothly. Set the blade height slightly above the top surface of the plastic to prevent chipping.

When the intended line to be cut has been indicated on the plastic, an application of wax or crayon over the line will provide lubrication and prevent rejoining of the plastic behind the blade from heat buildup.

Plastic sheet up to 1/4-inch in thickness can also be cut as glass is. It is scored with a plastic cutting tool (Red Devil makes one) instead of a glass cutter. Use a straightedge guide and draw the cutter from one side of the sheet to the other. For thinner plastic, under 3/16-inch thick, make 5 or 6 successive cuts in the same groove. Make 7 to 10 cuts for plastic from 3/16 to 1/4-inch thick. After the line has been cut, place the panel over a 3/4-inch dowel, with the dowel directly under the scored line. Hold the long side of the panel to the table with one hand and apply downward pressure to the short side. Start making the separation at one end of the scored line and move your hands down the sheet, applying pressure to make the separation move along the line until the two pieces come apart.

This is an effective cutting technique if the cut is being made more than 1-1/2-inches in from the edge of the plastic. Cuts less than 1-1/2-inches from the edge are not practical using this method, and sawing is generally used. Patterned Plexiglas sheet cannot be cut this way, either.

Drilling plastic. Standard twist drill bits in a hand drill can be used for drilling plastic. Use regular metal drill bits at slow speeds with moderate pressure. Lubricating the bit with wax helps. Watch carefully for signs of a plastic accumulation on the bit. Plastic makers recommend specially ground drills — Hanson Special Purpose High Speed Twist Drills — which are de-

signed to clear accumulated materials from the bit. However, you should invest in these only if you do a lot of plastic drilling.

Edging finishing. The edges of acrylic sheet are finished in a three-step process:

1. Smooth finish. Round the corners and smooth the edges, eliminating any uneven cuts, by filing with a medium or fine metal file. To eliminate saw marks, scrape the edge with the back edge of a hacksaw blade.

2. Satin finish. This is in preparation for cementing. Sand the edge with successively finer grits, beginning at 150 and working down to 320. Use a sanding block or rest the work on the table of a disc sander so the edges remain square. If you round the edges it will result in bubbles in the cemented joint.

3. Transparent finish. Continue sanding with finer grits (400-500), and then buff the edge with a Dremel cloth polishing wheel in a Moto-Tool, using Dremel No. 421 Polishing Compound. This process also can be done on the Moto-Shop, using the cloth buffer and Dremel polishing compound.

Capillary cementing. This method of cementing is an easy and neat way to glue acrylic plastic pieces together. (Remember that glazing grade of plastic sheet cannot be capillary cemented.) To do this, finish the edges to the "satin" stage just described. Then remove the protective paper from the plastic and place the pieces to be glued in the position you want, holding them in place with masking tape.

The solvent (adhesive) used in this procedure can be bought at the shop where you bought the plastic stock. One brand is IPS Weld-On. A special "hypodermic" applicator, sold where the adhesive is purchased, is used to run the solvent along the joints, which should be kept horizontal. The solvent works its way into the joint by capillary action. Allow it to dry thoroughly before removing the masking tape.

Thickened or paste cements, such as IPS Weld-On #16, can produce weather resistant joints in both glazing and non-glazing types of plastic. This cement is applied from the tube to both edges to be joined. Place the edges together carefully and clamp until the cement sets in 2 hours.

Clearing scratches from plastic. Minor surface scratches can be removed by polishing with a 400-600 grit sandpaper or with the fine abrasive disc in the Moto-Tool. Follow the sanding with a buffing, using a polishing wheel and Dremel polishing compound.

Wash plastics with a mild soap or dishwashing detergent. Do not use window cleaning fluids, scouring powders, alcohol, acetone, or gasoline on them. Mineral spirits can be used to take off paint.

Soft metals

Some grades of soft metals such as aluminum, brass, copper and bronze can be worked in your compact workshop. These materials can be sawed, drilled, polished and shaped with the Moto-Tool and proper accessories and can even be turned on the Moto-Lathe, with certain limitations as to size, as explained in Chapter Five.

Purchasing bar stock, rods and small blocks of these metals depends to a degree on your location. Well-equipped hardware stores often carry some sizes of rod, bar and angle stock. Another source could be local machine shops, who may be willing to sell from their stock, or can tell you where they buy their supplies. In major cities, check the Yellow Pages under the type of metal you want, and call the listed suppliers to learn if they sell in small quantities.

Be careful of what you buy, however. Some "soft" bronzes and aluminums are as hard as steel, and other alloys can be as gummy as a marshmallow if cut with a high speed cutter. Tell your supplier what you intend to do with the metal and how you intend to work it. Let him suggest an alloy that will work properly. If still in doubt, buy a small amount and try it before buying a large supply that you can't use.

Working metal. Dremel high speed cutters, tungsten carbide cutters, and small engraving cutters can be used for engraving, grinding and shaping many soft metals. The polishing accessories all may be used on metals.

When shaping or smoothing with any abrasive accessory or with the Disc/Belt Sander, soft metals will cause a fast accumulation of metal between abrasive particles. The sanding surface will lose its abrasiveness when this happens. Sometimes the accumulation can be removed with a stiff brush.

Abrasives

In general, coarse abrasives are used to remove material and shape a workpiece. Fine abrasives are used to smooth and finish the workpiece. The best way to bring a workpiece to a truly fine finish is to sand it three or four times, beginning with a moderately coarse paper and working down to the finest paper for the last sanding.

Abrasive papers. Sand is seldom now used to make sandpaper, but most people call it sandpaper anyway. Abrasives now used are, garnet, silicon carbide, aluminum oxide, emery and flint. Flint is considered the lowest quality.

You can buy *open-grained* and *closed-grain* papers. Open grained papers are used when sanding paint, soft metals, and other material likely to clog the paper by ac-

ABRASIVE PAPER CHART

Common Name	Grit		Number	Typical Uses
Superfine	600 400	500 360	10/0 9/0	Final wood polish
Extra Fine	320	280	8/0	Final sanding of finish
Very Fine	220		6/0	Sanding between coats
Fine	180 120	150 100	5/0 4/0	Sanding before sealer or primer is applied
Medium	80 50	60	1 0 1/0 1/2	Rough sanding or shaping. Rust removal.
Coarse	40 30	36	1-1/2 2 2-1/2	Rough sanding. Wood removal, paint removal
Very Coarse	24	20	3 3-1/2	Heavy wood removal. Removing many paint coats

cumulating between the grains. Open-grained paper has the abrasive particles spread wide, while close-grained paper has them close together. Use the open-grain for removing unwanted finishes and similar projects. Use the closed-grain for most average sanding jobs.

You can buy both dry and wet paper. Most jobs need only dry paper, but for final rubdowns in furniture finishing, use the wet paper with either oil or water to produce that handrubbed effect.

Finally, when buying sandpaper, consider the thickness of the paper. Thicker papers are less flexible, not easily bent around corners, and subject to cracking and uneven folding. They are best used in power sanders. The thinner papers are better for hand and sanding block use.

Adhesives

Sometimes you hear about "all-purpose glues," but in fact, there really is no such thing. The reason is that, with each type of material to be glued, you are dealing with a different kind of surface (porous, non-porous, etc.), and with each adhesive, you have a different kind of action in relation to that surface.

There are numerous categories of adhesives, with many varieties and brands in each category. In addition, there are a number of special purpose adhesives. Some of the more common adhesives are:

White glue, and its cousin, the yellow furniture glue. Inexpensive and easy to use, these glues work on wood, paper, cloth, leather, cardboard and cork. They set reasonably fast after application, dry clear, provide a strong bond, and are not toxic or flammable. Water, high humidity and heat can weaken the bond of this adhesive, and it doesn't work well on metals, rubber, non-porous materials or plastics.

Urea resin glue. Comes as a powder and is mixed in small quantities to be used within 4 hours. It is strong and nearly waterproof. Used in furniture work, it is light in color and excess amounts are easy to wash off. It must be applied at room temperature and requires 16 hours or more to harden.

Hide glue. An old favorite, available in flakes to be mixed with water and heated and also ready mixed. Very strong, but not water-proof.

Epoxy adhesive. These are the strongest glues available and will bond most materials. They are best used on non-porous materials such as ceramic tile, metals, masonary, chinaware and hard plastics. Epoxy is brittle and doesn't do well on plastic materials. It is resistant to moisture, gasoline and most chemicals.

Contact adhesive. This is used for applying plastic laminates to wood, veneers and wall tiles. Some types are flammable, others are not. Best used on flat surfaces and where large surface areas are to be bonded. Does not do well in weight or pressure bearing situations such as joints.

Clear cements. These dry quick and clear, and work on ceramics, book bindings, costume jewelry and other things where the glue joint might be visible.

Cyanoacrylate glue. This is the stuff that glues your fingers together instantly if you aren't careful. It works with great speed, and a drop will do the job. For use on glass, ceramics, plastics, metal and rubber. In many cases, it replaces the clear glue mentioned earlier.

Another specialized adhesive is panel or construction adhesive, used by carpenters to put up paneling, attaching furring strips to concrete walls, put up ceiling tiles, mount shelf brackets on cement walls and dozens of other jobs formerly reserved for nails or other fasteners. Applied with a caulking gun from a tube the size of a tube of caulking compound, these adhesives are good to know about for building and remodeling applications. They are not used for furniture or typical craft projects.

Butyl and silicon rubber based adhesives are another specialized category. They resist shock, mois-ture and vibration, and are available in small tubes and in cartridges for caulking guns.

The four most important rules in gluing. There are four rules that will virtually guarantee success in all your gluing jobs.

1. Always read and heed the instructions on the tube or container. This holds true even if you have been using a product for some time. The manufacture wants you to be successful in using his product, and the label gives the best and latest information to help assure it. Labels often change as new uses are discovered or new formulations adopted. So always read the label.

2. Always clamp every glue job. Find some way or some type of clamp (there are a dozen or more varieties) to firmly clamp or apply pressure to the glued area until the glue sets. The greatest reason for glue failures, according to experts, is the lack of clamping.

3. Allow enough time for the glue to set. The second greatest reason for failure in glue jobs is born of the impatience of the craftsman. Most of us find it difficult to wait the required number of hours for a glue (or a paint or anything else) to set completely. Many glues look and feel dry after a short time but still require time to set hard. Pay serious attention to the drying times specified on the label, and then let the glue set a little longer than that — especially if the day is humid.

4. Make sure all surfaces to be joined are clean, dry and free of oil or grease. Most glues will not work well if foreign materials are present.

Fasteners

It is critical to use the right size and kind of fastener when assembling any project. In most cases, you will be concerned with joining wood, and therefore with the use of nails or screws, the most common fasteners.

Nails. Nails are sold by the penny system, which dates back some 400 years to the way nails were sold in London at that time. The letter "d" stands for a penny in the English money system. In today's nail system, the "d" actually represents 1/4-inch of nail length.

The 2d (or two-penny) nail is 1-inch long. The 3d nail is 1/4-inch longer, or 1-1/4-inches. The 4d nail is 1-1/2-inches, and so on. See the chart for a full listing.

For design purposes, plan to use a nail that is three times the thickness of the piece of wood it will go through. Thus, nailing a 1-inch board requires a nail 3-inches long for maximum strength.

Some woods have a tendency to split when nails are driven into them. When nailing hardwoods, softwoods which tend to split, for fine finishing work, and always when nailing near a board edge, bore a pilot hole. The hole can be the same size as the nail to be driven, or slightly smaller.

Screws. There is no doubt that, given a choice between a nail and a screw, you should select the screw if you want strength. They will hold better under all circumstances.

The correct size of screw is important. About 2/3 of the length of the screw should be in the second or receiving piece of wood. Thus, to fasten a 3/4-inch board the screw should be 2-1/4-inches long.

Common Nails

Penny size	Length	Dia. (wire gauge)	Approx. No. per lb.
2	1″	15	830
3	1-1/4″	14	528
4	1-1/2″	12-1/2	316
5	1-3/4″	12-1/2	271
6	2″	11-1/2	168
7	2-1/4″	11-1/2	150
8	2-1/2″	10-1/4	106
9	2-3/4″	10-1/4	96
10	3″	9	69
12	3-1/4″	9	63
16	3-1/2″	8	49
20	4″	6	31
30	4-1/2″	5	24
40	5″	4	18
50	5-1/2″	3	14
60	6″	2	11

Finishing Nails

2	1″	16-1/2	1351
3	1-1/4″	15-1/2	807
4	1-1/2″	15	584
5	1-3/4″	15	500
6	2″	13	309
8	2-1/2″	12-1/2	189
10	3″	11-1/2	121
16	3-1/2″	11	90
20	4″	10	62

Most Commonly Used Screw Sizes

Shank Number	Length
0, 1, 2, 3	1/4″
2, 3, 4, 5, 6, 7	3/8″
2, 3, 4, 5, 6, 7, 8	1/2″
3, 4, 5, 6, 7, 8, 9, 10	5/8″
4, 5, 6, 7, 8, 9, 10	3/4″
6, 7, 8, 9, 10, 11	7/8″
6, 7, 8, 9, 10, 11, 12, 14	1″
6, 7, 8, 9, 10, 11, 12, 14, 16	1-1/4″
6, 7, 8, 9, 10, 11, 12, 14, 16, 18	1-1/2″
7, 8, 9, 10, 11, 12, 14, 16, 18	1-3/4″
8, 9, 10, 11, 12, 14, 16, 18, 20	2″
10, 11, 12, 14, 16, 18, 20	2-1/4″
12, 14, 16, 18, 20	2-1/2″
14, 16, 18, 20	2-3/4″
16, 18, 20	3″
16, 18, 20	3-1/2″
18, 20	4″

The diameter or gauge of screws is indicated by numerals ranging from 0 to 24. At the hardware store, a box marked 7—1-1/2, for example, means that the box contains screws of No. 7 gauge, 1-1/2-inches long. Check the screw chart in this chapter to see the actual diameter of each gauge number.

You can select from three different types of screw heads: flat, round, and oval. Flathead screws can be driven flush to the surface or countersunk. Round and oval head screws usually are driven to the surface only. In addition to these standard heads, the Phillips head is also frequently used.

The Use of Materials and Supplies

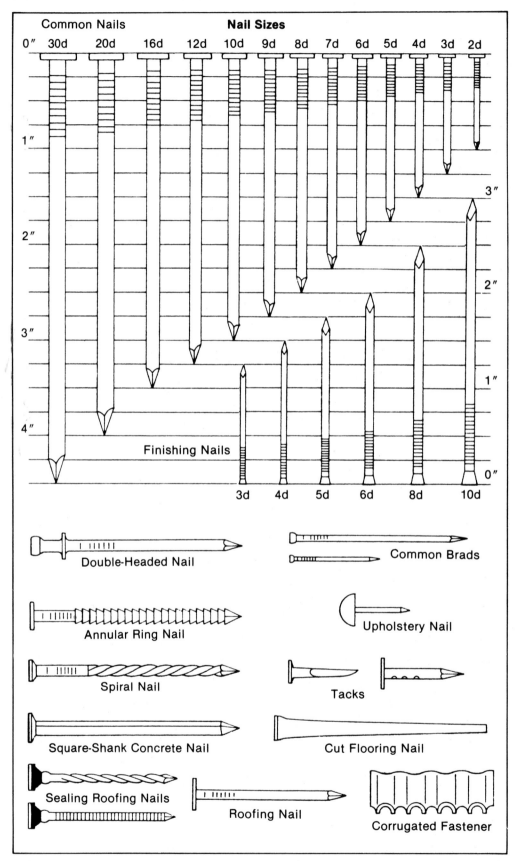

Common Nails

Nail Sizes

0" 30d 20d 16d 12d 10d 9d 8d 7d 6d 5d 4d 3d 2d

1"

2"

3"

4"

Finishing Nails

3d 4d 5d 6d 8d 10d

3"

2"

1"

0"

Double-Headed Nail

Common Brads

Annular Ring Nail

Upholstery Nail

Spiral Nail

Tacks

Square-Shank Concrete Nail

Cut Flooring Nail

Sealing Roofing Nails

Roofing Nail

Corrugated Fastener

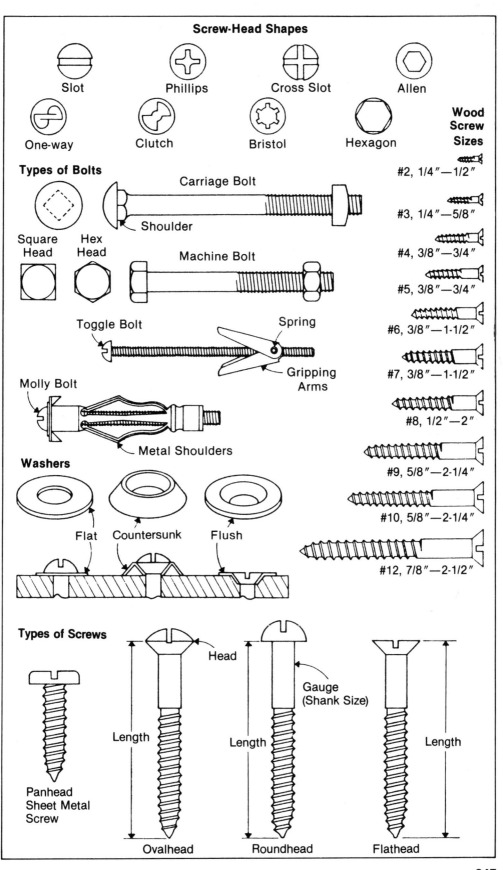

Screw-Head Shapes

Slot · Phillips · Cross Slot · Allen

One-way · Clutch · Bristol · Hexagon

Types of Bolts

Carriage Bolt

Shoulder

Square Head · Hex Head

Machine Bolt

Toggle Bolt · Spring

Gripping Arms

Molly Bolt

Metal Shoulders

Washers

Flat · Countersunk · Flush

Wood Screw Sizes

#2, 1/4″—1/2″

#3, 1/4″—5/8″

#4, 3/8″—3/4″

#5, 3/8″—3/4″

#6, 3/8″—1-1/2″

#7, 3/8″—1-1/2″

#8, 1/2″—2″

#9, 5/8″—2-1/4″

#10, 5/8″—2-1/4″

#12, 7/8″—2-1/2″

Types of Screws

Head

Gauge (Shank Size)

Length · Length · Length

Panhead Sheet Metal Screw

Ovalhead · Roundhead · Flathead

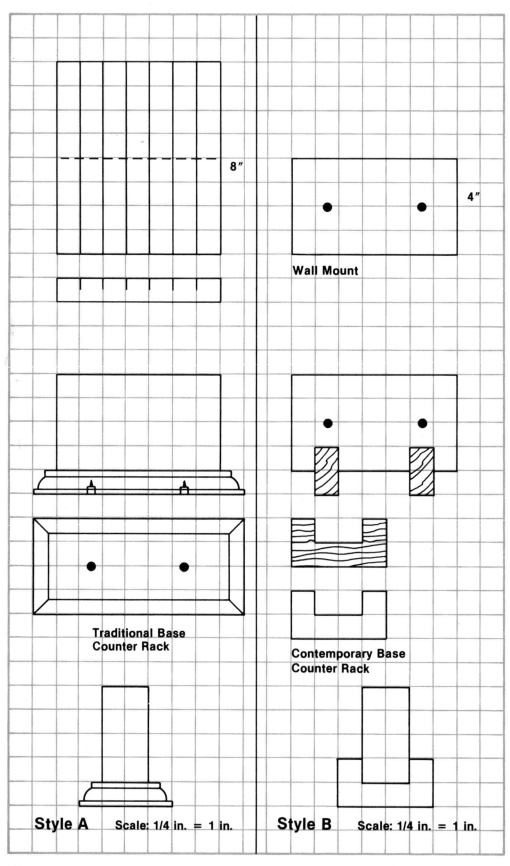

8″

Wall Mount

4″

**Traditional Base
Counter Rack**

**Contemporary Base
Counter Rack**

Style A Scale: 1/4 in. = 1 in.

Style B Scale: 1/4 in. = 1 in.

Project 11

KNIFE RACK

A good, sharp set of steak or carving knives can be kept safely and conveniently in this hardwood knife rack.

Materials:
Oak or other hardwood, 9 × 14 × 1-in.
Oak or other hardwood, 4 × 9 × 1 for base, or 2 blocks of 2 × 4 × 4-in. for block legs
Flathead screws
Waterproof glue
Linseed oil

Tools:
Table saw, Disc/belt sander, Clamps, Screwdriver

This is a project you must vary to suit your own requirements. The racks shown were designed to hold 6 steak knives with 4-in. blades. If your knife set has more knives or the blades are a different size, redesign the block, making it to the necessary dimensions. You also can design a similar block for carving knives by enlarging the block and the knife slots and tapering the block to accommodate knives of differing lengths, from short to long.

Begin by cutting the workpiece to the needed dimension on the table saw. See Detail A. Next, plan the knife slots about 1-in. apart across the block and determine the width of the slots. Again using the table saw, make blind grooves the length of the board, with each groove half as deep as the planned width of the knife slots. The number of passes for each groove depends on how wide the knife blades to be stored are. Usually, each groove should be 2 or 3 saw passes wide, but for large carving knives, could be 4 or more passes. Next, saw block in half, as indicated in Detail A. Glue the halves together so that the grooves

match and form knife slots. Using the disc/belt sander, put a good finish on the block. Start sanding with a coarse belt, then graduate to increasingly finer belts until wood is smooth. Two different bases which can be constructed are shown in Details B and C. Sand the base you make smooth and join it to the rack with countersunk flathead screws driven up from the bottom of the base. For a natural finish, apply linseed oil, rubbing it in, allowing it to stand for several hours, and then wiping thoroughly. If you choose, you can stain the wood before oiling.

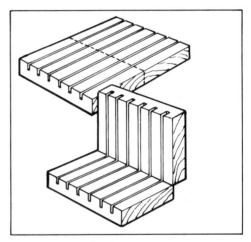

DETAIL A. Knife slots are groove cuts made on table saw. Block is then cut in half and glued together as shown.

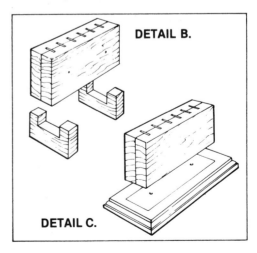

DETAIL B.

DETAIL C.

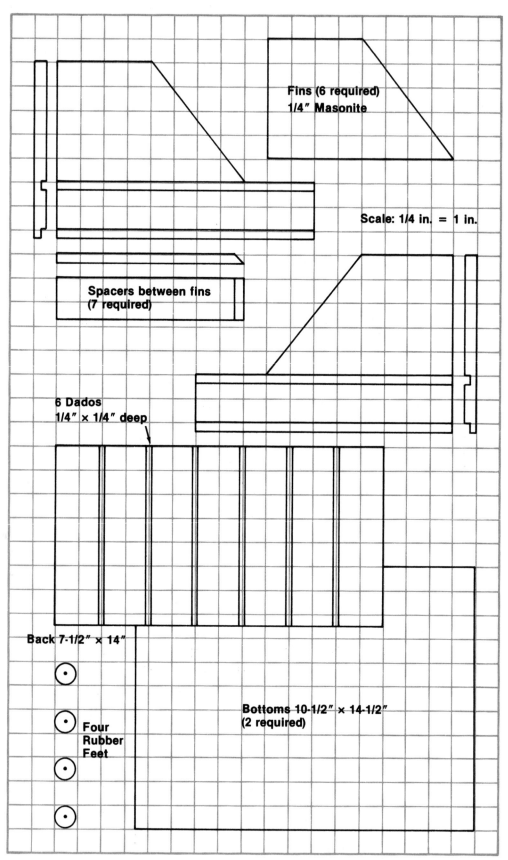

Fins (6 required)
1/4" Masonite

Scale: 1/4 in. = 1 in.

Spacers between fins
(7 required)

6 Dados
1/4" × 1/4" deep

Back 7-1/2" × 14"

Four
Rubber
Feet

Bottoms 10-1/2" × 14-1/2"
(2 required)

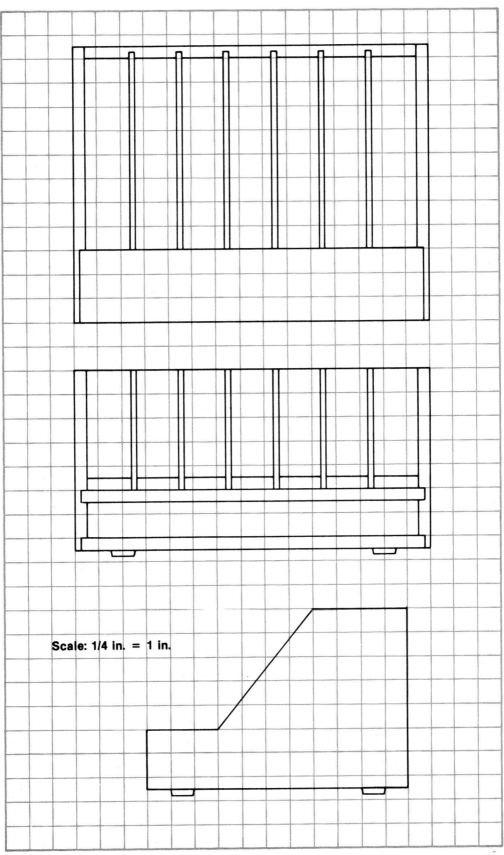

Scale: 1/4 in. = 1 in.

CHAPTER TWELVE

How to Design and Lay Out A Project

An idea is only an idea until it is translated into a plan. Here you find out how to plan, to scale the plans, make plan drawings, and use templates.

All ideas for projects of any kind goes through a series of steps. In the first step, the idea blossoms in your mind. In the second step, you mentally develop the idea, adding to it, refining it, considering such items as materials and tools needed, etc. At some point, you are satisfied with it, and want to proceed to translate it into actuality.

At this stage, many craftsmen begin work. They see the idea clearly enough to begin production without a plan. This is satisfactory for simple projects, but can be a mistake when the project is complex. If many pieces must be joined and if measurements are important, then the best procedure is to first put the idea on paper.

As you draw plans for the project, you will find better ways to make it work, better means of fitting the pieces together, and perhaps even good additions or variations for it.

Plans need not be elaborate, nor do you have to be an artist to draw a good plan. The plan should show necessary detail, such as the way pieces are to be joined, dimensions of each part, fittings and fasteners to be used, etc.

Tools for drawing

Drawing boards. A drawing board which tilts toward you is the best surface for making plans. But boards are expensive. A dining room or kitchen table works, but isn't really convenient, since the paper must lie flat on it. However, you can make an inexpensive but workable table top drawing board using hardwood plywood.

The size of the board depends on storage space available and the size of the drawings you intend to make. For most people, a board of 1/2-inch plywood that measures 18 × 24 is minimum, ranging up to 24 × 36 or larger. Buy the plywood board in the size you prefer and sand the edges smooth.

The board should have a bottom lip on it. This can be a wood strip 1/4 × 1-inch, screwed to the edge of the plywood so that it projects above the board surface. This lip will keep pencils and other drawing materials from falling.

This board is used on a table, tilted at an angle so the work is held up in front of you. It is supported by two wooden triangles, also made of

1/2-inch stock, attached to the bottom. The hypotenuse of each triangle should be as long as the drawing board sides.

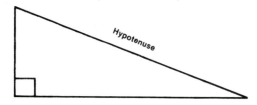

The angle between the hypotenuse and the long side or bottom side of the triangle determines how the board will sit. Most people find an angle of 20 degrees to be right, but if you want the board tilted up more, increase this angle to 25 or even 30 degrees. You can use trial and error, trying one set of triangles and then changing to another if these aren't suitable.

The triangles can be attached to the bottom side of the drawing board with piano hinges so they can be folded up for storage. Put rubber feet on them to protect the table surface and to keep the board from sliding as you work. These rubber feet can be purchased at hardware stores.

T-square. The most important drawing tool on a board is the T-square. You can buy one for your table, or make one. The T-square consists of a long arm that extends all the way across the drawing board, with a block of wood or metal making the T across the top. This block, mounted on the cross arm at exactly 90 degrees, rides up and down the side of the board. When it is held against the side of the board, the cross arm is exactly parallel to the base of the drawing board. It is important that the side of the drawing board which the T-square rides on is perfectly straight.

The T-square makes it easy to draw perfectly straight lines and to be certain that lines are square with the edges of the board.

Other drawing tools. You will be able to handle most plan drawings if you include the following items in your drawing kit: a set of divider points, an 8-inch plastic 45-45-90 degree triangle, a plastic irregular curve guide, and a 6-inch protractor. Add an art gum eraser, pencil sharpener and hard and soft pencils. These are all available at art supply and stationary stores.

Drawing paper can be held on the surface of the board by bits of masking tape at each corner of the paper. Before putting the masking tape down, use the T-square to square the paper with the bottom of the board.

Graph paper, ruled in squares, is convenient to use in planning because with it you can quickly draw parts in scale. Each square (graph paper usually is ruled in 1/4-inch squares) is allowed to represent a specified scale dimension — one square equals one inch, one square equals one foot, etc. Thus, a 24 × 24-inch chess board drawn on graph paper using a scale of 1/4-inch to 1-inch, would be 6 × 6-inches.

Often, the best method is make initial sketches in scale on graph paper. When you are satisfied, you can expand to full size drawings by enlarging by the squares.

Enlarging by squares

Projects in magazines and books often are presented in squared scale drawings. To build projects from these drawings, you enlarge the original drawing by redrawing it on the plan with larger squares.

The standard procedure is to divide a sheet of paper into squares larger than those on the original drawing. These squares should be sized to produce a full-sized plan of the project. Thus, if the magazine plan shows a 4-inch design on 1/4-inch squares, and you want the

When joining dots on enlarged plan, make the new drawing smooth by using an irregular curve guide and a straightedge.

final project to be 12-inches long, you prepare a sheet with 3/4-inch squares on it.

Note that the increase in size of any drawing is directly related to the ratio of the sizes of the squares. If the squares on the small drawing are 1/4-inch, then 1-inch squares on the larger drawing will make the final plan four times the original size. When you make a plan drawing from unscaled photos or art, you can begin by laying a grid of 1/4-inch squares over it, and then enlarge by transferring it to a plan with 1/2, 3/4, or 1-inch squares, as you want.

Each vertical and horizontal line on the original plan and the corresponding lines on the larger drawing are numbered, creating grids.

Transferring the plan. To transfer the plan from the smaller drawing to the larger one, note where each line on the small drawing crosses either a vertical or horizontal line on the small grid. Locate that same point on the larger grid and place a dot there. Continue to make these dots until all intersecting points have been located. Then join the dots. Use a straightedge and drawing tools such as the irregular curve guide and compass to make the lines connecting the dots smooth, and keep checking the original art

to see that your lines agree with it.

If a plan has identical left and right sides, it is necessary only to enlarge one side. Then fold the finished drawing along the centerline of the pattern, then cut the drawing out with a scissors, cutting through both layers of paper. The result is a full-sized pattern, identical on both sides.

When making patterns, it is a good idea to glue the paper to lightweight cardboard to make it easier to handle and to trace. If you expect to make many pieces from the pattern, glue it to 1/8-inch hardboard for durability and cut it out on a scroll saw.

You can turn any printed picture or drawing into a scale drawing by laying a plastic grid over it, locating one horizontal and one vertical line at the approximate center of the drawing. You can buy plastic sheets already printed with grids in different sizes, or make your own by drawing them on thin tracing paper or plastic food wrap. For the latter, make the lines with a china marking pencil (grease pencil) with a sharpened point.

Tape the grid over the drawing or photo, number the horizontal and vertical lines as previously described, and make the plan drawing.

The pantograph. Another way to copy and enlarge plans or drawings is to use a pantograph, a device consisting of several hinged arms which can be adjusted to enlarge a drawing to a number of different scales. Inexpensive pantographs can be purchased at most art stores. When using a pantograph, the planner steers a point on one arm along the lines in the original art while he presses down on a pencil attached to another arm. The interplay of the hinged arms automatically causes the drawing by the pencil to be enlarged.

Templates. A template is a full-sized but reversed cutout made from the plan. Templates are made to be held directly against the workpiece as a check to see that the wanted shape is being achieved. To make a template, you make a full-sized drawing of the part and then cut it out of the paper. The cutout adjacent to the plan of the part is a reverse view of the part, and becomes the template.

Templates should be glued to cardboard so they can be held accurately against the workpieces.

Cross-sectional templates are used for shapes such as model ship hulls, where the outside dimensions of the workpiece change continuously. In model ship work, cross-sectional views of the hull are drawn at intervals along the plan where dimensions change. Templates are then made from one-half of each cross-sectional drawing and held against the work as the hull is shaped.

Engineering a project

When planning to build a project, designing is one important feature and engineering is another. Engineering, for most small projects, consists of three major considerations: strength, working parts, and joints.

Strength. If you are designing a 24 × 24-inch Parsons Table for chess and checker playing, how strong does it have to be? The legs obviously do not need to be made out of 4 × 4 lumber. On the other hand, they should not be made out of 1/2 × 1/2 lumber, either.

The point is this: As you develop any project, give consideration to the need for strength of the various parts. Make a conscious effort to design each part to do its job — bear weight, support other parts, endure friction, etc. As a general rule, it is better to make a design too strong than not strong enough. The important thing is to think of the need for strength as you lay out the original plan.

Working parts. Sliding doors, hinged lids, articulated joints — all these are moving parts, and should be given careful thought in the design stages. Consider the location of hinges, for example, and the swing of doors, the throw of any moving parts. Is there room for each part to work without interference? After you have made the initial design sketches, study them specifically for operation of all moving parts.

Joints. The majority of work done in the compact power tool shop is woodwork, so this section is concerned chiefly with wood joints. When joining wooden parts, it is necessary to make joints that are strong enough to carry any weight, survive typical use, and have the desired appearance. There are dozens of different types of wood joints, each designed to meet specific applications.

The plain butt joint, for example, is made by butting the end of one piece of wood against another. It has little strength, depending almost entirely on the glue or fastener used in making the joint. Its chief use is in spacing — that is, a wood part used as a spacer between two other parts, and bearing no weight or pressure, could be joined by means of a butt joint. If the part is expected to bear weight, then a stronger joint should be used — a butt dowel joint, for example, or a mortise and tenon.

To help you design the right kinds of joints into your wood projects, a chart of many common wood joints is included in this chapter. Study the different drawings for a few minutes to become familiar with joint terminology, and at the same time, look at the obvious strength factors in each. Even without great design experience, you can select joints for your projects which will do the job after looking these drawings over.

Try to select joints that are strong enough, but that are not so complicated as to make the project too difficult to make. Most of these joints can be made on the table saw, with a router, or with hand tools, including sharp wood chisels and a hammer.

Developing skills

Start out at the drawing board with simple designs. Learn how to develop front views and side views of the project. Learn to make expanded detail views of complex parts of a project. Practice turning flat drawings into three-dimensional views. Each of these parts of plan drawing can be learned through practice, if you work on simple projects at first.

The great advantage in being able to draw plans is that you will be able to refine and develop your projects while still on the drawing board — and before you get into the workshop. Good working plans cut down on failures and improve the quality of your work.

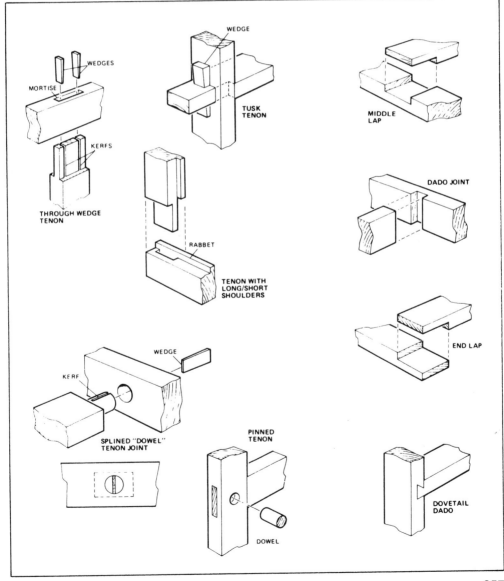

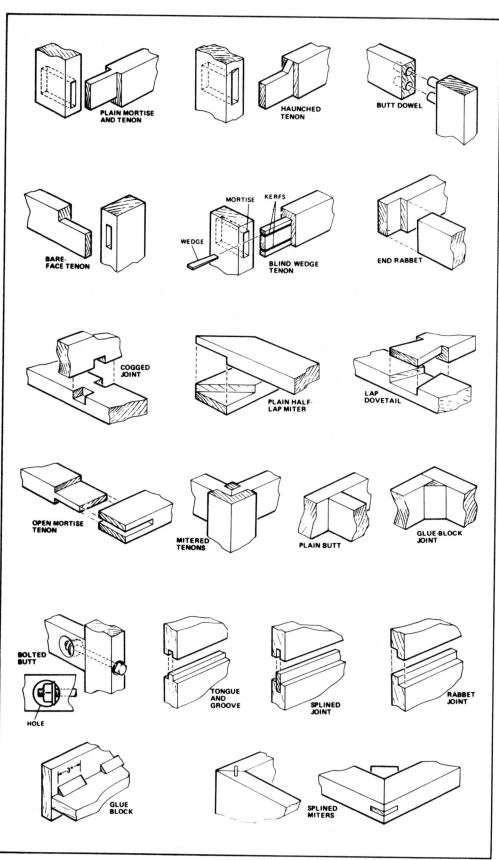

Project 12

GLASS ENGRAVING
Using any appropriate photograph or drawing, make etched glass silhouettes to hang on the walls of a child's room.

Materials:
12 × 12-in. glass pane
1/2 × 1-in. oak or pine for frame
Finishing nails
White glue
Stain sealer

Tools:
Dremel Engraver
Moto-Tool with silicon carbide grinding accessories
Table Saw

Fasten the photograph or drawing to be copied on the back of the glass pane, facing through the glass. See Detail A. Use the engraver to follow the outline of the image, thus transferring the design to the glass. See Detail B. You can frost areas of the design and also highlight areas by grinding with silicon carbide grinding points in the Moto-Tool. For additional effect, paint the engraved area, then wipe it, leaving paint only where glass was frosted. You also can turn glass over and paint back in desired color to highlight image, (See Detail C) or apply a piece of backing paper to make design stand out. This is a highly indivldualistic project. Each engraver will achieve a different creative result, even using the same picture pattern, because of the individual ways each etches the glass. Experiment to find ways you prefer to create silhouettes and highlighting. Use table saw to cut framing material to 12-in. lengths. Cut a slot the thickness of the glass in one edge of each piece, as shown in Detail D, then cut miters on ends of all pieces and join into a frame around the glass, as seen in Detail E.

DETAIL A. Place art or photo under glass, facing up. Secure art to glass and glass to table with masking tape.

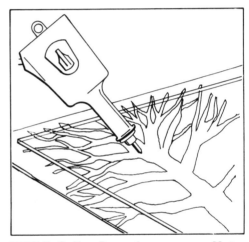

DETAIL B. Use Dremel engraver or Moto-Tool with silicon carbide grinding points to etch lines of photo.

DETAIL C. By painting back of glass in dark color, design on front can be made to stand out.

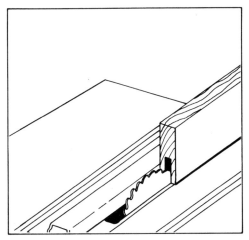

DETAIL D. Rip a dado groove in the edges of the framing pieces to hold the glass in place.

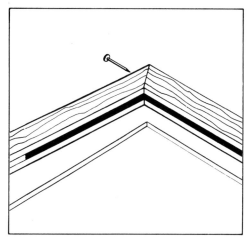

DETAIL E. Complete the frame by mitering the corners of the frame as shown here and securing with finishing nails.

Index

NOTES

NOTES